An Aging India: Perspectives, Prospects, and Policies

An Aging India: Perspectives, Prospects, and Policies has been co-published simultaneously as *Journal of Aging & Social Policy*, Volume 15, Numbers 2/3 2003.

An Aging India: Perspectives, Prospects, and Policies

Phoebe S. Liebig, PhD
S. Irudaya Rajan, PhD
Editors

An Aging India: Perspectives, Prospects, and Policies has been co-published simultaneously as *Journal of Aging & Social Policy*, Volume 15, Numbers 2/3 2003.

NEW YORK AND LONDON

An Aging India: Perspectives, Prospects, and Policies has been co-published simultaneously as *Journal of Aging & Social Policy*™, Volume 15, Numbers 2/3 2003.

First published in 2003 by The Haworth Press, Inc.
10 Alice Street, Binghamton, NY 13904-1580 USA

Published 2015 by Routledge
711 Third Avenue, New York, NY 10017
2 Park Square, Milton Park, Abingdon, Oxon OX14 4RN

Routledge is an imprint of the Taylor and Francis Group, an informa business

© 2003 by The Haworth Press, Inc. All rights reserved. No part of this work may be reproduced or utilized in any form or by any means, electronic or mechanical, including photocopying, microfilm and recording, or by any information storage and retrieval system, without permission in writing from the publisher.

The development, preparation, and publication of this work has been undertaken with great care. However, the publisher, employees, editors, and agents of The Haworth Press and all imprints of The Haworth Press, Inc., including The Haworth Medical Press® and Pharmaceutical Products Press®, are not responsible for any errors contained herein or for consequences that may ensue from use of materials or information contained in this work. Opinions expressed by the author(s) are not necessarily those of The Haworth Press, Inc. With regard to case studies, identities and circumstances of individuals discussed herein have been changed to protect confidentiality. Any resemblance to actual persons, living or dead, is entirely coincidental.

Cover Design by Lora Wiggins
Cover Photography by Phoebe S. Liebig, PhD
Shiva Sculpture Photographed by Bernard D. Conrad
(at: <bdcom@earthlink.net>)

Library of Congress Cataloging-in-Publication Data

An aging India: perspectives, prospects, and policies/Phoebe S. Liebig, S. Irudaya Rajan, editors.
    p. ; cm.
    "Co-published simultaneously as Journal of aging & social policy, volume 15, numbers 2/3 2003."
    Includes bibliographical references and index.
    ISBN 0-7890-2239-7 (hard : alk. paper) – ISBN 0-7890-2240-0 (softcover : alk. paper)
    1. Aged–India. 2. Aging–India. 3. Aged–Services for–India. 4. Aged–Government policy–India. [DNLM: 1. Aged–India. 2. Public Policy–India. WT 30 A26855 2003]
I. Liebig, Phoebe S. II. Rajan, S. Irudaya (Sebastian Irudaya), 1959- III. Journal of aging & social policy.
HQ1064.I4A355 2003
                                                      2003013523

ISBN-13: 978-0-7890-2240-0 (pbk)

An Aging India: Perspectives, Prospects, and Policies

CONTENTS

INTRODUCTION

An Aging India: Perspectives, Prospects, and Policies   1
   Phoebe S. Liebig, PhD
   S. Irudaya Rajan, PhD

FOUNDATIONS OF AGING IN INDIA

Demography of Indian Aging, 2001-2051   11
   S. Irudaya Rajan, PhD
   P. Sankara Sarma, PhD
   U. S. Mishra, PhD

Perspectives of Research on Aging in India   31
   P. V. Ramamurti, PhD

ECONOMICS, HEALTH, AND SOCIAL NETWORKS

Economic Security for the Elderly in India:
  An Overview   45
   S. Vijaya Kumar, PhD

Health Status and Health Care Services
  Among Older Persons in India   67
   Vinod Kumar, MBBS, MD

Aging, Disability, and Disabled Older People in India   85
   Indira Jai Prakash, PhD

SOCIAL AND FAMILIAL RELATIONS

Social Networks of Old People in India:
   Research and Policy   109
     John van Willigen, PhD
     N. K. Chadha, PhD

Issues of Elder Care and Elder Abuse in the Indian Context   125
     D. Jamuna, PhD

CURRENT INTERVENTIONS

Geriatric Hospitals in India, Today and in the Future   143
     K. R. Gangadharan, Dip. SSA

Old-Age Homes and Services: Old and New Approaches
   to Aged Care   159
     Phoebe S. Liebig, PhD

The Role of Non-Governmental Organizations
   for the Welfare of the Elderly: The Case of HelpAge India   179
     Maneeta Sawhney, MPhil, PhD candidate

ADVOCACY AND POLICY

Senior Grassroots Organizations in India   193
     P. K. B. Nayar, PhD

Towards a Policy for Aging in India   213
     S. D. Gokhale, PhD, MSW

Index   235

ABOUT THE EDITORS

Phoebe S. Liebig, PhD, is Associate Professor of Gerontology and Public Administration at the University of Southern California. She is the author of numerous articles in policy-related journals and is co-editor of two books, one on international aspects of housing and the other on long-term care policies in the state of California. Dr. Liebig is a Fellow of both the Gerontological Society on Aging and the Association for Gerontology in Higher Education.

S. Irudaya Rajan, PhD, is Associate Fellow at the Centre for Development Studies (CDS), Thiruvananthapuram, Kerala, India. Currently he is Coordinator, Population and Development Program, at CDS. Formerly, he was a Doctoral Fellow at the International Institute for Population Sciences, Mumbai, and recipient of the Gold Medal (First Rank) for the best student in Demography during 1982-83. He is a lead author of the book, *India's Elderly: Burden or Challenge?,* published by Sage Publications. Currently, he is coordinating a major project on Economics of Pensions in South Asia: Special Focus on India, Sri Lanka, and Bangladesh. He has co-authored/co-edited seven books and several articles in international journals on aging-related issues and has been a consultant for World Bank.

Acknowledgments

As is so often the case, credit for this enterprise goes to many individuals. First, a debt is owed to my father, Marshall Harvey Stone, who inspired a love of India because of his many trips there and who died in Chennai. Special thanks are due to Michael Zarky who accompanied me on my three trips to India and smoothed many paths, especially during the four months of my Fulbright there. Thanks also are due to Vinaya Mehrohtra, whose visit to southern California in the mid-1990s helped trigger my research topic, and to his many associates in Mumbai. Special accolades go to the staff at the Center for Research on Ageing and the Department of Psychology at Sri Venkateswara University in Tirupati, especially Drs. P. V. Ramamurti and D. Jamuna and then research assistant, now Dr. K. Lalitha.

Additional acknowledgements are made of the intellectual and practical help provided by numerous Indian colleagues and friends, particularly T. K. Nair, M. S. Kulkarni, Parul Dave, John Kottakayam, P. K. Muttagi, T. V. Ramprasad, Indira Khadambi and her family, Dr. Alladi Ramakrishnan and his family, the Joseph family of Chennai, and several Aurovillians in Pondicherry; the Fulbright program staff in the United States and New Delhi; various practitioners, state and national policymakers and ordinary folk who shared their views about aging in India; and the leaders of more than 20 aging advocacy groups and non-governmental organizations, especially HelpAge India personnel in Bangalore, Calcutta, Chennai (Madras), Delhi, Kochi (Cochin), Madurai, and Thiruvananthapuram (Trivandrum).

Finally, particular thanks go to my co-guest editor, S. Irudaya Rajan, without whose persistence and being "our man in India" this project would never have been completed; to all our authors who responded with grace and fortitude to the requests of multiple reviewers; to Francis Caro and Robert Morris, co-editors of the *Journal of Aging & Social Policy,* who saw the merit of this project; and last, but certainly not least, to the two managing editors, first Jill Norton, and then Robert Geary, for their constant help and encouragement, despite the lengthy gestation of this project.

Phoebe S. Liebig
Editor

INTRODUCTION

An Aging India: Perspectives, Prospects, and Policies

Phoebe S. Liebig, PhD
University of Southern California

S. Irudaya Rajan, PhD
Centre for Development Studies
Thiruvananthapuram, Kerala, India

This volume is the result of ideas developed in several communications between the two co-editors, Drs. Liebig and Rajan, after completion of Liebig's Fulbright to India in 1997. By the late fall of 1998, a proposal to create a special book on aging in India was accepted by the *Journal of Aging & Social Policy*. Sponsorship of Dr. Liebig's research by Dr. P. V. Ramamurti and the Center for Research on Ageing, S. V.

[Haworth co-indexing entry note]: "An Aging India: Perspectives, Prospects, and Policies." Liebig, Phoebe, S., and S. Irudaya Rajan. Co-published simultaneously in *Journal of Aging & Social Policy* (The Haworth Press, Inc.) Vol. 15, No. 2/3, 2003, pp. 1-9; and: *An Aging India: Perspectives, Prospects, and Policies* (ed: Phoebe S. Liebig, and S. Irudaya Rajan) The Haworth Press, Inc., 2003, pp. 1-9. Single or multiple copies of this article are available for a fee from The Haworth Document Delivery Service [1-800-HAWORTH, 9:00 a.m. - 5:00 p.m. (EST). E-mail address: docdelivery@haworthpress.com].

© 2003 by The Haworth Press, Inc. All rights reserved.
http://www.haworthpress.com/store/product.asp?sku=J031
10.1300/J031v15n02_01

University at Tirupati, led to encounters with many leaders in the field, thereby expediting the selection of the authors whose work appears here.

AN AGING INDIA–A RATIONALE

Why look at an aging India? Numerous reasons abound. Much of our knowledge of aging societies is based on developed nations in Western Europe, North America, and increasingly, Asia. However, the demographics of aging also challenge developing countries in South America, Africa, and Asia. Of paramount interest for the World Bank and the United Nations are the issues of aging in what was formerly labeled the Third World. This includes China and India, two of the oldest societies in the world, both of which are undergoing extraordinary changes in modernization, urbanization, and globalization in a very brief time span, accompanied by explosive growth in their aging populations. Together, China and India will account for 38% of the world's elders age 60+ by the year 2025. Even more to the point is the rapid aging of the elderly in these two nations. More than 75% of all persons age 75 and older live in four countries: China and the United States have the largest proportion of this age group, followed by India and Japan. Still, the gerontological community knows far more about aging in China, Japan, and the United States than we do about India, which is a gap that needs to be filled.

Another set of reasons for becoming better versed about an aging India stems from characteristics shared by that nation and the United States. India is the world's largest democracy, with a written Constitution partly modeled on that of its North American counterpart. Similarly, India is a highly diverse society along several dimensions: geography, religion, language, and socioeconomic status, due to its growing middle-class. Like the United States, Australia, and Canada, India shares a common British heritage and operates under a federated system of government. Finally, because of migration to other parts of the world, a substantial number of Indians now reside in America, bringing their traditions with them, including family care for elders.

However, India is unlike the United States and is beset by a number of issues beyond population aging. Like most developing nations, it is undergoing major social and economic challenges. These include changes in the traditional family and in the role of women that affect elder care, and transitions from centralized planning and a model of British socialism to a gradual blending in of market capitalism. At the same time, India is still largely an agricultural economy with high rates of poverty for all age groups. As of 1997, the proportion of people below the poverty line was 39.9%, likely a severe underestimation (Sainath, 1998).

Policy Framework

Unlike many other developing nations, India has made a remarkably successful transition from colonial status to independence in 1947. While adoption of the British parliamentary system (similar to Australia and Canada) and strong leadership have been vital factors, another has been the principle of federalism, initiated by the Government of India Act of 1935, which established a quasi-federal union of autonomous provinces. This principle was maintained in the 1950 Constitution, with the states reorganized to make boundaries conform more with the geographic distribution of linguistic and cultural groups, similar to Canada (Verney, 1995). The division of powers between the central and state governments is set forth in three lists in the Constitution's seventh schedule. The union list gives the national government exclusive authority over 97 domains, including defense, banking, and income taxes, while the state list gives states authority over 66 matters, such as health, education, welfare, agriculture, and local government–all of particular importance to the aged and their families. The national government also has major responsibility for the welfare of various disadvantaged members of society, including elders, subject to its economic capacity. The concurrent list allows the two levels of government to share authority in 47 areas (e.g., civil and criminal law). However, unlike the U.S. Constitution, residual powers are vested in the central government, and a 1976 amendment to the Indian Constitution substantially increased the power of the central government over the states (Ray & Kincaid, 1988).

In addition (and in contrast to the U.S. experience), the national government exercises considerable financial power, because it levies and collects most taxes. The 25 Indian states are highly dependent on transfers from Delhi for nearly 60% of their expenditures, compared with the 20% received by the American states and their local governments from Washington, D.C. (Verney, 1995). Tax revenues are distributed among the states for their exclusive use according to a formula recommended every five years by a National Financial Commission (Ray & Kincaid, 1988). The central government, like the U. S. government, also has authority to make grants-in-aid for any public purpose and must generally rely on the states to implement and administer national domestic policies. This "pragmatic decentralization" has also enhanced the constitutional goal of promoting local self-government, empowering marginalized sections of rural society (Arora, 1995). The Panchayat Act of 1991-92 constituted panchayats (village governments) as a third tier of government, with a list of 29 subjects to be transferred to them from state governments, including programs of economic development and social justice. This constitutional framework provides the scenario under which prospects and policies for India's elderly occur, particularly the National Policy on Older Persons (NPOP), enacted in 1999.

OVERVIEW OF THE ARTICLES

We have organized the articles based on the issues and topics they address. Many topics of interest were not included. Space and time considerations prevented the inclusion of separate articles on the role of the media, mental health and aging, gender, and education and training. These topics are mentioned briefly in various articles. A more exhaustive approach must await the development of a handbook on aging in India.

Foundations of Aging in India

The two articles in this section provide a foundation for those that follow.

Aging Population. "Demography of Indian Aging, 2001-2051," by S. Irudaya Rajan, P. Sankara Sarma, and U. S. Mishra, presents an overview of population aging in India, comparing it with other nations. The authors discuss life expectancy trends, dependency ratios, and various socioeconomic characteristics (e.g., literacy, marital status) of Indian elders for the first half of this century. A final section analyzes policy implications for family support, social security, geriatric health care, and the promotion of elders as societal resources.

Research on Elders' Needs. In "Perspectives of Research on Aging in India," Dr. Ramamurti describes the current situation in research on the status and needs of older persons, stressing the importance of science as the basis for policy and planning, for understanding what constitutes quality of life for elders, and for mounting appropriate interventions. He notes the greater output in the social and behavioral sciences and the recent basic biomedical research. He also points out the methodological problems arising from conducting research in many different languages, the lack of effective intervention models, and the need for more governmental and non-governmental funding, a refrain familiar to audiences in the United States.

Economics, Health, and Social Networks

A second cluster of articles on economics, health, disability, social networks, and family care builds on the first two articles.

Economic Security. S. V. Kumar, in "Economic Security for the Elderly in India: An Overview," stresses the lack of any widespread social insurance mechanism for elders, 40% of whom live below the poverty line. Existing pensions cover former public employees and industrial workers, about 10% of the work force. State old-age assistance and a similar recent national program targeting poor elders without family support provide inadequate income. Dr. Kumar recommends that policies be developed for rural elders who need income support beyond what their families can provide, a difficult task given India's current economic capacity.

Health Status of Elders. In "Health Status and Health Care Services Among Older Persons in India," Dr. Vinod Kumar describes the health status of the Indian aged with their "double disease burden" of degenerative illnesses and infectious diseases, a major cause of death, and provides detailed information on their mortality, morbidity, and disability profile. No separate system of geriatric services exists. Village-based primary health care is the current source of health services for all ages and is seen as the appropriate setting for rural geriatric care.

Disabled Elders. In "Aging, Disability, and Disabled Older People in India," Indira Jai Prakash focuses on younger persons growing older with disabilities. The author emphasizes the issues of mental health, especially depression, and of gender, noting the double stigma of being female and disabled. Under the Persons with Disability Act of 1994 and the NPOP in 1999, the concerns of these two groups are handled separately, a situation requiring attention in India, as well as the United States (see Liebig & Sheets, 1998).

Social and Familial Relations

The third set of articles focus on the social and familial relations of Indian elders.

Links with Non-Kinship Groups. Van Willigen's and Chadha's article, "Social Networks of Old People in India: Research and Policy," is centered on social networks–links with non-kinship groups–as vital components of life satisfaction among the elderly. Such networks are important sources of social support for elders–beyond the family, which has been the primary research emphasis in India. The authors suggest the need for government policies that encourage the creation and maintenance of robust social networks of older persons. However, they recognize that gender-biased laws reflecting a cultural pattern of male dominance produce negative impacts on the outcomes of social aging processes for Indian women throughout the life course, especially in old age.

Gender, Elder Care, and Abuse. The recurring theme of gender is raised in D. Jamuna's article on elder care and abuse, "Issues of Elder Care and Elder Abuse in the Indian Context." As in the United States, elder care is the province of female family members, but daughters-in-law are the primary caregivers in India, followed by spouses; care in old-age homes is a last resort. Studies on caregiver stress bespeak a need for home help. There is, however, little empirical evidence of elder abuse, despite economic strains on families caring for their elders. Dr. Jamuna indicates that incentives to strengthen family care are needed, for example, food subsidies. Professional care services are not likely to succeed in India.

Current Interventions

A fourth group of articles focuses on current interventions in health, housing, and social services and the role of NGOs in developing such services.

Heritage Hospital. K. R. Gangadharan's "Geriatric Hospitals in India, Today and in the Future" features a case study of Heritage Hospital in Hyderabad. Few geriatric facilities or trained health-care personnel exist. Heritage is one of the few comprehensive programs of geriatric care encompassing both acute and long-term care units, extended home care services, other home- and community-based care via "service clubs," community outreach, training, and consultation. Heritage Hospital is fast becoming a model in India and could become a model for other developing nations.

Old-Age Homes. Next is Phoebe S. Liebig's article on "Old-Age Homes and Services: Old and New Approaches to Aged Care." Old-age homes for the destitute are not new to India; however, community-based services (e.g., day care centers, Adopt-a-Granny) and for-pay homes are new. Most community-based programs serve small numbers of the poor, primarily in urban/suburban areas, relying on unstable funding (e.g., "in-kind" donations of services, food, supplies) and fund-raising by their sponsoring NGOs. The recent growth of these homes and services raises debates about their appropriateness for India. Still, the NPOP stresses the roles to be played by NGOs and panchayats in such provision, a monumental task requiring more governmental aid than may be possible, given the need.

HelpAge India. Maneeta Sawhney's article, "The Role of Non-Governmental Organizations for the Welfare of the Elderly: The Case of HelpAge India," describes the goals and activities of HelpAge India, the premier NGO in creating programs for elders since 1978. A major focus is on development via income generation, micro credit, and other programs to strengthen participation of elders in society. Via a network of 24 regional offices, HelpAge fundraising, research, advocacy, communications, and publications emphasize rural health, old-age homes, and long-lasting programs to be sustained by elders themselves, in keeping with the goals of the NPOP of senior empowerment.

Advocacy and Policy

Two articles on advocacy and policy make up the final section.

Pensioner and Senior Citizen Associations. P. K. B. Nayar's "Senior Grassroots Organizations in India" focuses on two groups. Pensioner associations, composed of state and central government retirees, began in 1934. The associations do not represent all pensioners but are quite successful in maximizing retirement benefits for their members. Senior citizen associations draw from middle- and upper-income elders and owe their origins in 1950 to Rotary International. Attempts to create an AARP model have not been successful, but the Indian Federation on Ageing and umbrella associations of senior groups in Mumbai, Delhi, and Kerala have been strong advocates for empowering elders. The NPOP bypassed existing senior groups in creating two new entities, the National Council for Older Persons and the National Association of Older Persons. While some existing groups are part of the latter, Dr. Nayar predicts it will be some time before Indian senior grassroots groups have the political clout of their U.S., Canadian, and British counterparts.

Policy Development, Past and Current. In "Towards a Policy for Aging in India," S. D. Gokhale provides an overview of past and current policy development for elders, which built on traditional values; some pre- and post- independence laws; and insertion of age-related concerns into several Five-Year Plans in the late 1980s and early 1990s. Influenced strongly by international activity on aging, the creation of a national policy evolved slowly due to the need to consult with the states. After many drafts and regional forums, the NPOP was enacted. The author describes the NPOP goals, reminiscent of the Older Americans Act, and the implementation section that focuses on the roles of NGOs, the states, and panchayats. Gokhale critiques the plan for its inadequate attention to the economic security of rural and female elders, its administrative and coordination problems, and the lack of an expenditure plan.

PURPOSES OF THIS VOLUME

This volume has several purposes. First and foremost is the goal of exposing a wider audience in North America and the world to the dimensions of aging in India, and of enabling readers to make comparisons between it and other aging societies, especially the United States. It differs from other volumes on an aging India in featuring Indian scholars and practitioners in a U. S. publication, rather than one published in India. Only two non-Indian authors are represented, both of them Fulbright scholars in 1997. Unlike other recent books on India and aging published in America, an anthropological focus is not dominant in the present collection. Rather, its emphasis is on the implications of various facets of India's aging society for policy and practice and, wherever appropriate, to draw attention to similarities and differences between the approaches employed in comparison with those employed in the United States.

The two co-editors hope this volume will serve to promote more dialogue on the topic of an aging India in its own right and as an example of approaches to the challenges and opportunities of aging that can be used elsewhere in the developing world. By exposing researchers and practitioners outside India to what is happening inside that nation, a foundation for more collaborative research between Indian gerontologists and their counterparts in other countries can be laid. Finally, it is hoped that this volume will be useful to instructors in India, the United States, and elsewhere, as students seek to understand better the international phenomena of aging.

REFERENCES

Arora, B. (1995). Adapting federalism to India: Multilevel and asymmetrical innovations. In B. Arora & D. Verney (Eds.), *Multiple identities in a single state: Indian federalism in comparative perspective* (pp. 71-104). New Delhi: Konark.
Liebig, P. S., & Sheets, D. J. (1998). Ageism, disability, and access to environmental modifications. *Technology and Disability, 8,* 69-84.
Ray, A., & Kincaid, J. (1988). Politics, economic development, and second-generation strain in India's federal system. *Publius: The Journal of Federalism, 18,* 147-167.
Sainath, P. (1998). *Everybody loves a good drought: Stories from India's poorest districts.* London: Headline Book Publishing.
Verney, D. (1995). Federalism, federative systems, and federations: The United States, Canada, and India. *Publius: The Journal of Federalism, 25,* 81-97.

FOUNDATIONS OF AGING IN INDIA

Demography of Indian Aging, 2001-2051

S. Irudaya Rajan, PhD

Centre for Development Studies
Thiruvananthapuram, Kerala, India

P. Sankara Sarma, PhD

Achutha Menon Centre for Health Science Studies
of the Sree Chitra Tirunal Institute for Medical Sciences and Technology,
Thiruvananthapuram, Kerala, India

U. S. Mishra, PhD

Centre for Development Studies
Thiruvananthapuram, Kerala, India

SUMMARY. India is the second largest country in the world, with 72 million elderly persons above 60 years of age as of 2001, compared to China's 127 million. One of the objectives of this paper is to assess the emerging scenario of elderly for the first half of the 21st century. Ac-

---

[Haworth co-indexing entry note]: "Demography of Indian Aging, 2001-2051." Rajan, S. Irudaya, P. Sankara Sarma, and U. S. Mishra. Co-published simultaneously in *Journal of Aging & Social Policy* (The Haworth Press, Inc.) Vol. 15, No. 2/3, 2003, pp. 11-30; and: *An Aging India: Perspectives, Prospects, and Policies* (ed: Phoebe S. Liebig, and S. Irudaya Rajan) The Haworth Press, Inc., 2003, pp. 11-30. Single or multiple copies of this article are available for a fee from The Haworth Document Delivery Service [1-800-HAWORTH, 9:00 a.m. - 5:00 p.m. (EST). E-mail address: docdelivery@haworthpress.com].

© 2003 by The Haworth Press, Inc. All rights reserved.
http://www.haworthpress.com/store/product.asp?sku=J031
10.1300/J031v15n02_02

cording to projections, the elderly in the age group 60 and above is expected to increase from 71 million in 2001 to 179 million in 2031, and further to 301 million in 2051; in the case of those 70 years and older, they are projected to increase from 27 million in 2001 to 132 million in 2051. Among the elderly persons 80 and above, they are likely to improve their numbers from 5.4 million in 2021 to 32.0 million in 2051. The increasing number and proportion of elderly will have a direct impact on the demand for health services and pension and social security payments. Mobilizing resources for geriatric care and providing sufficient maintenance for the elderly will emerge as a major responsibility for heath-care providers and pension economists. *[Article copies available for a fee from The Haworth Document Delivery Service: 1-800-HAWORTH. E-mail address: <docdelivery@haworthpress.com> Website: <http://www.HaworthPress.com> © 2003 by The Haworth Press, Inc. All rights reserved.]*

KEYWORDS. Elderly in India, population aging, literacy among the aged, old age dependency

INTRODUCTION

Population aging is an obvious consequence of the process of demographic transition. The developed regions of the world have already experienced its consequences, while the developing world is facing a similar scene. Although the proportion of elderly–defined in terms of those aged 60 and above in a population–seems small in some of the developing countries, those countries have more elderly persons in absolute terms because of their large population bases. While the recent emphasis on studies pertaining to the elderly in the developing world is attributed to demographic transition, the deteriorating conditions for the elderly are a result of the fast-eroding traditional family system in the wake of rapid modernization, migration, and urbanization. Projected increases in both the absolute and relative sizes of the elderly populations in many third world countries is a subject of growing concern for social policy (Treas & Logue, 1986; Grigsby, 1993; World Bank, 1994). These increases are the result of changing fertility and mortality over the last 40 to 50 years. The combination of high fertility and falling mortality during the 20th century has ensured large and rapid increases in elderly populations as successively larger cohorts enter the span of old age. Furthermore, the recent sharp decline in fertility is bound to lead to an increasing proportion of future elderly. Moreover, given that these demographic changes have been accompanied by rapid and profound socioeconomic change, cohorts might differ in their experiences as they become aged.

The number of elderly in the developing countries has been growing at a phenomenal rate; in 1990, the population of those aged 60 years and above in the developing countries exceeded that of the developed countries. Most of this growth will take place in developing countries and over half of it will be in Asia (World Bank, 1994). Obviously, the two major population giants of Asia, India (Irudaya Rajan, Mishra, & Sarma, 1996; 1999) and China (Irudaya Rajan, 1994) will naturally contribute a significant proportion to this growing elderly population.

AGING:
GLOBAL SCENARIO

The population of the world in 1995 was 5.7 billion, and it is expected to reach 10.8 billion by 2050. Between 1950 and 2150, the world population will have increased fourfold. Interestingly, between 1995 and 2000, it is estimated that 81 million people have been added to the world population each year (United Nations, 1998). The likely future scenario (assuming medium fertility) of world population is shown in Table 1.

The percentage of elderly in the world population will increase rapidly from 9.5 in 1995 to 20.7 in 2050 and to 30.5 in 2150 (Table 1). In absolute numbers, this will mean an increase from 542 million in 1995 to 1.9 billion in 2050 and to 3.3 billion in 2150. Although the number of children below 15 years in 1995 was estimated to be 3.3 times higher than the aged 60 and above, the elderly are expected to surpass the number of children by 2050.

Among the elderly, the number of the oldest old–those aged 80 or over–will increase more rapidly. According to the projections, the number of those aged 80 and over will multiply by a factor of 17 between 1995 and 2150; from 61 million in 1995 to 320 million in 2050 and to 1054 million by 2150.

According to the assessment of the United Nations, only Western Europe in the whole world had a proportion of elderly above 15% in 1950. In 2000, all three regions of Europe except Eastern Europe registered a proportion above 20%. In the next 50 years, the proportion of aged is expected to grow more rapidly. As of today, Southern Europe has the highest proportion of elderly (21.5%) and is expected to reach 37.2% by

TABLE 1. Global Scenario of Aged, 1995-2150

Year	Population (billion)	% aged 60+	% aged 65+	% aged 80+
1995	5.687	9.5	6.5	1.1
2000	6.091	9.9	6.8	1.1
2025	8.039	14.6	10.8	1.7
2050	9.367	20.7	15.1	3.4
2075	10.066	24.8	19.1	5.3
2100	10.414	27.7	22.0	7.1
2125	10.614	29.2	23.6	8.6
2150	10.806	30.5	4.9	9.8

Source: United Nations, 1998. World Population Projections to 2150. Department of Economic and Social Affairs, Population Division.

2050. In the developing countries, one in every 12 persons is now elderly; the ratio is expected to become one in five by 2050, equaling that in the developed countries. The latter is projected to reach one in three by 2050.

Although Asia as a whole accounts for only 9% of elderly, there are variations among the various regions (Table 2). As of the year 2000, Eastern Asia leads with 11%; the corresponding proportion for other regions is only 7%. By the year 2050, one in four persons in Eastern Asia, one in five in South Central and Eastern Asia, and one in six in Western Asia are expected to be elderly. Out of 36 countries under study, not a single country had a proportion of elderly above 10% in 1950. Presently, seven countries in Asia have crossed that level, and the proportion is already 23% in Japan. For more details on Japan's elderly and social policy, see Bass, Morris, and Oka, 1996.

By 2050, the proportions of elderly in 33 Asian countries, except Afghanistan, Oman, and Yemen, are projected to be above 10%. In 10 countries, the proportions are likely to exceed 20%, with six having 25% elderly, and two as large as 35%. Hong Kong is predicted to lead with 39% of elderly, followed by Japan. The two most populous countries in the world, China and India, will share the major proportion of the world's elderly. Currently, one in 10 Chinese is an elderly person, and this ratio is expected to reach one in four by 2050; similarly, one in 12 Indians is elderly, and this ratio is likely to be one in five in 2050. In absolute terms, India's elderly population is expected to increase from 76 million in 2000 to 327 million in 2050, and that of China is expected

TABLE 2. Aging in Asia, 1950-2050

Country	Percentage Aged 60 and above			
	1950	2000	2025	2050
Asia	6.7	8.7	14.4	21.9
Eastern Asia	7.4	11.0	19.6	26.9
China	7.5	10.0	18.5	26.2
Hong Kong	3.7	15.0	32.4	38.9
Japan	7.7	22.6	32.1	36.0
Mongolia	5.5	5.6	10.0	20.2
Republic of Korea	5.4	10.5	21.8	28.8
South Central Asia	6.1	7.0	11.3	19.5
Afghanistan	3.4	4.6	6.1	9.9
Bangladesh	6.2	5.2	9.0	19.9
Bhutan	5.8	5.2	6.3	10.6
India	5.6	7.6	12.6	21.3
Iran	8.3	5.8	8.0	16.5
Maldives	8.2	5.0	5.9	12.1
Nepal	7.1	5.4	7.1	13.5
Pakistan	8.2	4.9	8.2	15.1
Sri Lanka	6.0	9.6	17.0	25.2
South Eastern Asia	5.9	7.2	12.5	21.2
Cambodia	4.5	4.8	8.7	14.6
Indonesia	6.2	7.4	12.7	21.6
Laos	4.6	4.8	6.0	11.0
Malaysia	7.3	6.5	12.5	21.1
Myanmar	5.5	7.0	10.8	18.8
Philippines	5.5	5.7	10.9	18.7
Singapore	3.7	10.4	27.8	29.1
Thailand	4.8	8.7	17.9	28.1
Vietnam	6.5	7.3	11.9	22.1
Western Asia	7.1	7.1	10.7	17.0
Bahrain	4.6	4.9	19.6	24.3
Cyprus	9.1	15.3	22.3	26.1
Iraq	4.3	4.9	7.5	14.7
Israel	6.3	12.7	18.1	24.4
Jordan	7.4	4.6	6.6	13.4
Kuwait	4.5	3.6	16.0	24.7
Oman	5.0	3.9	5.5	8.4
Qatar	5.7	4.8	24.1	19.8
Saudi Arabia	5.6	4.6	8.8	13.3
Syria	6.8	4.7	7.7	18.1
Turkey	5.9	8.7	14.7	23.9
Emirates	5.7	5.0	22.7	23.4
Yemen	6.2	3.7	4.3	8.8

Source: United Nations, 1998. World Population Prospects. The 1996 Revision, Department of Economic and Social Affairs.

to increase from 127 million to 397 million during the same period (United Nations, 1998).

THE ELDERLY IN INDIA

According to the 1991 census, India had an elderly population of 56 million. Among the 25 Indian states and seven union territories, Uttar Pradesh led with 9 million elderly, followed by Maharashtra (5.5 million), Bihar (5.2 million), and Madhya Pradesh (4.3 million). The small elderly population was in Lakshadweep. The old-old (70+) numbered 20 million, with the states of Uttar Pradesh and Maharashtra having the major share (see Table 3).

The proportion of elderly persons in India rose from 5.63% in 1961 to 6.58% in 1991 (Irudaya Rajan, Mishra, & Sarma, 1999). Given the differences in mortality and fertility across Indian states and union territories (see Irudaya Rajan, Mishra, & Ramanathan, 1993; Zachariah & Irudaya Rajan, 1997; Mari Bhat & Irudaya Rajan, 1990; Guilmoto & Irudaya Rajan, 1998), the highest proportion of elderly is found in Kerala (8.77%) and the lowest (3.55%) in Andaman and Nicobar Islands. The proportion of old-old was 2.4% in 1991. As expected, Kerala had the highest (3.46%) proportion of old-old.

India is one of the few countries in the world where males outnumber females. This phenomenon among elderly is of prime importance because female life expectancy at ages 60 and 70 is slightly higher than that of males. However, at any given age, there are more widows than widowers. Reasons for this unusual phenomenon need to be identified in the wider context. Since the beginning of the 20th century, life expectancy at birth among Indian males was higher than that for females until the first half of the 1990s. Besides this unusual demographic pattern of excess female mortality at infant and childhood ages, the analysis is further hampered by the phenomenon of age exaggeration among the aged. Thus, the finding of more males in old age does not reveal a true picture of the situation among elderly persons (see Mari Bhat, 1992). In India, the sex ratio of the aged as well as the old-old favors males. Only nine states and union territories reported a sex ratio above 100, indicating an excess of females over males in old age. Reasons for more males in old age may consist of under-reporting of females, especially widows; age exaggeration; low female life expectancy at birth; and excess female mortality among infants, children, and adults (Sudha & Irudaya Rajan, 1999; Mari Bhat, Navaneetham, & S. Irudaya Rajan, 1995). Notwith-

TABLE 3. Demographic Profile of the Aged, 1991 Census

States	Population(000's)		Percentage to total population		Sex ratio (f/m)*100	
	(60+)	(70+)	(60+)	(70+)	(60+)	(70+)
Andhra Pradesh	4306	1425	6.47	2.14	102	106
Arunachal Pradesh	37	12	4.23	1.42	83	90
Assam	1186	448	5.29	2.00	81	76
Bihar	5227	1803	6.05	2.09	86	85
Goa	74	27	6.34	2.27	131	141
Gujarat	2540	966	6.15	2.34	107	113
Haryana	1230	528	7.47	3.21	93	81
Himachal Pradesh	402	164	7.79	3.18	89	87
Jammu & Kashmir	432	163	5.78	2.18	77	75
Karnataka	3041	1149	6.76	2.56	101	105
Kerala	2549	1006	8.77	3.46	115	121
Madhya Pradesh	4254	1583	6.43	2.39	98	100
Maharashtra	5453	1934	6.91	2.45	101	105
Manipur	109	40	5.94	2.19	88	92
Meghalaya	82	29	4.62	1.64	83	86
Mizoram	34	12	4.93	1.77	96	105
Nagaland	65	28	5.40	2.31	71	69
Orissa	2217	794	6.98	2.51	99	98
Punjab	1532	625	7.56	3.08	83	78
Rajasthan	2666	917	6.06	2.08	98	103
Sikkim	19	6	4.59	1.51	75	78
Tamil Nadu	4073	1408	7.29	2.52	92	90
Tripura	192	87	6.96	3.17	97	100
Uttar Pradesh	9250	3403	6.65	2.45	81	77
West Bengal	4087	1500	6.00	2.20	96	96
Andaman & Nichobar Islands	10	3	3.55	1.18	67	78
Chandigarh	29	11	4.52	1.73	83	87
Dadra Nagar Haveli	6	2	4.40	1.24	122	140
Daman & Diu	6	2	6.32	2.43	150	168
Delhi	444	154	4.71	1.63	85	86
Lakshadweep	3	1	5.22	1.68	92	93
Pondicherry	56	21	6.90	2.55	108	105
All India	55606	20252	6.58	2.40	94	93

Source: Irudaya Rajan, Mishra and Sarma, 1999.

standing the several analytical and statistical problems, it cannot be disputed that the preponderance of females in extreme old age needs to be brought to the attention of planners and policymakers.

According to the 1991 census, 78% of the Indian elderly lived in rural areas. The percentage of aged in rural areas was 7.22 compared to 5.37 in urban areas. Detailed analysis indicates that states and territories have shown a similar type of rural-urban pattern. Over the last 20 years, the rural share of elderly has increased steadily; four-fifths of Indian elderly are found in rural areas (Irudaya Rajan, Mishra, & Sarma, 1999).

Available research on population aging suggests that fertility plays a predominant role in inducing the aging process, compared to mortality. In India, there has been a substantial reduction in mortality compared to fertility since 1950. For instance, while the crude birth rate for India declined from 47.3 during 1951-61 to 22.8 in 1996, the crude death rate fell steeply from 28.5 to 8.4 during the same period. India is expected to have a faster decline in fertility in the immediate future compared to mortality because mortality is already at a low level. The aging process in India will, therefore, be faster than in other developing countries. Moreover, the transition from high to low fertility is expected to narrow the age structure at its base and broaden the age structure at the top. In addition, improvement in life expectancy at all ages will allow more old people to survive, thus intensifying the aging process. See Figure 1 (Irudaya Rajan & Mishra, 1995).

Moreover, the aging process is intensified owing to increased survival of elderly persons beyond ages 60 and 70, as shown in Table 4. As the table shows, males are expected to live 17 years beyond age 60 and 10 years beyond age 70; the corresponding years for females are 18 and 11, respectively, by the year 2021 (Irudaya Rajan & Mishra, 1995).

Both young and total dependency ratios have shown a consistent decline over time; however, old-age dependency ratios exhibit an increase. According to the 1991 census, the ratio was 11.8. The child dependency ratio was 67.0. In understanding dependency among the old, it is assumed that all those 60 years and older are dependent. But the available data indicate that many Indian elderly are self-sufficient or still working and therefore cannot be treated as dependent. Old-age dependency estimated on the basis of non-workers shows a much lower value than the one estimated on the basis of age only; the ratio drops from 11.8 to 7.42. Further, non-workers in the Indian census include renter/pensioners, beggars, and those in household duties who may otherwise be considered economically productive. Exclusion of these

FIGURE 1. Population Pyramids of India

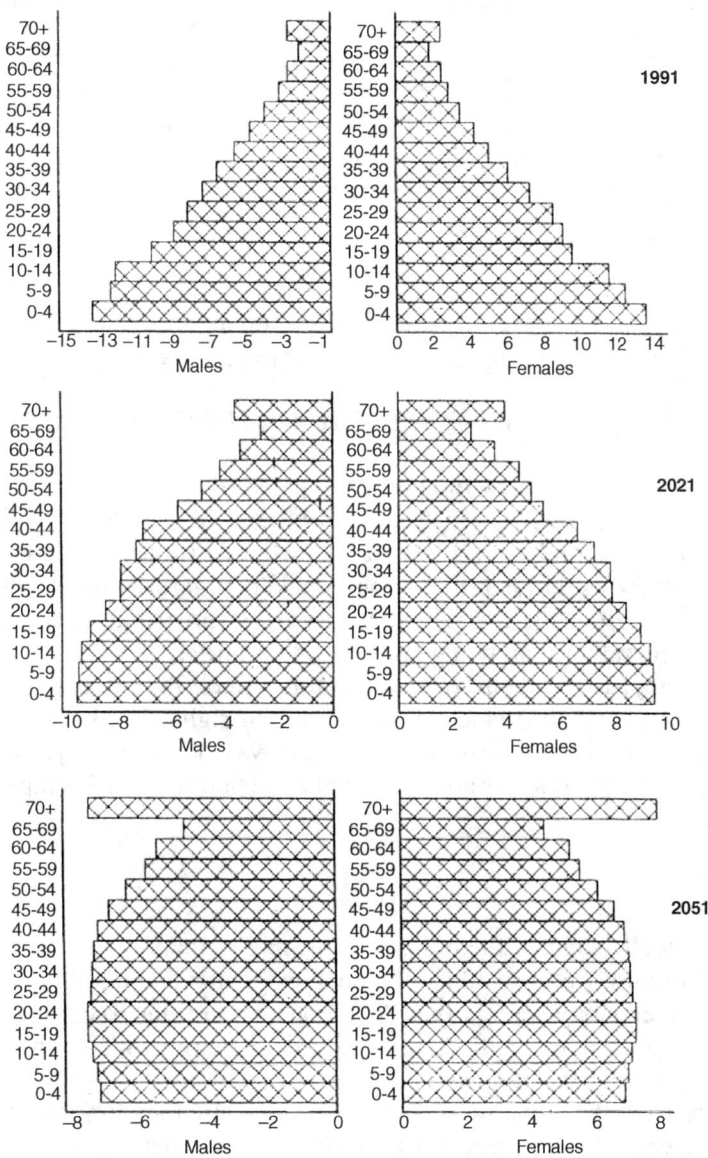

TABLE 4. Expectation of Life at Ages 60 and 70 for India

Year	Male		Female	
	e60	e70	e60	e70
1971	13.80	8.57	14.75	9.10
1981	14.25	8.83	15.31	9.42
1991	15.01	9.27	16.23	9.97
2001	15.74	9.70	17.05	10.45
2011	16.29	10.03	17.75	10.87
2021	16.75	10.32	18.18	11.14

Source: Estimated by the authors.

non-workers further reduces the old age dependency to 4.56. (For more details, see Irudaya Rajan, Mishra, & Sarma, 1999.)

SOCIAL AND ECONOMIC CHARACTERISTICS

Besides the numbers and proportions of elders, it is also pertinent to understand various characteristics of elders, such as level of literacy, marital status, and work status as revealed from the Indian censuses. These analyses will enlighten policymakers regarding the needs of the elderly and indicate the remedial measures for making older persons real assets rather than being considered liabilities.

Literacy, a prominent social indicator, reflects the extent to which the older people can be made conscious of their rights. Furthermore, marital status provides an insight into elders' way of life. Lastly, the nature of elders' economic dependence can be viewed from their employment status.

Literacy

The well-being of the elderly is intimately linked with their educational records because education enables greater adaptability to changing socioeconomic conditions. A "literate," according to the Indian census, is a person having the ability to read and write with an understanding in any regional language.

The data show the dismally low level of literacy among the aged, with greater discrepancy between the level of literacy in the general population and in the aged. Low-level literacy among the older population is understandable since they have spent much of their lives prior to the advent of accelerated socioeconomic development in the country. With a low overall literacy level in the country, the differential between younger and older generations has yet to narrow. The rural elderly seem to be more disadvantaged in this respect, as both quantity and quality of educational facilities in rural areas have been quite inferior compared to those in urban areas in the past. Older women are the least literate because of the existing gender differentials in literacy levels in the general population. Higher educational levels are most uncommon among the elderly. The literacy rate among elderly females in 1991 was 12.68%-30.76% and 7.51% in urban and rural areas, respectively. Of 100 elderly rural women, there were only eight literates! The trends between the 1961 and 1991 censuses reveal the following points: Literacy levels among elderly persons are low. Levels are extremely low in rural areas and especially so among women. In 1961, only Kerala had a rural female literacy of 15%. It is noteworthy that half of the female elderly in Kerala are literate. Many states and union territories had literacy levels below 5%. The situation has, however, changed considerably after 30 years as shown by the 1991 census. As of 1991, six states and union territories had elderly female literacy levels above 25% and only two states (Arunachal Pradesh and Rajasthan) had a literacy rate below 5%.

Surprisingly, between 1961 and 1991, the literacy levels among rural elderly women trebled not only in India in general, but in most states and union territories. Planners and policymakers should take note of the increasing literacy levels among elderly because the future elderly are expected to demand more social, financial, and health services compared to the present generation of old persons. Though the current literacy level among the aged is low, the future elderly are expected to be more literate and hence more demanding in terms of their rights and privileges.

Marital Status

Marital status of the elderly gains prominence from the consensus that married persons fare better than singles on a number of dimensions, for example, economic, social, emotional, and care-giving (Myers, 1986). A major concern is the increasing proportion of women in general and those widowed in particular. A much smaller proportion of men are widowed compared to women in extreme old ages. This gender disparity in widowhood is due to the longer life of women compared to men and the universal tendency for women to marry men older than themselves. Also, widowed men are much more likely to remarry.

Though the relationship between elderly well-being and their marital status cannot be spelled out precisely, any change in this status deserves special attention.

According to the 1991 census, married males accounted for 80.7% of the population against 44.2% for females. However, 54.0% of elderly women were widows versus 15.5% widowers. The gap in widowhood narrows among the old-old (70+). More than 67% of women aged 70 and above were widows in India as of 1991.

Work Status

Some studies have attempted to explain the consequences of the aging phenomenon on the basis of the conventional dependency ratios. A more satisfactory approach in this respect, however, is to base our conclusions on field surveys on work status according to assets, including land. Sample surveys conducted in rural India reflect a greater degree of financial insecurity among the aged. Inadequate financial resources have been indicated as one of the major problems of the Indian elderly (Desai, 1985). The financial inadequacy seems to be of a higher degree for female elderly compared to their male counterparts (Dak & Sharma 1987; Nandal, Khatri, & Kadian, 1987).

Another significant finding is the loss of economic independence with increased age (Kaur, Grover, & Aggarwal, 1987). In many situations, rural elderly continue to work, though their number of working hours decreases with increasing age (Singh, Singh, & Sharma, 1987). While examining economic sufficiency in another context, the same authors established that financial problems are more common among widows and among elders in nuclear families. They also indicated that economic insecurity is related to class and caste. Another observation in this regard by Punia and Sharma (1987) finds economic insecurity to be the sole concern of the elderly in barely sustainable households in rural India. The major sources of worries consist of social strain and economic dependence. The worries about social relations are greater compared to economic concerns for those who live in nuclear families or live alone (Shah, 1993). They worry about what will happen to them in case of sickness or disability. On the other hand, financial worries have their bearing on the social class to which they belong.

According to the National Sample Survey Organization (NSSO) 1986-87 study, 34.02% of the rural elderly were financially independent compared to 28.94% of their urban counterparts (NSSO, 1991). Of course, the situation varies from state to state. In Maharashtra, the dependence of rural elderly was 33% compared to 46% among the urban elderly (Dandekar, 1993). Aged females, especially those residing in the urban areas, were most dependent (Dandekar, 1996).

Analysis of labor force participation among the elderly is important from the point of view of understanding their economic dependence, given the fact of inadequate social security. The predominant rural character of the population, coupled with opportunities for insufficient wage and salaried employment, compel people to prolong their working lives as long as it is physically possible. Even in the case of self-employment, economic necessity forces many to continue work as long as they are able, although perhaps at a reduced pace. Analysis of the employment pattern of the working elderly shows that, on the whole, their work participation rates were on the decrease between 1961-91, irrespective of rural or urban residence. However, participation continues to be significantly higher in rural areas compared to urban areas.

Rates among elderly persons declined by 10 units between 1961 and 1981. With the reduction, there were 9 units and 7 units for rural and urban areas, respectively. However, between 1981 and 1991, the decline was only 1%. Detailed analysis indicates that, comparatively, more elderly men participate in economic activities than women. This may partly be due to the definitional problems related to women's work in the census (Leela Gulati, Irudaya Rajan, & Ramalingam, 1997). Surprisingly, however, the share of old age workers in agriculture has been on the increase over time, both in rural and urban areas. Almost 80% of aged workers in India worked in the agricultural sector in 1991.

Detailed investigation indicates that around 62% of elderly males work as cultivators, whereas 70% of females work as agricultural laborers. For the first time, in the 1981 census, the data on main workers were classified by marital status. It showed that 58% of widowed elderly worked as main workers in rural areas and 69% in urban areas. Confronted with the burden of maintaining themselves, elderly persons in India continue to work, even after reaching 60 years of age. In one of the group discussions among the rural elderly in India, we were told, "for us there is only one retirement, not from work, but from the world" (Irudaya Rajan, Mishra, & Sarma, 1999).

The Indian census also provides economic data on non-workers by categories such as household workers, beggars, students, pensioners, renters, and others. Although there are problems with defining non-workers, some crude observations can be made. As of 1991, around 40% of Indian women were involved in household duties indicating their active participation in maintaining and caring for their children and grandchildren. Another 5% are pensioners, 0.5% work as beggars, and 0.1% live in institutions for the aged and indigent. In a recent study conducted by the senior author, it was observed that there were 134 old age homes providing accommodation for 5000 elderly in Kerala (Irudaya Rajan, 2000). Only 56% of women and 67% of men were reported as dependents, and therefore need social assistance and support in their old age. According to the same census, the number of persons who required social assistance was found to be very low in West Bengal, followed by Tamil Nadu and Gujarat; the highest number was reported in Haryana, Punjab, and Rajasthan. For instance, the highest number of pensioners was reported in West Bengal, followed by Tamil Nadu and Gujarat. Surprisingly, only 23% of men and 4% of women receive pensions in Kerala. The highest number of women pensioners is found in Tamil Nadu, followed by Gujarat and West Bengal.

EMERGING AGING SCENARIO, 2001-2051

One of the major objectives of this paper has been to assess the emerging aging scenario of India in the first half of the 21st century (2001-2051). Towards this end, we have projected the elderly population of 25 states and seven union territories by dividing the country into six major regions: south, west, central, east, north, and northeast. Table 5 gives the distribution of the elderly falling in the 60+ category, and Table 6, those falling in the 80+ category. The tables profile the region-wise elderly classified by ages 60 and above and 80 and above in terms of size, proportion, and gender. The age pyramids present the emerging age structure of India, as seen in Figure 1.

A few comments on the projections are called for. We have used the 1991 census age structure as the base population, and the assumptions on fertility and mortality are based on the past trends as revealed from the Sample Registration System in India. The projection period ranges from 1991 to 2051. Given our assumptions regarding mortality, the projections are likely to be valid.

India's elderly population aged 60 and above is expected to increase from 71 million in 2001 to 179 million in 2031 and further to 301 million in 2051. The proportion is likely to reach 12% in 2031 and 17% in

TABLE 5. Number, Proportion, and Sex Ratio of Elderly (60+), 2001-2051

Region	Absolute Numbers (millions)					
	2001	2011	2021	2031	2041	2051
South	18.60	25.49	34.64	46.28	59.32	69.73
West	10.59	14.66	20.60	27.56	35.29	43.66
Central	16.17	21.03	28.13	37.09	50.86	69.88
East	15.03	20.86	29.36	38.77	51.39	67.33
North	8.23	11.17	15.92	22.17	30.04	39.01
Northeast	2.16	3.09	4.67	6.72	9.10	11.35
India	70.78	96.30	133.32	178.59	236.01	300.96
Region	Proportion					
	2001	2011	2021	2031	2041	2051
South	8.3	10.2	13.0	16.8	21.4	25.8
West	7.5	9.1	11.5	14.4	17.7	21.7
Central	6.4	6.8	7.5	8.4	9.9	11.9
East	6.8	8.0	9.9	11.7	14.4	17.8
North	6.6	7.4	9.0	11.1	13.6	16.5
Northeast	5.6	6.8	9.0	11.6	14.5	17.2
India	7.1	8.2	9.9	11.9	14.5	17.3
Region	Sex Ratio (m/f*1000)					
	2001	2011	2021	2031	2041	2051
South	954	966	942	897	927	939
West	980	1005	1000	974	1005	985
Central	1114	1069	1020	995	1084	1072
East	1070	1074	1030	975	1014	1018
North	1067	1070	1048	1025	1063	1028
Northeast	1139	1139	1084	985	978	993
India	1036	1034	1004	964	1008	1007

Note: According to the 1991 census, India was administratively divided into 25 states and 7 Union Territories. To make the discussion more meaningful, we have classified the 32 units into 6 regions geographically. Population projections are made by the authors.
South: Andhra Pradesh, Kerala, Karnataka, Tamil Nadu, Pondicherry, and Lakshadweep (6)
West: Goa, Gujarat, Maharashtra, Daman and Diu, and Dadra Nagar Haveli (5)
Central: Madhya Pradesh and Uttar Pradesh (2)
East: Bihar, Orissa, West Bengal, and Andaman & Nicobar Islands (4)
North: Delhi, Haryana, Himachal Pradesh, Jammu Kashmir, Punjab, Rajasthan, and Chandigarh (7)
Northeast: Arunachal Pradesh, Assam, Manipur, Meghalaya, Mizoram, Nagaland, Tripura, and Sikkim (8)

2051. As of 2001, South India has the highest number of elderly persons above 60 years and maintains its lead in the next 40 years (19 million in 2001 to 70 million in 2051). In fact, one-fourth of India's elderly persons live in South India, indicating the low fertility and high expectation of life at birth in the region (Guilmoto & Irudaya Rajan, 1998; Irudaya Rajan & Zachariah, 1998). The lowest numbers are expected in North-

TABLE 6. Number, Proportion, and Sex Ratio of Elderly (80+), 1991-2051

Region	Absolute Numbers (millions)					
	2001	2011	2021	2031	2041	2051
South	1.42	2.19	3.03	4.38	6.28	8.77
West	0.81	1.21	1.68	2.47	3.67	4.99
Central	1.21	1.68	2.21	3.09	4.42	6.02
East	1.08	1.64	2.28	3.39	5.98	6.73
North	0.70	0.95	1.24	1.87	2.90	4.22
Northeast	0.15	0.21	0.31	0.49	0.82	1.25
India	5.37	7.88	10.75	15.69	23.17	31.98
	Proportion					
Region	2001	2011	2021	2031	2041	2051
South	0.6	0.9	1.1	1.6	2.3	3.2
West	0.6	0.6	0.9	1.3	1.8	2.5
Central	0.5	0.5	0.6	0.7	0.9	1.0
East	0.5	0.6	0.8	1.0	1.4	1.8
North	0.6	0.6	0.7	0.9	1.3	1.8
Northeast	0.4	0.5	0.6	0.9	1.3	1.9
India	0.5	0.7	0.8	1.0	1.4	1.8
	Sex Ratio (m/f*1000)					
Region	2001	2011	2021	2031	2041	2051
South	859	781	760	765	700	644
West	848	803	819	812	752	713
Central	1199	1040	980	898	820	797
East	1067	928	919	878	785	724
North	1052	894	893	882	838	826
Northeast	1104	986	991	1021	967	904
India	998	884	866	843	774	732

Note: According to the 1991 census, India was administratively divided into 25 states and 7 Union Territories. To make the discussion more meaningful, we have classified the 32 units into 6 regions geographically. Population projections are made by the authors.
South: Andhra Pradesh, Kerala, Karnataka, Tamil Nadu, Pondicherry, and Lakshadweep (6)
West: Goa, Gujarat, Maharashtra, Daman and Diu, and Dadra Nagar Haveli (5)
Central: Madhya Pradesh and Uttar Pradesh (2)
East: Bihar, Orissa, West Bengal, and Andaman & Nicobar Islands (4)
North: Delhi, Haryana, Himachal Pradesh, Jammu Kashmir, Punjab, Rajasthan, and Chandigarh (7)
Northeast: Arunachal Pradesh, Assam, Manipur, Meghalaya, Mizoram, Nagaland, Tripura, and Sikkim (8)

east India. In fact, Central India, with the second highest number of elderly in 2001, is projected to increase its population at the same rate as South India by 2051. East India also follows South and Central India and is expected to reach 67 million in 2051.

Only South India is projected to reach 10% by 2011, while West India is expected to have an elderly population above 10% in 2021. However, except Central India, all other regions of India are projected to reach above 10% in 2031. Around 2051, South India is expected to have an elderly population above 25%, followed by West India with above 20%. Another three regions (East, North, and Northeast) will be above 15%, with the lowest expected in Central India. Excess elderly females are noted only in South India throughout the period under study.

The number of elderly persons above 70 years of age (old-old) is likely to increase more prominently than those 60 years and above. The old-old are projected to increase five-fold between 2001 to 2051 (from 27 million in 2001 to 132 million in 2051). Their proportion is expected to rise from 2.7 to 7.6. Although we have found excess males in the group aged 60 and above, the old-old sex ratio is very much favorable to females. In 2051, South India is expected to lead with the highest number (34 million) of old-old, followed by East and Central India, and the lowest is expected in the Northeast. However, the proportion of old-old is expected to be highest in South India, followed by West India and the lowest in Central India. South and West India are projected to have excess females throughout the study periods: other regions show excess females only in some periods.

The oldest-old group (80+) in India is expected to grow faster than any other age. In absolute numbers, it is likely to increase six-fold from 5.4 million in 2001 to 32.0 million in 2051. As expected, South India will lead with the highest numbers and proportions of oldest-old in the next half of the 21st century. From 2011 onwards, all regions are expected to have excess oldest-old females.

The old-age dependency ratio for India and the different regions within the country are almost similar in 1991 except Northeast India. However, the trend is expected to be different in 2051; 100 persons in the age group 15-59 will have to support 42 persons above 60 and more in South India. The ratios are 35 for West India and 28 for India as a whole. As of 2001, India has 20 elderly per 100 children, and the index is expected to reach 80 in 2051. South India and West India are expected to have more elderly persons over 60 compared to children. The projected indices are 172 and 127, respectively.

IMPLICATIONS FOR POLICY

The family as a single unit is likely to change. The old-age dependency will increase more quickly than the decline in child dependency. It will require a great deal of adjustment at the family level to accommodate and care for the elderly. While daughters and daughters-in-law are replacing their role as caregivers to their parents by working outside the home, a new challenge for elderly care will be posed. Day care centers, geriatric hospitals, and old-age homes are likely to play a major role in the living arrangements for the elderly (Irudaya Rajan, 2000).

The elderly are likely to become more vulnerable in the absence of a familial support network; thus, they will need a strong social security system. The current elderly who have not made adequate provision for old age may be in for a great deal of frustration during their old age. Social security measures for the prospective elderly may thus become imperative.

The increasing number and proportion of elderly will have a direct impact on the demand for health services. Currently, the Government of India runs various health programs targeted primarily at the needs of mothers and children. The primary health-care system is not geared up to meet the future challenges arising from an increase in chronic diseases. Conditions like hypertension and diabetes, which have higher incidence among the aged, will pose an increasing burden to the elderly themselves and to their families. Mobilizing additional resources for geriatric care will emerge as a major responsibility of health-care providers in countries like India. Achieving this without affecting maternal and pediatric care will be a challenge

AUTHOR NOTES

S. Irudaya Rajan is Associate Fellow at the Centre for Development Studies, Thiruvananthapuram, Kerala, India.

P. Sankara Sarma is Associate Professor of Health Sciences at the Achutha Menon Centre for Health Science Studies of the Sree Chitra Tirunal Institute for Medical Sciences and Technology, Thiruvananthapuram, Kerala, India.

U. S. Mishra is Research Associate at the Centre for Development Studies, Thiruvananthapuram, Kerala, India.

Dr. Irudaya Rajan can be contacted at the Centre for Development Studies, Trivandrum, Kerala, India (E-mail: sirajan@vsnl.com).

REFERENCES

Bass, Scott, A., Morris, R., & Oka, M. (Eds.) (1996). *Public Policy and Old Age Revolution in Japan.* Binghamton, NY: The Haworth Press, Inc.

Dak, T. M., & Sharma, M. L. (1987). Changing status of the aged in north Indian villages. In Sharma, M. L. & Dak, T. M. (Eds.), *Aging in India.* New Delhi: Ajanta Publications, pp. 43-55.

Dandekar, K. (1993). The aged, their problems and social intervention in Maharashtra. *Economic and Political Weekly*, *27*(23), pp. 1188-94.
Dandekar, K. (1996). *The Elderly in India*. New Delhi: Sage Publications.
Desai, K. G. (1985). Situation of the aged in India. *Journal of the Indian Anthropological Society*, *20*(3), 201-09.
Grigsby, J. (1993). Paths for future population aging. *The Gerontologist*, *31*(2), 195-203.
Guilmoto, Christophe Z., & Rajan, S. Irudaya (1998). *Regional Heterogeneity and Fertility Behaviour in India*. Working Paper No. 290. Trivandrum: Centre for Development Studies.
Irudaya Rajan, S., Mishra, U. S., & Mala Ramanathan (1993). Two child family in India: Is it realistic? *International Family Planning Perspectives*, *19*(4), pp. 125-128 & 154.
Irudaya Rajan, S. (1994). China's One Child Policy: Implication for Population Aging. *Economic and Political Weekly*, *29*(38), September 17, pp. 2502-06.
Irudaya Rajan, S., & Mishra, U. S. (1995). Defining old age: An Indian assessment. *Journal of United Nations Institute on Aging*, *5*(4), pp. 31-35.
Irudaya Rajan, S., Mishra, U. S., & Sarma, P. S. (1996). INDIA: National Aging Trends. In United Nations. *Life Long Preparation for Old Age in Asia and the Pacific*. New York: United Nations, pp. 79-104. ST/ESCAP/1684.
Irudaya Rajan, S., & Zachariah, K. C. (1998). Long-term implications of low fertility in Kerala, India. *Asia-Pacific Population Journal*, *13*(13), pp. 41-66.
Irudaya Rajan, S., Mishra, U. S., & Sarma, P. S. (1999). *India's Elderly: Burden or Challenge?* New Delhi: Sage Publications.
Irudaya Rajan, S. (1999). Aging and Social Security. In Prakash, B. A. (Ed.), *Kerala's Economic Development: Issues and Problems*. New Delhi: Sage Publications, pp. 49-71.
Irudaya Rajan, S. (2000). *Home Away from Home: A Survey of Old Age Homes and Inmates in Kerala*. Thiruvananthapuram: Centre for Development Studies Working Paper No. 306.
Kaur, Malkit, Grover, R. P., & Aggarwal, K. (1987). Socio-economic profile of the rural aged. In Sharma, M. L. & Dak, T. M. (Eds.), *Aging in India*. New Delhi: Ajanta Publications, pp. 67-75.
Leela Gulati, Irudaya Rajan, S., & Ramalingam, A. (1997). Women and work in Kerala: A Comparison of the 1981 and 1991 Censuses. *Indian Journal of Gender Studies*, *4*(2), pp. 231-52.
Mari Bhat, P. N., & Irudaya Rajan, S. (1990). Demographic transition in Kerala revisited. *Economic and Political Weekly*, *25* (35 & 36), September 1-8, pp. 1957-1980.
Mari Bhat, P. N. (1992). Changing demography of elderly in India. *Current Science*, *63*(8), October 25, pp. 440-48.
Mari Bhat, P. N., Navaneetham, K., & Irudaya Rajan, S. (1995). Maternal mortality in India: Estimates from a regression model. *Studies in Family Planning*, *26*(4), July/August, pp. 217-232.
Myers, G. C. (1986). *Cross-National Patterns and Trends in Marital Status Among the Elderly*. Paper presented to the conference on aged populations and the gray revolution, Universite Catholique de Louvain, Belgium, October.
Nandal, D. S., Khatri, R. S., & Kadian, R. S. (1987). Aging problems in the structural context. In Sharma, M. L. & Dak, T. M. (Eds.), *Aging in India*. New Delhi: Ajanta Publications, pp. 106-16.

National Sample Survey Organisation (1991). Socio-economic profile of the aged persons: NSS 42nd Round (July 1986-June 1987) *Sarvekshana, 15*(2). New Delhi: Author.

Punia, D., & Sharma, M. L. (1987). Family life of rural aged women. In Sharma, M. L. & Dak, T. M. (Eds.), *Aging in India*. New Delhi: Ajanta Publications, pp. 57-66.

Shah, V. P. (1993). *The Elderly in Gujarat*, Department of Sociology, Gujarat University, Ahmedabad (Mimeographed).

Singh, K., Singh, R., & Sharma, M. L. (1987). Problems of aged women in Haryana. In Sharma, M. L. & Dak, T. M. (Eds.), *Aging in India*. New Delhi: Ajanta Publications, pp. 134-144.

Sudha, S., & Irudaya Rajan, S. (1999). Female demographic disadvantage in India 1981-1991: Role of sex-selective abortions and female infanticide. *Development and Change, 30*(3), 585-618.

Treas, J., & Logue, B. (1986). Economic development and the older population. *Population and Development Review, 12*(4), pp. 645-673.

United Nations (1998). *World Population Projections to 2150*. Department of Economic and Social Affairs, Population Division. New York: Author.

World Bank (1994). *Averting the Old Age Crisis: Policies to Protect the Old and Promote Growth*. Oxford: Oxford University Press.

Zachariah, K. C., & Irudaya Rajan, S. (1997). Kerala's demographic transition: An overview. In Zachariah, K. C. & Irudaya Rajan, S. (Eds.), *Kerala's Demographic Transition: Determinants and Consequences*. New Delhi: Sage Publications, pp. 17-29.

Perspectives of Research on Aging in India

P. V. Ramamurti, PhD

Center for Research on Aging
Sri Venkateswara University, Tirupati, India

SUMMARY. Any social action plan, scheme, or program for welfare or intervention can be formulated only on the basis of data generated by research findings. Empirical data forms the backbone of the formulation of policy. This paper outlines the summary of the Indian research effort in the area of aging. An examination of the research trends shows both strengths and weaknesses. The generation of large and varied pieces of data across disciplines is a strength, while the absence of methodological rigor, integration of research effort, and the building of theory are the lacunae. The needs of the elderly, elder-care issues, State vs. family care, elder abuse, interventional and action plan research are some areas that need accentuation. Documentation of data, creation of databases, and a national body for overseeing research are requirements that cannot be delayed any longer. *[Article copies available for a fee from The Haworth Document Delivery Service: 1-800-HAWORTH. E-mail address: <docdelivery@haworthpress.com> Website: <http://www.HaworthPress.com> © 2003 by The Haworth Press, Inc. All rights reserved.]*

KEYWORDS. Indian elderly, aging policy, research on aging, elder abuse

---

[Haworth co-indexing entry note]: "Perspectives of Research on Aging in India." Ramamurti, P. V. Co-published simultaneously in *Journal of Aging & Social Policy* (The Haworth Press, Inc.) Vol. 15, No. 2/3, 2003, pp. 31-43; and: *An Aging India: Perspectives, Prospects, and Policies* (ed: Phoebe S. Liebig, and S. Irudaya Rajan) The Haworth Press, Inc., 2003, pp. 31-43. Single or multiple copies of this article are available for a fee from The Haworth Document Delivery Service [1-800-HAWORTH, 9:00 a.m. - 5:00 p.m. (EST). E-mail address: docdelivery@haworthpress.com].

INTRODUCTION

"Knowledge is power" is an old adage. The knowledge of aging empowers us to provide for a better quality of life for the aged. Sound knowledge generated through sustained research alone can form the basis for scientific formulations of policy and planning that are data-driven. Therefore, the importance of research on aging can hardly be overstressed.

India is in the throes of a temporally compacted demographic transition. The Indian population has been growing fast. It has nearly trebled in the last 50 years (1950-2001), while the number of elderly has increased by four times in the same period (see Table 1).

By the year 2021, the elderly population is likely to double. The average life expectancy (at birth), which was about 39 in 1951, is now around 65, and it may become 70 in the next 20 years. The birth rate is expected to decrease to 15 (by 2021) from 45 in 1951. These figures indicate a phenomenal growth in the elderly population, with the probability of many of them living to a ripe old age. At the same time, with the crude birth rate sharply dropping, it is expected that the number of younger carers (adult children) will be greatly reduced. This phenomenon of demographic transition, the predominantly rural-based elderly population, the out-migration of children of aged parents from the villages to the towns, cities, and other countries, and the low educational level of most of these elderly who are living in conditions of poverty and poor hygiene have made the lot of the elderly difficult and deplorable.

Thus, India, despite being a country with a tradition of good elder care, is facing many affronts that seem to threaten the status of the elderly. In view of these developments, only research on the elderly in In-

TABLE 1. Total Indian Population and the Elderly Population (in Millions) 1950-2025

Group	1951	1991	2001	2021
Total	356.0	827.2	964.1	1228.8
60+	20.1	60.5	81.4	177.5
Percent	5.62	7.31	8.44	14.45

Source: Sharma, S.P. & Xenos, P. Ageing in India: Demographic Background and Analysis (Based on Census Materials. Occasional papers, Census of India, 1997).

dia will provide basic information on various facets of the life and living of this fast-growing population.

The functions of aging research in India would be three-fold. First, research is expected to provide basic normative data on the overall status and needs of the elderly. This could form the basis for policy and planning. Second, research is aimed at understanding the ingredients of a good quality of life for the elderly. Third, research is to be directed towards the formulation, execution, and evaluation of appropriate interventions to improve the lot of the elderly.

India is a land of varied subcultures with scores of languages and myriad dialects. Carrying out studies across the length and breadth of this country is no easy task. While conducting surveys involving different language groups, the investigator translates and adapts the test or schedule to be used to the regional language, ensuring semantic equivalence. While dealing with illiterate persons, the investigator interviews them and records the responses. Despite standardization of interviewing and recording procedures, some variation in interviewer effect on responses cannot be entirely ruled out.

EARLY RESEARCH ON AGING

Although interest in India in the prevention of aging is ancient, its scientific study is of recent origin. Ayurveda, "The Science of Life," is an ancient Indian system of medicine. It mentions various plant and vegetable preparations that have favorable effects on rejuvenation and on improving cognition and memory, while generally promoting health and longevity. Many of these preparations, like the "Ginseng" of China, have evoked modern pharmacological interest for their roles in retarding aging changes.

On the psychosocial aspects, there are the prescriptions of Sage *Manu* (the Hindu law giver) in his *Dharmashastra* with regard to the do's and don'ts in old age. Manu suggests disengagement and gradual noninvolvement in the family and mundane activities during old age, while trying to lead a very simple life, close to nature, with limited needs. The process of aging and old age have been considered integral parts of the process of development of the life course, set against the backdrop of births and rebirths. According to Manu (Manu Smriti, 1932), the life course is divided into several stages. They are Balya (childhood), Brahmacharya (adolescence and youthhood), Grishastha (wedded adulthood), Vanaprastha (early old age), and Sanyasa (late old age). Old age is supposed to begin at 60 years. Its onset is celebrated as "Shastipurthi" or the completion of 60 years. It also marks the completion of the stage of establishing a family and rearing children. The stage of Vanaprastha is a period when the individual gradually disengages from the bonds of family life and trains himself for the next stage, Sanyasa. During Sanyasa there is a complete renunciation of bondage, and time is spent in prayer and penance, preparing to die (i.e., for the release of the soul from the mortal body). Many ancient writers and poets have discussed at length the problems of old age. But scientific interest in aging is a 20th-century, post-independence (1947) phenomenon.

It was in the 1950s for the first time that a few articles on aging appeared in journals (e.g., Amesur, 1959; Ramamurti, 1956), followed by a few scientific studies in the early 1960s (Ramamurti & Parameswaran, 1963, 1964). The early doctoral theses in psychosocial gerontology also appeared in the late 1960s and 1970s (Anantharaman, 1976; Marula Siddaiah, 1970; Paintal, 1971; Ramamurti, 1968). The 1970s also saw a wider range of articles covering the fields of biology and the various social sciences, such as psychology, sociology, anthropology, and social work. This constitutes the pre-1982 era (Ramamurti & Jamuna, 1984, 1993a, 1993b, 1995).

The United Nation's "Vienna Declaration" of the International Year of the Elderly in 1982 spurred research activity in aging in India. The founding of the Association of Gerontology (India) in 1982 and the Geriatric Society of India, already established in 1979, brought Gerontologists in India together. The teaching of aging as part of the Master's Course was first started in the Department of Psychology at the Sri Venkateswara University in 1978 and was later raised to the level of a Masters specialization in 1989. A Center for Research on Aging was started at the same University in 1983. Soon, a string of conferences, seminars, and research projects was organized that heralded a general awareness in aging that gradually built up research interest countrywide (Ramamurti, 1996; Ramamurti & Jamuna, 1993a, 1993b).

THE TRENDS

As of today, more than a 1000 academic articles in refereed journals, more than 50 major research projects, and a score of PhDs have occurred in the area of aging. Three refereed journals and three popular magazines exist on aging. Funding agencies like the University Grants Commission (UGC), the Indian Council of Medical Research (ICMR), the Indian Council of Social Science Research (ICSSR), and the Department of Welfare, Government of India consider aging as one of their priority areas. The University Grants Commission (UGC) has offered Special Assistance for Research in Aging and Life Span Development to the Department of Psychology, S. V. University, and the Department of Zoology (Biochemistry Laboratory), Benares Hindu University for aging research. In 1999, the International Year of the Elderly, a national policy on aging was formulated by the Ministry of Welfare, Government of India (now the Ministry of Social Justice and Empowerment), with a National Council for Older Persons (NCOP) created to monitor the implementation. The ICMR, which was the first to constitute a task force on aging, has also developed a research agenda on aging. With these developments, Indian research on aging is fast coming of age.

Biomedical Research

The research output in the social and behavioral sciences predominates when compared to the biological and medical fields. This may be because there are more researchers in the social and behavioral sciences, and social issues of aging are comparatively of greater common concern. There is a host of biological changes with aging that are universal. Biological research in aging is likely to hold good across cultures except to the extent to which cultural factors may modify age-related biological changes. Biological research in the area of aging in India started with the work of Kanungo and his team at the Biochemistry Laboratory, Department of Zoology, Benaras Hindu University in the 1960s (Kanungo & Singh, 1965). These studies mostly pertained to aging changes at the molecular level and the role of genes. The work has been continuing since the 1960s, resulting in a significant contribution by the Benaras group to the understanding of aging (Kanungo, 1975, 1980, 1994; Thakur, 1984).

Other places where significant contributions in the field of biology have been made are Guru Nanak Dev University, Amritsar (Mahajan et al., 1991); University of Gwalior (Patro, 1991; Patro et al., 1991); Kurukshetra University (Sharma et al., 1991); Jawaharlal Nehru University, New Delhi (Singh & Sriram, 1996); Central University of Hyderabad (Subba Rao, 1993; Subba Rao & Bhaskar, 1996); and Aligarh Muslim University, Aligarh (Hasan, 1985, 1996). The research covered areas such as gene aging, DNA repair, nutrition and aging, the role of free radicals in aging, the role of neurotoxins, the role of gonadotropic hormones, etc. However, the research effort in the biology of aging needs to be diversified to cover other areas.

Basic medical research in India in the area of aging is very recent. Inasmuch as most medical professionals treat disease conditions in the elderly along with those in other age groups, the elderly get care anyway. No special efforts were made to carry out in-depth research by any institution concerned with geriatric conditions. However, the Indian Council of Medical Research (ICMR) constituted a task force to investigate morbidity in the aged (Rao, 1986, 1990). A geriatric outpatient service and a geriatric ward were created at the Government General Hospital, Madras. Recently, a course in geriatrics was started at the Madras Medical College for the first time in the country (Natarajan, 1997). A geriatric counseling center was also started in the All India Institute of Medical Sciences, Delhi (Kumar, Dey, & Nagarkar, 1993). Very recently (1999), the ICMR formulated a national plan of research and policy in medical aspects of aging at a meeting convened in collaboration with the World Health Organization (WHO). The ICMR noted that, at the moment, the organization of medical and health services for the elderly is poor and recommended a series of steps. However, a survey of medical research in the area of aging in India gives the impression that it is still in an embryonic stage (Bela, 1994a, 1994b). Prioritizing research efforts and interventions in the area of geriatrics and a National Health Policy for the elderly are needed to emphasize the preventive aspects of disease and the general promotion of health in the elderly as a positive goal in itself. The WHO on its part has been urging the developing countries for a long time to act in this regard.

Behavioral and Social Sciences

Though behavioral and social aspects of aging are amenable to cultural and environmental influences, they differ from culture to culture. The research output in the areas of the behavioral and social sciences in India has far outweighed that of the biological and medical sciences. The investigations came chiefly from the disciplines of psychology, sociology, social work, and anthropology. Overall, more than a 1000 articles have been published covering these areas since 1960. The ICSSR (New Delhi); the National Institute of Public Cooperation and Community Development (NIPCCD), New Delhi; the Center for Research on Aging (CEFRA), S. V. University, Tirupati; and more recently, HelpAge India (New Delhi) are continuing to document the publications in the behavioral and social sciences. The work in the field of behavioral sciences has been reviewed since 1984 (Bali, 1995; Ramamurti & Jamuna, 1984, 1993a, 1995, 1999). Research in the social and behavioral sciences is fast spreading through the length and breadth of the country. Recently, HelpAge India, through a series of four regional seminars, reviewed the research work on aging in the country and came out with a consolidated report on the state of the art in research on aging in India (*R & D Journal, HelpAge (India)*, 1999).

In the behavioral and social sciences, all aspects of aging have not been uniformly researched. Some areas have been well-covered, certain others were moderately covered, while in a few areas the coverage has been inadequate. The areas fairly well or moderately covered are problems of adjustment and coping, retirement, life satisfaction, the elderly in the family, caregiving, social supports, attitudes, intergenerational interactions, leisure utilization roles, techno social changes and the family, elder care across subcultures, impact of demographic changes, quality of life, and widowhood problems (Jamuna, 1999; Ramamurti & Jamuna, 1999).

The following areas need more research: mental health; disability; family ties; health behavior; personality characteristics; motivation; frustration; tolerance levels; loneliness; psychosocial, economic and other needs; elder abuse; the elder as a resource and human resource development; euthanasia; meaning in life and values; psychological morbidity of various types; cognition and memory; longevity-related variables; housing needs and living arrangements; the economic status of the elderly in the country; the human resource potential of the elderly; and service needs of the elderly (Jamuna, 1999).

THE STRENGTHS AND WEAKNESSES

As is evident from this overview of developments, interest in aging research in India is only a few decades old. There is no doubt that the research effort is gathering momentum. Its major strength is that it is still in its infancy, which provides the distinct possibility of planning and determining its course of development. It is possible to lay down a plan, determine the priorities and emphases, and control the course of its future development. This must be a national exercise to be carried out by an expert body empowered to initiate, monitor, and make necessary course corrections on the basis of periodic evaluations of its progress. Also, since aging is multidisciplinary, there must be coordination and cooperation in drawing up themes of research that could be interdisciplinary or at least complementary.

The review of developments in the field of aging also points to certain broad lacunae. A significant drawback of these studies is that a majority of them were carried out on insufficient, unrepresentative samples in small pockets of the country. On many aspects, there are no national data that can be used to represent the status of the country, even in a remote sense. Therefore, organizations like the UGC, ICSSR, ICMR, DST, and the Welfare Department need to organize national surveys on representative populations of the elderly. Only such data can be used as a basis for policy planning or for drawing up intervention and rehabilitation programs. This is an urgent requirement. Also, these agencies need to take up projects of applied or action research in the community.

Many of the conditions observed in the elderly have their roots in the earlier years. Therefore, for a better understanding of the phenomena and to be able to work with elders effectively, we need knowledge on how they originate and how they develop over the years and come to be what they are in old age. In other words, there is the need to have a life-span approach in the understanding of these conditions as they pertain to India. Research has to emphasize developmental studies that trace characteristics as individuals grow old. Such research is better carried out by organizations or a team of persons rather than by single individuals. Also, since various disciplines are involved in the study of these characteristics, it would be useful if interdisciplinary teams could undertake such work across a phase of the life span.

A further examination of the existing studies, particularly in the social and behavioral sciences, reveals that many studies suffer from shortcomings that exclude them from being seen as valid and reliable. Some of these are discussed as follows. For any set of findings to be useful for application and adoption, they must be representative of the population parameter they are supposed to cover. Procedures of sampling adopted heretofore leave much to be desired. Standard procedures, such as stratified random sampling of a population parameter, are essential to ensure representativeness. Also, the procedure adopted in sampling in a given study needs to be described in detail so that the reader can evaluate the procedure and make a decision regarding its applicability and use.

The tools used in data collection should enable the investigator to cull the critical information needed by him. The tools need to have fairly good validity and reliability for use on a desired population. Casually constructed instruments without following psychometric procedures, or instruments standardized on populations in countries other than India and the subculture in question, generate invalid and unreliable data.

In Indian research, there has been a continuing problem of proper dissemination of research findings. In view of the absence of international journals on aging published in India, the articles get published in Indian journals of diverse disciplines that do not have a wide circulation or do not emphasize aging problems.

There is no well-established central documentation or database facility to get at aging research in India. As a result, many investigators in the field of aging in India are often unaware of the amount of published work. With journals published abroad being prohibitively costly, even institutions are unable to purchase them within their allotted budgets. This has become a significant handicap to many Indian researchers, particularly in the social and behavioral sciences. This situation needs to be urgently redressed. Online database facilities are beginning to be made available at a few centers. It is only the annual academic meetings in the field of aging (e.g., Association of Gerontology, India) that provide a forum and a meeting place for gerontologists to exchange information.

Yet another weakness of social science research to date has been that the important basic research findings with potential implications for welfare never reach the service providers, caregivers, and policymakers. Development of appropriate strategies for the dissemination of knowledge for successful aging is an important need. Many students, who work on aging for their Masters degree or PhD or those who take up funded projects, stop their work on completion of the project and the writing of the report. Many useful studies remain on the shelves. They are not disseminated through publications and consequently do not become available to users. Sometimes the works get published in obscure journals that are unavailable to practitioners.

THE FUTURE

Any program directed towards a better quality of life for the elderly or their general welfare must be based on research. Research, too, must have a direction and a driving force; otherwise, it will be like a rudderless ship drifting aimlessly on the high seas. Promotion of longevity that is disability-free and with a good quality of life that would be a resource rather than a liability to the community is the goal of gerontological research. Funding organizations must ensure that the research proposals they support meet these objectives.

Indian research on aging has an insufficient and unorganized output. A quick comprehensive profile of the Indian elderly is simply not available at this time. For example, we do not have data on the various needs of the Indian elderly, so we cannot fashion our programs appropriately. We lack national data on the prevalence of the variety of morbidities in the elderly in India, their contexts, and associated factors. We have to develop safe and effective models of interventional research that would serve the cause of the elderly. In a country where two-thirds of the elderly are poor and where the government simply cannot afford to prioritize funded elder care, what strategies must be adopted to buttress the sagging potential of the family to continue as the primary caregiver? What are the priorities for short-term and long-term interventions? These are research questions, among many others, that the directors of research and planners of research policy must address in the immediate future.

The national policy on the elderly, prepared in consultation with experts in the field and promulgated by the Ministry of Social Justice and Empowerment, has stressed the importance of research, particularly policy-relevant research, on the elderly. The policy has underscored the role of governmental and non-governmental agencies to fund and organize research on the elderly, plan and execute interventions, and make available the data thus collected to the policy-making bodies. The policy suggests that research on aging may be prioritized by the different funding agencies in a coordinated fashion. A National Council of Older Persons (NCOP) has been constituted to deal with all matters pertaining to the elderly, including research. Several other Ministries, including the Ministry of Health and Ministry of Human Resource Development, have been asked to facilitate studies of relevant aspects of aging in the institutions under their control. In view of these developments, it is expected that research on aging in India will get the necessary push.

The scope for future Indian research on aging is tremendous. Qualified manpower to handle the research may be a current shortcoming, but with encouragement, incentives, and prioritizing, the situation should correct itself in the near future. Thanks to the media, there is a fast-growing awareness of the problems of aging in India. The major research funding organizations have appreciated the importance of aging research and put aging as an area of thrust. Of course, aging needs a lobby in parliament. We also need a political will to give a head start for aging research. With these possibilities, the research effort can improve. Scientific effort, backed by organized, goal-directed research, is the only way to ensure a livelier longevity.

AUTHOR NOTES

Professor P. V. Ramamurti, after a distinguished academic career including a Fulbright fellowship to work at the Andrus Gerontology Center, University of Southern California, Los Angeles, in 1983, is presently Professor Emeritus and Honorary Director, Center for Research on Aging, Department of Psychology, S. V. University, Tirupati, India. As a pioneer in the area of aging research in India, he was responsible for introducing, for the first time in India, the subject of aging as a Master- and Doctoral-level specialization at his university. He has to his credit a score of research projects, and more than a hundred publications in the area of aging. He has been involved as an Expert Consultant for the formulation of National Policy for Older Persons, India, and is a member of the National Council for Older Persons. He is also a member of the Expert consultant group for preparing an agenda for aging research at the United Nations. Widely traveled, Professor Ramamurti is recipient of several national and international Awards for his contribution to aging.

Professor P. V. Ramamurti can be contacted at the Center for Research on Aging, Department of Psychology, S. V. University, Tirupati–527 502–India (E-mail: ramu14@nettlinx.com).

REFERENCES

Amesur, C. A. (1959). Welfare services for the aged and the infirm. *Indian Journal of Social Work, 20*(3), 157-162.

Anantharaman, R. N. (1976). *Psychology of aging: A study of adjustment.* Doctoral dissertation, Bangalore University, Bangalore.

Bali, Arun P. (1995). Status of gerontology and geriatric research in India. An overview and guidance for further research. *Research & Development Journal, 1*(2), 17-29.

Bela Shah (1994a). Geriatric research in India: ICMR's perspective. In Vinodh Kumar (Ed.). *Aging–Indian perspective and global scenario. Proceedings of the International Symposium on Gerontology & 7th AGI Conference,* New Delhi, 24-94.

Bela Shah (1994b). Ageing in India. In C. R. Ramachandran & Bela Shah (Eds.). *Public Health Implications of Ageing in India,* New Delhi, 84-88.

Hasan, M. (1985). Age related changes in various regions of the brain: Correlation with neurotoxilogical alterations. *Ann. Natl. Acad. Med. Sci. (India), 21,* 69-91.

Hasan, M. (1996). Mitochondria, free radicals and aging. In Vinodh Kumar (Ed.). *Aging–Indian perspective and global scenario. Proceedings of the International Symposium on Gerontology & 7th AGI Conference,* New Delhi, 419-422.

Jamuna, D. (1999). Challenges of changing socio-economic and psychological status of the aged. *R&D Journal, HelpAge (India), 5*(1), 5-13.

Kanungo, M. S. (1975). A model for aging. *J. Theo. Biol., 53,* 253-261.

Kanungo, M. S. (1980). *Biochemistry of Aging.* London: Academic Press.

Kanungo, M. S. (1994). *Genes and Aging.* Cambridge: Cambridge University Press.

Kanungo, M. S., & Singh, S. N. (1965). Effect of age on the isoenzymes of lactic dehydrogenase of the heart and brain of the rat. *Biochem. Biophs. Res. Commun., 21,* 454-459.

Kumar, V., Dey, A. B., & Nagarkar, K. (1993). Ageing: Current perspectives. In P. M. Dalal (Ed.). *Current Concepts in Internal Medicine.* Bombay: Assoc. Physicians of India, 155-162.

Mahajan, S., Garg., S. K., & Sharma, S. P. (1991). AT Pase and NADH-Dehydrogenase activities in ageing caryedon Serratus oliver. In Rameshwar Singh & G. S. Singhal (Eds.). *Perspectives in Ageing Research.* New Delhi: Today & Tomorrow Pubs., 57-59.

Manu-Smriti. (1932). Stages of life course. In M. Ganganath Jha (Ed.), *Manu Bashya of Medhatithi.* Calcutta: Calcutta Asiatic Society of Bengal.

Marula Siddaiah, H. M. (1970). The declining authority of old people. *Indian Journal of Social Work, 27*(2), 175-185.

Natarajan,V. S. (1997a). Geriatrics: A new discipline. *Indian Journal of Community Guidance, 4*(1), 63-70.

Paintal, H. K. (1971). *Study of social and emotional adjustment to aging in medical men.* Doctoral dissertation, NIMHANS, Bangalore.

Patro, I. K. (1991). Lipofuscinolysis by four neurotropic agents: A comparative study. In Rameshwar Singh & G. S. Singhal (Eds.). *Perspectives in Ageing Research.* New Delhi: Today & Tomorrow Pubs., 133-136.

Patro, N., Sharma, S. P., & Patro, I. K. (1991). Meclophenoxate and myocardial lypofuscin. In Rameshwar Singh & G. S. Singhal (Eds.). *Perspectives in Ageing Research.* New Delhi: Today & Tomorrow Pubs., 137-139.

R & D Journal, HelpAge (India) (1999). *5*(1), 5-13.

Ramamurti, P. V. (1956). Interest in music among the young and the elderly. In B. Kuppaswamy (Ed.). *Proceedings of the Regional Conference of Psychology,* Mysore, University of Mysore.

Ramamurti, P. V. (1968). *A study of some factors related to the adjustment of urban aged men.* Doctoral dissertation, S.V. University, Tirupati.

Ramamurti, P. V. (1996). The psycho-social scenario of the elderly: Problems, priorities and perspectives. *Research and Development Journal, 3*(1), 3-9.

Ramamurti, P. V., & Jamuna, D. (1984). Psychological research on the aged in India. *Journal of Anthropological Society of India, 19*(3), 269-286.

Ramamurti, P. V., & Jamuna, D. (1993a). Psychological dimensions of aging in India. *Indian Journal of Social Science, 6*(4), 309-331.

Ramamurti, P. V., & Jamuna, D. (1993b). India. In Erdman B. Palmore (Ed.). *Developments and Research on Aging: An International Handbook.* Westport: Greenwood Press, 145-158.

Ramamurti, P. V., & Jamuna, D. (1995). Perspectives of geropsychology. *Indian Psychological Abstracts & Reviews, 2*(2), 208-267.

Ramamurti, P. V., & Jamuna, D. (1999). Frontiers of ageing. In S. D. Gokhale et al. (Ed.). *Ageing in India.* Bombay: Somaiya Pubs. Pvt. Ltd, 205-215.

Ramamurti, P. V., & Parameswaran, E. G. (1963). A study of bilateral transfers on a mirror drawing task in the old and the young. *Journal of Psychological Researches, 7*(2), 1-3.

Ramamurti, P. V., & Parameswaran, E. G. (1964). A study of the figure reversals in the old and young. *Journal of Psychological Researches, 8*(1), 6-8.

Rao, Venkoba A. (1986). *Depressive Disorders.* New Delhi: ICMR.

Rao, Venkoba A. (1990). *Health Care of the Rural Aged.* New Delhi: ICMR.

Sharma, S. P., & Xenos, P. (1997). *Aging in India: Demographic Background and Analysis.* New Delhi: Census of India.

Sharma, S. P., Gupta, S. K., James, T. J., & Patro, I. K. (1991). Influence of centrophenoxine on protein malnourishment. Induced lipid peroxidation and lipfuscion in rat spinal cord. In Rameshwar Singh & G. S. Singhal (Eds.). *Perspectives in Ageing Research*. New Delhi: Today & Tomorrow Pubs., 117-125.

Singh Rameshwar, & Sriram, A.V. (1996). Ascorbic acid and αtocopherol in the ageing rat brain hippocampus and the effect of amino guanidine. In Vinodh Kumar (Ed.). Aging–Indian perspective and global scenario. *Proceedings of the International Symposium on Gerontology & 7th AGI Conference*, New Delhi, 439-441.

Subba Rao, K. (1993). Genomic damage and its repair in young and aging brain. *Molecular Neurobiology, 7*, 23-48.

Subba Rao, K., & Bhaskar, M. S. (1996). Alterations in DNA structure in ageing neurons. In Vinodh Kumar (Ed.). *Aging–Indian perspective and global scenario. Proceedings of the International Symposium on Gerontology & 7th AGI Conference*, New Delhi. 415-418.

Thakur, M. K. (1984). Age related changes in the structure and function of chromatin–a review. *Mech. Age. Dev, 27*, 263-286.

ECONOMICS, HEALTH, AND SOCIAL NETWORKS

Economic Security for the Elderly in India: An Overview

S. Vijaya Kumar, PhD

Council for Social Development, Hyderabad, India

SUMMARY. The basic concept of social security is not new in India. Traditionally, a sort of moral economy existed to provide security to older destitute and other vulnerable groups in society. However, gradually, traditional support systems are disappearing, and state-based social security systems have come into existence. Under standardized economic security policies, government is covering retirement benefits for those in the organized sector; economic security benefits for those in the unorganized sector; and old-age pension for rural elderly. These are contributory as well as non-contributory programs. Besides life insurance approaches, savings-linked insurance and *Annapurna* (food security) are other important programs. However, in terms of coverage, program quality and effectiveness have been largely criticized by social security experts, suggesting immediate reforms to old-age programs. *[Article copies available for a fee from The Haworth Document Delivery Service: 1-800-HAWORTH. E-mail address: <docdelivery@haworthpress.com> Website: <http://www.HaworthPress.com> © 2003 by The Haworth Press, Inc. All rights reserved.]*

KEYWORDS. Tradition, contributory, non-contributory, formal, informal, reforms

INTRODUCTION

Economic security for the elderly in India is in transition. Traditional systems of support and concepts of retirement are gradually giving way to new approaches. While there is no widespread social insurance mechanism as is found in the United States and many other developed nations, the Indian states and Central Government have developed a limited number of retirement income programs. As of 1997, nearly 23.8 million of India's more than 70 million elderly had some kind of pension coverage (Government of India, 1999). The extent to which these programs are effective in providing economic security, especially for the significant numbers of the elderly poor, is an important issue as India becomes a rapidly aging society.

TRADITIONS OF ECONOMIC SECURITY AND RETIREMENT

Before the latter part of the 20th century, the traditional support systems of the joint family, kin, and community provided economic security for older Indians. The primary responsibility of the joint family system of multi-generational co-residence has been to protect its dependent members. This system has provided income, health care, and personal, physical, and emotional security for all family members, including the elderly. Old age was viewed as a stage of wisdom, maturity, prestige, and power, with respect accorded to elderly persons, especially to the oldest male. By contrast, older women, especially widows, were less revered under the patrilineal system. A variety of factors, however, such as urbanization, migration, and industrialization, have weakened these traditional customs and bonds.

The concept of social security, as assistance and insurance, is not new for India. It began in the post-Vedic period, with various rules laid down for the regulation of guilds, whose main purpose was collective security for life, prosperity, and freedom from want and misery (Irudaya Rajan, 1999). In addition, the disabled and elderly destitutes–those with no income and no families to provide support–were looked after by the community. Traditionally, a sort of "moral economy" existed to provide security to older destitutes and other vulnerable groups in society. Even poor families without any productive assets, such as cultivatable land, were able to provide such security through barter and exchange or under the Jajmani system. Under this system, poor families provided services to rich families and, in turn, received daily food and clothes once or twice a year (Vijaya Kumar, 1995).

The idea of retirement as a life stage also is not new. Of the four stages (ashramas) of the life span, two focused on old age: vanaprastha, covering the years of 60 to 80, was the age of retirement; sanya or the time of renunciation, covered the years 80 to 100. Each of the four stages included specific roles and had its own code of conduct. From birth to death, an individual was socially and economically protected, according to this ancient tradition.

Retirement for most older Indians, however, has not been and is not the norm today. Those working in the "organized sector" (primarily government employees), who constitute 10% of the working population, are subject to mandatory retirement. For the Central Government, retirement at age 60 is required and at ages 55-60 for nearly all state government employees.

Almost 90% of workers are found in the agricultural sector where there is no retirement age. Rural elderly continue to work but they reduce the number of hours worked, especially with increasing age (Singh, Dak, & Sharma, 1987; Singh, Singh, & Sharma, 1987). About 40% of older men are cultivators, while 65% of older women are agricultural laborers, with widows predominating. Only 16.5% of rural elders get any kind of pension or retirement benefit, compared to 48.2% in urban areas (Irudaya Rajan, Mishra, & Sarma, 1999).

ECONOMIC STATUS OF THE ELDERLY: A BRIEF OVERVIEW

The majority (about 80%) of India's elders still reside in rural areas; 40% live below the poverty line, with nearly 33% just above it (National Sample Survey Organization [NSSO], 1998). As revealed in some small-scale surveys, inadequate financial resources are a major problem of Indian elders, with a higher degree of economic insecurity among older women (Irudaya Rajan, Mishra, & Sarma, 1999). The most vulnerable are those who do not own productive assets, have little or no savings or income from investments made earlier, have no pension or retirement benefits, and are not taken care of by their children; or they live in families that have low and uncertain incomes and a large number of dependents (Bose, 1996; Vijaya Kumar, 1990). Levels of economic security also are related to social class and caste (Punia & Sharma, 1987). Annual per capita income of all Indians, while up from 10,919 rupees (approximately $275) in 1996-1997, is still only about $440 today.

Nearly half of the elderly are fully dependent on others, while another 20% are partially so (NSSO, 1998). An earlier report revealed that 34.02% of rural elders were financially independent versus 29.94% of urban elders (NSSO, 1991). For elders living with their families–still the dominant living arrangement–their economic security and well-being are largely contingent on the economic capacity of the family unit. Particularly in rural areas, families suffer from economic crisis, as their occupations do not produce income throughout the year. The tendency is to spend more on their growing children, while minimizing expenditures on aged parents; thus, financial security for the elderly in rural families is very limited (Bali, 1995; Vijaya Kumar, 1990).

Women are more likely to be dependent on others (NSSO, 1998). They have limited control over family income, as well as their own earnings; only 8% of women are heads of household (Irudaya Rajan et al., 1999). Women are also more vulnerable because of greater longevity, lower literacy rates (especially in rural areas), and the higher incidence of widowhood among aged females (Bose, 1996; Irudaya Rajan et al., 1999). Of the elderly who report they are dependent, 70% are women (Irudaya Rajan, 2001).

SOCIAL AND ECONOMIC SECURITY POLICIES IN INDIA

Historically, social security and pension policy development in India can be divided broadly into three periods: the colonial period, post-Independence prior to the late 1980s, and developments in the 1990s. India has a set of standardized economic security policies formulated by the government for the benefit of the elderly population. These policies can also be divided into three categories: retirement benefits for those in the "organized sector," economic security benefits for those in the "unorganized sector," and old-age pensions for rural elderly.

Colonial Period

The British brought with them the concept of retirement benefits for employees. Colonial administrators were paid old-age pensions to which they were entitled as employees of the British government. This benefit was made available to all government employees in India, including the native-born. It would have been viewed as discriminatory if pensions had only covered employees who were British citizens and not those of Indian origin (Parduman Singh, 1998). This pension system for government employees was created in 1881 by the Royal Commission on Civil Establishment. It was retained by the new Government of India after independence was gained in 1947, as was a workmen's compensation program enacted in 1923. This pattern of providing pensions for government employees, before enacting a comprehensive social security program, mirrors the development of retirement income policies in the United States. Pensions were created for state and national civil servants before Social Security was enacted.

Post-Independence

Prior to independence, no such benefit as an old-age pension existed for industrial workers or for workers in general. The Adarkar Report of 1944, however, laid the groundwork for a social security system in India (Irudaya Rajan et al., 1999). A few years later, specific mention was made about social security in the new Constitution in Article 41 of the Directive Principles of State Policy. It states. "The State shall, within the limits of its economic capacity and development, make effective provision for securing the right to work, to educate and to public assistance in case of unemployment, old-age, sickness and disablement, and in other cases of underserved want." Social security was made the concurrent responsibility of the Central (national) and state governments. In addition, Articles 42 and 47 deal with social security issues for the elderly, while other sections of the Constitution focus on labor welfare, including conditions of work, Provident funds, liability for worker's compensation, invalidity (i.e., disability), and old-age pension and maternity benefits. These declarations embraced a modern concept of social security: The state should make itself responsible for ensuring a minimum standard of material welfare to all its citizens. A social security system aims to help individuals in times of dependency and interruption of earnings such as childhood, old age, maternity, sickness, accident, medical care, and unemployment–what have been termed the "contingencies of life" by the International Labor Organization.

From the late 1940s through the 1960s, economic development issues were key for the new nation, as laid out in a series of Five-Year Plans. The pension policies that evolved during this time reflected those overarching concerns and focused primarily on pension and welfare benefits for the organized sector work force. This sector includes the employees of the Central and state governments, of local government bodies, and of major enterprises in basic industries (e.g., manufacturing, mining). These groups of employees constitute approximately 30 million workers and nearly one in every 10 members of the total Indian work force of 314 million (Vijaya Kumar, 2000).

Retirement Benefits for the Organized Sector: Civil Service Employees

In Article 309 of Part IV of the Constitution, the recruitment and conditions of service are delineated for Central and state government employees, including retirement benefits. These benefits are designed to provide a secure life after retirement through non-contributory and contributory approaches. The benefits available on a non-contributory basis are: a pension program, cashing out unused leave at the time of retirement, pension dearness relief (cost of living adjustments), service and death-with-retirement gratuities, and the Central Government health service program. The contributory approach comprises group insurance, Contributory Provident Fund, and General Provident Fund.

Non-Contributory Programs. Under the pension program, non-industrial employees of government departments are covered, with benefit payments governed by the Central Civil Service Pension Rules of 1972. Persons who retire after 33 years of regular service are eligible to receive a full pension, at rates ranging from 43% to 50% of their final salary, according to the following formula: Pensioners are credited with 50% on the first 1,000 rupees of salary counted for the pension (c. $22); 45% on the next 500 rupees; and 40% of the remaining monthly salary, up to an overall ceiling. Those who have not completed 33 years are also eligible to receive a pension, but it is calculated proportionately to their years of service (Irudaya Rajan et al., 1995). This program is financed from Government of India general revenues.

In addition, government employees who are disabled for reasons related to their official duties are eligible for a disability pension. Furthermore, they can retire from service on an invalidity (disability) pension due to any bodily or mental infirmity that permanently incapacitates them and does not permit continued active service.

"Dearness relief," or cost-of-living adjustments, for pension benefits is provided to government employees. From time to time, a retired pensioner will get this kind of adjustment on his/her pension at the rate of 2.5% of the total pension. This relief is subject to a minimum of 2.50 rupees (or approximately $.05) to a maximum of 12.50 rupees (c. $.28) for each increase of eight points in the consumer price index for industrial workers. This kind of ad hoc adjustment is also characteristic of many U. S. public employer pension plans and, to a far lesser extent, private employer plans.

Two gratuity programs also are in force. Government employees who retire before a minimum of 10 years of qualifying service are not entitled to a pension; instead, they are paid a "service gratuity." This payment is earned; it is not a "tip." Payment is made at the rate of a half-month's salary for every completed six months of qualifying service and is given in lieu of a pension. This is similar to lump-sum pension distributions in the United States.

The retirement/death gratuity is another benefit for civil servants. Under this program, anyone who has completed five years of qualifying service and is eligible for the service gratuity or pension upon retirement will be paid at the rate of one-fourth of salary for every period of six months of qualifying service. This is subject to a maximum of 16.5 months' salary or 50,000 rupees (c. $1,112), whichever is less.

Similarly, if a government employee dies while in service, a death benefit is paid to his family, usually a minimum of 12 times the employee's salary at the time of death. For those who die after one year of service but before completing five years, the benefit equals six times the employee's salary at the time of death. If death occurs within the first year of service, the benefit is equal to twice the salary level at the time of death. For those employees who die after completing five years of qualifying employment but with less than 20 years of service, the benefit is 12 times the salary level.

Another type of economic benefit for civil servants is the cashing out of unused leave. Under this scheme, earned leave, up to a maximum of 180 days, can be paid out at retirement. Similar provisions exist in U.S. public employee pension systems.

After retirement, Central Government employees can avail themselves of medical care at a Central Government health program facility. Under this program, the government reimburses the retiree for medical expenses. This coverage is extended to dependent members of the pensioner, such as the spouse, unmarried daughter, and dependent son. Like all the other non-contributory programs, the employee/retiree does not pay anything; the entire cost is borne by the government.

Contributory Programs. In contrast with the programs described above, the cost of the following programs is on the employee. The Central Government Employees Group Insurance program is a relatively new benefit, having been introduced in 1982. Under this program, an employee who dies while in service is entitled to a certain fixed amount. The benefit ranges from a sum of 10,000 rupees (c. $223) to 80,000 rupees (approximately $1,778). The amount paid is dependent primarily on the service cadre/rank to which the employee belongs. If the employee retires after 35 years of service, he/she is entitled to an amount ranging from 23,000 rupees (approximately $512) to 187,000 rupees (or $4,156).

The two Provident funds cover different categories of employees. The Contributory Provident Fund, which is regulated by the Contributory Provident Fund (India) Rules of 1962, covers those employees who are industrial staff of government establishments, persons employed on a contract basis for a specific period, and science and technology professionals who entered government service at a relatively older age. Under this program, these employees must contribute a specific minimum amount, but they are free to contribute as much as they can. Income tax exemptions are allowed for the amounts contributed, similar to Individual Retirement Accounts in the United States. The government also makes a contribution, based on the amount of monthly salary earned by the contributing employee.

The General Provident Fund is in force for central and state government employees and is similar to programs for employees of banks, insurance companies, universities, and other public and private establishments. Government employees who opt for this retirement savings program are required to contribute a minimum of 6% of their pay. The accumulated funds earn interest tax-free, as well as an incentive bonus of 11% interest annually. These tax incentives resemble those in the United States designed to motivate workers, primarily those in the middle- and upper-income groups, to save for a more comfortable retirement.

Retirement Benefits for the Organized Sector: Non-Civil Service Employees

Similarly, benefits for other organized sector workers cover employees of factories, mines, oil fields, plantations, port and railway companies, and shops and other establishments with 10 or more employees. Benefits include workman's compensation, a coal mines Provident fund program, gratuity, employees Provident fund, Assam tea plantation Provident fund, and maternity benefits. The Coal Mines Provident Fund and Bonus Scheme Act and the Employees State Insurance Act were enacted in 1948, soon after independence. The Provident funds and maternity benefits were established between the early 1950s and 1970s.

Non-Contributory Programs. These social security programs include workman's compensation, maternity benefits, and gratuity. The first program, enacted in 1923 before independence, is designed to protect workers in hazardous occupations (e.g., construction, mining) by paying compensation for accidents occurring in the workplace. Compensation also is payable for certain occupational diseases contracted by workers during the course of their employment, similar to payments to U. S. miners for black lung disease. State governments can extend the scope of the Act to include any class of workers whose occupations are considered hazardous.

Maternity benefits were enacted in 1961 and apply to women working in factories, mines, plantations, or the service industry, and in shops and establishments with 10 or more workers. State governments can extend the provisions of the Act to other establishments, subject to Central Government approval. The medical bonus is 250 rupees; benefits are average daily wages for three calendar months or 10 rupees per day, whichever is higher.

The Payment of Gratuity program has been in force nationwide, except for Sikkim and plantation estates in Jammu and Kashmir, since 1972. It covers most industrial workers and employees of shops and establishments with more than 10 workers, whose monthly wages do not exceed 2,500 rupees. It does not cover administrators, managers, or civil employees of the Central and state governments. A benefit is paid to an employee who terminates employment after five years of continuous service; this requirement does not apply in the case of death or disablement. For every year of service, the rate of payment is 15 days' wages based on final salary, up to a maximum of 20 months. The monetary ceiling is 50,000 rupees.

Contributory Programs. With the exception of two programs (family pension and employees' insurance), all contributory programs were enacted within 10 years after independence. The Coal Mines Fund requires both the employer and employee to contribute a minimum of 8% of the employee's wage. The employee can contribute more, but the employer is not obligated to do so. The Fund provides post-retirement benefits for coal miners.

The Employees' State Insurance program applies to all factory workers in India, except state factory employees and those earning more than 1600 rupees monthly. Under this program, workers are covered in case of sickness, injury on the job, and maternity from the age of 14 onward. Considered a pioneering measure in social insurance in India because it represents the beginnings of a more comprehensive system, it is funded via both employer and employee contributions plus grants, donations, and gifts from the Central and state governments, local authorities, and other organizations. It is administered by the Employees' State Insurance Corporation via a network of regional and local offices. The Corporation also provides medical care for beneficiaries and their families through its own hospitals.

In the 1950s, Provident funds were established for industrial workers and tea plantation workers. The Employee Provident Fund is financed by employer-employee contributions to provide retirement benefits for industrial workers. A compulsory program, 195,000 factories or establishments nationwide (except for Sikkim, Jammu, and Kashmir) were covered as of 1990. The employee's minimum contribution of 10% is matched by the employer; a retired or dismissed employee is entitled to the full employer's share, regardless of the length of service. Employees receive 12% annual interest on their deposits. The Fund is administered by the Central Board of Trustees via 16 regional offices; the Board is appointed by the Central Government. Employees can also draw on this fund through non-refundable advances to sustain themselves and family members during illness, disability, and accidents, and to meet educational, social, and family obligations, such as marriage.

The Tea Provident fund covers only those laborers working in Assam, whose total salary does not exceed 500 rupees per month. This fund is also an employer-employee contributory plan to provide retirement benefits. Employees can contribute more than the 8% required of them and their employer.

Some wider-ranging programs were created for organized-sector employees in the 1970s, including the Employees' Family Pension and the Employees' Deposit-Linked Insurance program. A special pension also was enacted for those who had fought for India's independence. The Family Pension program facilitates long-term protection for the family of a worker who dies in service; it is compulsory for members of the Employees' Provident Fund. It is financed by a transfer of a portion of the employee's share of the Provident fund, representing 1.6% of pay. That payment is matched by both the employer and by the Central Government; the latter pays for administration of the program.

Three types of benefits are provided: a family survivor pension, life insurance, and retirement income with withdrawal privileges. If the worker dies during service before age 60, a pension is paid to a surviving family member. The monthly amount paid is calibrated to the salary level of the deceased, and ranges from 250 rupees for the survivor of a worker who earned 300 rupees per month, to a maximum of 750 rupees for a salary that exceeded 1,600 rupees per month.

A retirement benefit for those age 60, who contributed at least one year to the family pension fund, is also based on the member's monthly salary. For lower salaried workers (up to 1,130 rupees), the monthly benefit ranges from 110 rupees (for one year of contributions) to 9,000 rupees (for 40 years of contributions). For higher-paid workers, monthly amounts range from 182-400 rupees (for one year of contributions) to 9,000-19,825 rupees (for 40 years of contributions). If the worker dies after retirement, a pension is paid to one family member for seven years or up to the date at which the member would have reached 65 years of age, whichever is shorter. A lump-sum life insurance benefit of 5,000 rupees is paid to the survivor of a worker who died in service and had contributed to the Family Pension Fund for at least a year.

As of March 1998, 23.2 million persons were covered under these several plans and programs. They include 4.2 Central Government employees and nearly 7 million state and union territory employees. Other groups include the coal miners (.81 million) and Jammu and Kashmir Provident Fund members (.145 million) (Vijaya Kumar, 2000).

Economic Security for the Unorganized Sector

In India, nearly 90% of the total work force is employed in the "unorganized sector"; the majority are agricultural workers. Workers in this sector are subject to numerous disadvantages. Wages are relatively low and there is no job security. Most do not have year-round work and labor turnover is high. Roughly 47 million work on a regular basis; 97 million are in casual or temporary employment (Vijaya Kumar, 2000).

Life Insurance Approaches. There is no social security system for the majority of Indian workers. Retirement benefits are provided via life insurance, a concept that was introduced by certain British companies during the colonial period. Since 1956, life insurance in India has come under the control of the Central Government. Social security for the unorganized sector comprises five types of insurance policies issued by the Life Insurance Corporation of India (LIC) and the LIC's Group Superannuation program. The Unit Trust of India also provides contributory programs for medical care, such as the Senior Citizens Unit Plan and the Group Medical Insurance program.

The main purpose of the LIC is to provide family protection in the event of the breadwinner's premature death. Some policies combine the element of savings for old age with family protection. Life insurance plans are provided on both an individual and group basis; the latter are offered to employer-employee groups. Premiums, which are deducted from employees' monthly salaries, have two components: risk and savings. The risk part provides insurance coverage, and the savings part accumulates at 10% annually. The accumulated savings are paid in retirement; in the case of death before retirement, the insurance sum is paid together with the accumulated savings.

The Group Superannuation program of the LIC guarantees regular post-retirement income under two kinds of plans: defined benefit and defined contribution. Under the latter, a fixed percentage of salary is made by the employer, which is accumulated for each employee until retirement. Most plans are of this type, in which the amount of pension paid out depends on the level of funds accumulated. The pension from the defined benefit plans is fixed in advance and generally based on a formula of service and salary at retirement, like plans of this type in the United States.

These plans allow retirees to opt for a lump sum as part of their pension and also a choice of annuity. These include payable for life, payable for a certain period (10, 15, or 20 years) and for life thereafter, and joint life last survivor with full or part reversion of the pension to the spouse. Another annuity plan permits a pension payable for life, with return of capital on death. This is very popular as the annuitant gets a pension as long as he survives; upon his death, the family gets a lump sum equal to the capital sum that was invested for purchase of the annuity.

One policy, Jeevan Akshay, is primarily for the self-employed (e.g., doctors, lawyers, shopkeepers). Persons over 50 are eligible to purchase this policy on their own lives and get a monthly pension. The minimum premium is 10,000 rupees, with multiples of 100 rupees thereafter; no maximum exists. Each 1,000-rupee premium yields a monthly pension of 10 rupees. The policy guarantees an insurance sum equal to the purchase price, along with a final bonus to the pensioner's heir. A choice of type of annuity is also available.

Savings-Linked Insurance. The other major type of plan is the savings-linked insurance plan for individuals, known as endowment plans; the sum assured is payable at maturity or earlier death. In some cases, the assured payment may be different. For example, in a Jeevan Mitra policy, the sum payable at death is double; in a Double Endowment policy, the amount paid at maturity is double. A Money Back policy provides security in old age through lump-sum benefits paid out over periodic intervals. For a policy of 1,000 rupees, the sum of 150 rupees is paid if the policy-holder survives five years, with a like sum paid on his/her surviving 10 years, and similar payments for subsequently surviving 15 and 20 years. The balance of 400 rupees is paid if the policy-holder survives the full term of 25 years.

Other plans are suited to special circumstances of a given individual. For instance, a Bhavishya Jeevan plan is a specially designed endowment plan for professionals who have limited spans of high income. Similarly, a Jeevan Griha plan, which is available in double and triple coverage, may be suitable for those obtaining a housing loan and who need collateral security for ensuring loan repayment in the event of premature death. This is similar to mortgage insurance in the United States.

Another LIC offering is the New Jeevan Dhara plan, a deferred annuity whereby an individual builds up funds during a deferment period, either through the payment of regular premiums or a single premium. The annuity vests when the deferment period is over. The policy-holder then has several payment options (e.g., payable for life, payable for a certain period, payable for life with return of capital upon death).

The Jeevan Suraksha plan for individuals is available in three versions: with life coverage, without life coverage, and endowment. Under life coverage, if the policy-holder's death occurs during the deferment period, at least 50% of the target pension is paid to the spouse. Once the annuitant retires, he/she receives a pension payable for 15 years certain and for life thereafter. An additional option is available: The full pension is paid to the principal annuitant, and upon his/her death, the spouse receives a 50% pension for life. The endowment type plan provides that if the death of the annuitant occurs during the term of the policy, the spouse can opt for a 25% sum, and the balance of the assured sum is utilized to pay a pension. Under this plan, policy-holders get an income tax rebate.

These various plans for workers in the unorganized sector are primarily funded by individuals; some also involve employer contributions. None involves direct government funding. These retirement income vehicles operate like Individual Retirement Accounts (IRAs), but generally without the tax incentives provided to American workers. Most are not suitable for agricultural workers because the contribution levels required are too high.

State Old-Age Assistance. For rural elders, who work as long as their physical ability permits them to be employed in the fields, there has not been any guaranteed retirement income except old-age pensions offered by state governments. As discussed below, the national government did not initiate this kind of program until the mid-1990s. The first state to set up this kind of program was Uttar Pradesh in 1957, followed by Andhra Pradesh and Kerala in 1960 and six other states in that decade. The majority of states and Union Territories (e.g., Delhi, Pondicherry) created their plans in the 1970s, with Assam being last in 1983. Initially, these monthly benefits ranged from 30 to 100 rupees, with 60 rupees being most common. Tamil Nadu also provided clothing rations twice a year.

Eligibility criteria vary, but key provisions are similar: destitutes of 60 or 65 years of age and physically handicapped destitutes, usually 45 years or older. Nearly half of the states require a minimum age of eligibility of 60; seven states mandate different ages for men and women, with the requirement higher for men (usually age 65), by five years. One state, Madhya Pradesh, requires women to be at least 50 and men, age 60. Rajasthan has the lowest age requirement for men: age 58, and the second lowest for women: age 55. Sikkim and Tripura have higher age limits, ages 70 and 80, respectively. Special provisions are generally made for the blind and for widows, often with no age restrictions. A few states have residency requirements and/or monthly income restrictions, usually between 25-50 rupees per month. These plans are characteristically administered by each state's or Union Territory's Social Welfare Department. They are similar to the old-age assistance provided by many of the American states before the passage of the Social Security Act.

In the early 1980s, four states (Andhra Pradesh, Gujarat, Kerala, and Tamil Nadu) also initiated old-age pensions for landless agricultural workers (similar to U. S. sharecroppers). Amounts range from 30-75 rupees per month; Tamil Nadu includes clothing rations twice annually and a one kilogram weekly ration of rice. The age of eligibility is 60, with Gujarat extending the same benefit to a disabled/handicapped individual age 45 or older. Income restrictions (of the individual and his family) and residency requirements occur in Gujarat and Kerala.

Tamil Nadu and Kerala developed other benefit programs for very low-income workers. The former developed special protections for deserted and widowed destitute women in 1975 and 1986. Both programs provide a monthly benefit of 35 rupees, plus a semi-annual clothing and weekly rice ration. Abandoned women must be at least 35 years old, and widows, at least age 40. A one-year residency in the state is required.

Kerala has an extensive social welfare system of more than 30 programs. Nearly half of them are fully financed by the state, including the agricultural workers pension described above, a widow's pension, and assistance to indigent craftsmen and artists, leprosy and cancer patients, and the unemployed. In 1992-1993, these programs consumed 2.77% of the state budget, compared with 1.02% expended by the national government for its welfare programs in 1991 (Irudaya Rajan et al., 1999, 184-185). Seven programs are targeted to workers in particular industries (e.g., cashew-growing, hand weaving, fishing) and are partly financed by the state. Eleven programs are operated by boards for specific groups of workers. The extensiveness of Kerala's program is unique among the Indian states.

In the 1990s, state old-age pensions were liberalized, in part due to the rise in the cost of living. The lowest two payments are provided by Assam (60 rupees) and Andhra Pradesh (75 rupees), or $1.50 and $1.87, respectively. The maximum benefit of 300 rupees (or approximately $7.50) is paid in Rajasthan and West Bengal. The average old-age pension is now 150 rupees per month or less than $4.00, well below the average per capita income for all Indians, but still capable of purchasing basic food supplies if bought through the public distribution system (Irudaya Rajan, 2001).

Since the early 1980s, every state has developed an old-age pension system. However, several studies (see Gulati and Irudaya Rajan, 1988; Eswara Prasad, 1995; Vijaya Kumar, 1995) concluded there were several problems in the disbursement of old-age pensions. These include a cumbersome application procedure, the use of inappropriate eligibility criteria, unusual delays in processing applications, and irregular payments. Some of these same problems have arisen with a recent Central Government program.

NATIONAL GOVERNMENT ACTIONS IN THE 1990s

The Central Government initiated two important programs in the mid- to-late 1990s to improve the economic security of very poor elders.

These were a National Old-Age Pension Scheme and the Annapurna program. In addition, a National Policy on Older Persons was promulgated in 1999. On August 15, 1995, the National Social Assistance Scheme was introduced. This program is a significant step towards the fulfillment of the Directive Principles in Articles 41 and 42 of the Constitution. Comprising three components, two are focused on families and maternal benefits; the third is the National Old-Age Pension Scheme (NOAPS) designed to help poor elders.

The National Old-Age Pension Scheme (NOAPS)

The NOAPS is fully sponsored by the Central Government, which lays down the norms, guidelines and conditions for implementation and provides assistance to the states and union territories to carry out the program. At the national level, the program is administered by the Ministry of Rural Development and Employment.

Applicants must be age 65 and destitute (i.e., have little or no regular means of subsistence from their own incomes or through financial support from family or other sources). Any state or union territory procedures currently in force to determine destitution may also be followed, subject to the review of the Central Government. The monthly amount is 75 Rs (or roughly $1.75) and is to be paid in not less than two installments per year. A ceiling on the number of old-age pensions was specified for each state and union territory, with the latter entities having the smallest number of entitlements (except Delhi and Pondicherry). States with the largest ceiling are Uttar Pradesh, Bihar, Maharashtra, Nadhya Pradesh, and Andhra Pradesh. The numerical ceiling for all of India was 5.4 million (Irudaya Rajan, Mishra, & Sarma, 1999), based on the assumption that 50% of the population below the poverty line in the age group 65+ would qualify for these old-age pensions (Irudaya Rajan, 2001). The current numerical ceiling has increased to 6.9 million, and the allowable expenditure has increased from $48 million to nearly $62 million. Many states have utilized over 90% of their allotment (Irudaya Rajan, 2001, 614).

The NOAPS is implemented in the states and union territories by village panchayats (councils) and municipalities. They are encouraged to involve voluntary agencies, to the extent possible, in getting benefits to those elders for whom the program is intended. Actions include determining the age of prospective beneficiaries who may not know their exact age. The panchayats and municipalities also are responsible for reporting the deaths of recipients to ensure payments are stopped in a timely fashion.

Although the states and union territories have taken steps to carry out the program, various institutional and procedural complications arose. The identification of appropriate lead departments, the development of district-wise distribution of targets, the creation of state and district-level committees, and opening separate program accounts are some of the administrative problems that developed. Procedural issues included identification of true beneficiaries, often a procedure lacking accuracy, and ways to disburse payments. Committees were constituted to discuss and solve these various problems in 1996. Despite these implementation difficulties, the NAOPS is now in operation all over India (Vijaya Kumar, 1999). Ministry of Rural Development reports indicate that the most vulnerable sections of Indian society (e.g., women, lower caste individuals) have benefited from this program. For example, the proportion of women beneficiaries increased from 30% to 37% in just one year (Irudaya Rajan, 2001).

The purpose of the NAOPS was to ensure that social protection everywhere in the country would be uniformly available without interruptions. It was intended that this Central Government assistance would not displace the states' own efforts and expenditures for their old-age pensions and that states could expand their own social assistance programs independently. However, most of the states are disbursing only the national assistance funds and have diverted their own resources to other programs. A similar dynamic occurs with the U. S. Supplemental Security Income program in which several states choose not to add a state-funded increment to the national benefit for the old, blind, and disabled.

Annapurna Program

On March 19, 1999, the Central Government announced another social security program for elderly destitutes. It is similar to the old Jajmani system and the programs in Tamil Nadu and Kerala described above, as well as Adopt-a-Granny programs run by non-governmental organizations such as HelpAge India. Under the program, an older person who is eligible for the NOAPS is given 10 kilograms of rice or wheat monthly, free of cost, through the existing public distribution system. Expected to benefit 6.6 million persons, it is administered by the Ministry of Rural Development with the help of the Ministry of Food and Civil Supplies. Implementation of the program has been slow;

after 18 months of operation, half the states and union territories had not started the program, and only 612 million of the 991 million allocated had been released (Irudaya Rajan, 2001).

Program restrictions may play a role in this lack of rapid implementation. For example, in Andhra Pradesh about 1.1 million persons are covered under the NAOPS; 20% of them, or a little over 40,000, are covered by the *Annapurna* program. Selecting one in five of those eligible may lead to great dissatisfaction among those elders not selected, especially at the village level where such selections would not be a secret. In addition, the state is required to shoulder a financial burden of approximately 4 million rupees per month to implement the program. These administrative issues may explain why many states and union territories have been reluctant to participate.

The combined national budget allocation for the NAOPS and *Annapurna* programs comes to .6%, compared to the 6% of Central Government revenue expended on pensions for its employees (Irudaya Rajan, 2001). Other than the data on Kerala's expenditures for social security and social assistance programs, little is known about the proportion of state and union territory budgets for these kinds of programs. A proposal has been made in the National Policy for Older Persons to develop a mandatory contributory pension plan for all self-employed and salaried persons in government and private sector employment; however, no time frame has been specified and the proposal says little about the more vulnerable sectors (e.g., women, rural areas). The same is true of the OASIS (Old Age Social and Income Security) project that recommends improving the rate of return and enhancing coverage and customer services related to the several Provident funds and the LIC annuity plans. However, these proposals do not provide income in old age for those who need it most.

CONCLUDING REMARKS

Social security experts and economists have criticized the implementation of India's income security programs. Normally, the primary objective of pensions is to assure employees that they will receive a certain income during their old age. However, one criticism of the public pension system is that the real return on the contribution made by the participants is lower than that available from other forms of investment. Furthermore, over the generations, pensions for retirees have been declining in real terms. Overall, the existing programs tend to reduce individual savings and the governments tend to spend more, thereby reducing their savings (Parduman Singh, 1998). Similarly, in the selection of beneficiaries and the general implementation of the NAOPS, several defective approaches were spotlighted, largely because of the administrative and procedural problems noted above.

Regarding certain contradictions in pension policy, the World Bank (1994) has recommended a three-pillar approach. The first pillar is a mandatory and publicly-managed system, financed through taxes, which would ensure a means-tested minimum guaranteed pension. The second pillar, also mandatory, would be managed privately and fully-funded through personal savings, the investments of which are regulated. The third pillar is a voluntary, fully-funded system, in which investments are not regulated. Thus, the second and third pillars are based on a defined contribution principle, having tighter links between contributions and benefits and which require the maintenance of individual accounts (Subrahmanya, 2000). The World Bank, while suggesting that the Central Government should reform its existing pension policies, has argued that reforms should be in the direction of a pay-as-you-go principle to a funded principle in which pensioners would be benefited by getting higher returns.

Apart from reforming existing pension programs, policymakers should focus on the 89-90% of the population who remain uncovered under any of the existing pension programs. Agricultural workers, artisans, marginal farmers, self-employed persons, and workers in small-scale organizations and industries need protection in their old age. In the future, this group may increase and could become one more socioeconomic problem for policymakers.

While formulating reforms to ongoing statutory or voluntary programs, policymakers should also consider certain key challenges associated with the aging of India's population in general:

1. Fiscal: examining the interaction among increasing government expenditures, growth of Gross Domestic Product, and the increasing dependency ratio;
2. Market responsiveness: facilitating labor markets to respond flexibly to changing demographics;
3. Active aging: encouraging people to remain active and independent as they age; and
4. Responsibilities: examining the balance between collective and individual responsibilities, the respective roles of the public and

private sectors, and ensuring that individuals are able and confident in making choices and taking responsibility for their lives.

A detailed and critical analysis of these four issues is essential to help bring about needed changes in existing policies.

Two additional issues require examination. Thus far, the pension measure adopted by the Indian government has been largely borrowed from western industrialized countries, where the vast majority of the work force is involved in the highly organized industrial sector. However, India is still an agrarian nation, where the majority of the work force is engaged in the unorganized sector. There is an immediate need to re-examine and re-modify India's social security models to reflect the needs of its population. In addition, attention must be paid to the role of advances in medical technology and its impact on increasing longevity. The post-retirement years will increase considerably, and ultimately this trend will create a greater demand for basic needs of the elderly, such as long-term health care and housing. To meet these demands, the elderly will need viable income security for this longer period of retirement. India's policymakers must keep this issue a priority when formulating pension policies for the 21st century.

AUTHOR NOTES

S. Vijaya Kumar is a Fellow of the Council for Social Development, Hyderabad, India. He has published several books including *Family life and socio-economic problems of the aged,* and has executed a number of research studies in aging, social security, migrant labor and rural development.

Dr. Kumar can be contacted at Council for Social Development, Plot No. 230, Shiva Nagar Colony, Hyderguda, Rajendranagar Road, Bahadurpura Post, Hyderabad 500 064, India (E-mail: vijayskumar99@hotmail.com).

REFERENCES

Bali, Arun P. (1995). The role of the family in elderly care. *Research & Development Journal,* 2(1).

Bose, A. B. (1996). Economic and social conditions of the elderly, with a special focus on women: Needs and capabilities of the elderly. *Implications of Asia's population future for older people in the family* (ESCAP Asian Population Studies Series #145). Bangkok: ESCAP.

Eswara Prasad, K. V. (1995). Social security for destitute widows in Tamil Nadu. *Economic and Political Weekly,* 30(15).

Government of India (1999). *National policy on older persons.* Delhi: Ministry of Social Justice and Empowerment.

Gulati, L., & Irudaya Rajan, S. (1988). *Population aspects of aging in Kerala.* Trivandrum: Centre for Development Studies.

Irudaya Rajan, S. (1999). Financial and social security in old age in India. *Social Change, 29* (1/2), 90-125.
Irudaya Rajan, S. (2001, February 24). Social assistance for poor elderly: How effective? *Economic and Political Weekly*, 613-617.
Irudaya Rajan, S., Mishra, U. S., & Sarma, P. S. (1995). An agenda for national policies on ageing in India. *Research and Development Journal, 1* (2), 38-53.
Irudaya Rajan, S., Mishra, U. S., & Sarma, P. S. (1999). *India's elderly: Burden or challenge?* New Delhi: Sage Publications.
National Sample Survey Organization (NSSO) (1991). Socio-economic profile of the aged person (NSS 42nd Round: July 1986-June 1987). *Sarvekshana, 15* (2).
National Sample Survey Organization (NSSO) (1998). *The aged in India: A socio-economic profile.* New Delhi: Government of India, Department of Statistics.
Parduman Singh (1998). *Protection for the elderly–At the threshold of the 21st century.* New Delhi: Friedrich Ebert Stiftung.
Punia, D., & Sharma, M. L. (1987). Family life of rural aged women. In M. L. Sharma & T. M. Dak (Eds.), *Aging in India* (pp. 145-151). New Delhi: Ajanta Publications.
Singh, A. K. P. J., Dak, T. M., & Sharma, M. L. (1987). Work and leisure among the aged males. In M. L. Sharma & T. M. Dak (Eds.), *Aging in India* (pp. 82-93). New Delhi: Ajanta Publications.
Singh, K., Singh, R., & Sharma, M. L. (1987). Problems of aged women in Haryana. In M. L. Sharma & T. M. Dak (Eds.), *Aging in India* (pp. 134-144). New Delhi: Ajanta Publications.
Subrahmanya, R. K. S. (2000). "Future of social security in India." Paper submitted to the Study Group of the National Commission on Labour. Bangalore: Social Security Association of India.
Vijaya Kumar, S. (1990). Old Age: A Challenge of life. *Journal of Indian Anthropological Society, 16* (3/4).
Vijaya Kumar, S. (1995). Ageing in India: An anthropological outlook. *Research & Development Journal, 2* (1).
Vijaya Kumar, S. (1999). *Quality of life and social security for the elderly in rural India.* Hyderabad: Council for Social Development.
Vijaya Kumar, S. (2000). "Social Security in Indian Context." Paper for discussion submitted to the Second National Commission on Labour, Ministry of Labour, Government of India, New Delhi.
World Bank (1994). *The old age crisis, policies to protect the old and promote growth: A policy research report.* New York: Author.

Health Status and Health Care Services Among Older Persons in India

Vinod Kumar, MBBS, MD

St. Stephen's Hospital, New Delhi

SUMMARY. India is characterized by significant rural-based living, population heterogeneity, financial constraints, and reverse sex ratio. Traditions of joint families, life-long physical activity, vegetarianism, and social and spiritual enrichment, all known to promote healthy aging, are widely prevalent. With the increasing pace of population aging, the health of older persons in India has been the focus of recent attention. Existing data indicate a significant morbidity among the aged, much of which may remain subclinical. Considerable variations in morbidity exist with respect to gender, place of residence (rural vs. urban), and socioeconomic status. Rapid demographic transition without a concomitant epidemiological transition is responsible for the dual load of infections and degenerative diseases in older persons, these being common causes of death. Most age-related morbidity is preventable. Health promotion and cost-effective interventions based on the primary health care approach over a lifelong course, especially at the village level, will greatly help towards achieving the goal of healthy aging. The rapidly changing socioeconomic scenario in India also calls for appropriate policy actions to achieve this goal. *[Article copies available for a fee from The Haworth Document Delivery Service: 1-800-HAWORTH. E-mail address: <docdelivery@haworthpress.com> Website: <http://www.HaworthPress.com> © 2003 by The Haworth Press, Inc. All rights reserved.]*

[Haworth co-indexing entry note]: "Health Status and Health Care Services Among Older Persons in India." Kumar, Vinod. Co-published simultaneously in *Journal of Aging & Social Policy* (The Haworth Press, Inc.) Vol. 15, No. 2/3, 2003, pp. 67-83; and: *An Aging India: Perspectives, Prospects, and Policies* (ed: Phoebe S. Liebig, and S. Irudaya Rajan) The Haworth Press, Inc., 2003, pp. 67-83. Single or multiple copies of this article are available for a fee from The Haworth Document Delivery Service [1-800-HAWORTH, 9:00 a.m. - 5:00 p.m. (EST). E-mail address: docdelivery@haworthpress.com].

© 2003 by The Haworth Press, Inc. All rights reserved.
http://www.haworthpress.com/store/product.asp?sku=J031

KEYWORDS. Aging, health, India, geriatric morbidity, primary health care, geriatric services

INTRODUCTION

India is beset with diverse health problems and has to cope with traditional diseases like tuberculosis, malaria, malnutrition, and poverty-related diseases, on the one hand, and more recent challenges like chronic degenerative diseases, substance abuse, HIV/AIDS, mental stress, and environmental pollution, on the other. Counter-productive health practices and inappropriate health behavior are prevalent among the population in large measure. Enormous efforts have been expended by the nation over the last several years to achieve acceptable levels of conventional health indicators set out in the Global Strategy for Health for All by the Year 2000.

The health of older persons in India has recently attracted the attention of health professionals and policymakers. This is mainly due to the rapidly rising number and proportion of older persons and an urgent need to care for them, despite financial constraints faced by the country. In India, earlier Five-Year Plans did not consistently recognize "the old" as a target group needing welfare services. However, after the Seventh Five-Year Plan, the Ministry of Social Justice and Empowerment (hereafter, the Ministry) constituted a separate subgroup to study the Welfare of the Aged (Sureender & Khan, 1996). A National Policy for Older Persons is now in place (Government of India, 1999), and recently, the Ministry sponsored a study group on Old Age Income and Social Security, popularly known as the OASIS committee, under the leadership of Dr. Surendra Dave. The committee submitted its final report in 2000 (Dave, 2000).

Accurate knowledge about mortality, morbidity, and disability profiles of the population is essential for understanding the mechanism and prevention of various diseases, as well as for planning health care facilities. At the Ministry's insistence, a nationwide survey on older persons was first conducted by the national Planning Ministry through its Sample Survey Organization in 1986-87, covering both urban and rural areas (National Sample Survey Organization [NSSO], 1991). A major objective of the survey was to assess the socioeconomic profile of India's elderly. The survey was repeated in 1995-96 (NSSO, 1998). The results of both surveys played a major role in formulating the National Policy for Older Persons.

Older persons are highly heterogeneous, and considerable variations in morbidity were found with respect to gender, place of residence, and socioeconomic status. A general appraisal of the health status of older Indians reveals a few pertinent points. First, a large proportion of geriatric morbidity remains occult due to ignorance and lack of access to health care facilities. Second, the extent and severity of the dual load of degenerative and infectious diseases among older persons in India, the so-called "double disease burden," is greatly determined by socioeconomic factors. Third, subtle differences exist between urban and rural elders due to environmental, cultural, and socioeconomic differences and to large vulnerable groups such as older females, neglected or handicapped elders, or the poor elderly who need more vigorous attention. Finally, numerous unhealthy lifestyle factors, such as smoking, seriously affect health in later life. Smoking has been frequently reported among older persons (Anklesaria et al., 1996), and it continues to contribute to mortality (Kumar & Nagarkar, 1996).

Both negative and positive determinants of health influence the quality and length of an individual's life. These determinants fall into the domain of the health sector, as well as social and economic spheres. Science has shown that positive health practices in a supportive environment can delay or even prevent much of this age-related morbidity. Health promotion and cost-effective interventions based on a primary health-care approach over a lifelong course will greatly help achieve the goal of healthy aging (Kalache, 1999). The rapidly changing socioeconomic and cultural scenario in India calls for appropriate policy actions and program development to ensure disability-free life expectancy and, therefore, a good quality of life in the later years.

DEMOGRAPHY OF AGING IN INDIA

Aging is a worldwide phenomenon. Globally, persons aged 60 and older are projected to increase from 376 million in 1980 to 1121 million in the year 2025, with more than 70% living in less-developed regions. India is worthy of special focus due to its vastness and its heterogeneity of population, interregional demographic variations, and reverse sex ratio. It is the second largest country in the world, both in terms of total population and that of individuals aged 60+. It is home to several cultures, religions, and languages, with more than two-thirds of the population living in villages. There is enormous diversity among older persons regarding social, economic, and educational status.

The 60+ population in India in 1901 was estimated at 12 million, rising to 20 million in 1951 (a 67% increase) and to 55 million in 1991 (a 155% rise) or 6.5% of the total population (Sharma & Xenos, 1992). In 2001, elders numbered 75 million or 7.7% of all Indians. This is expected to increase to 179 million in 2031 and 301 million in 2051; the proportion of elders will be 12% and 17%, respectively (Rajan, Mishra, & Sarma, 1999). However, an increase in the number of persons 70 and above (the "old old") is likely to be even greater. They are projected to increase approximately five times between 2001 and 2051, from 27 million to 132 million. The "oldest old" (80 years and older) will grow faster than any other age group, increasing six-fold from 5.4 million in 2001 to 32 million in 2051 (For more details, see "Demography of Indian Aging, 2001-2051" by Dr. S. Rajan et al. in this collection).

Average life expectancy at birth and at age 65, which used to be markedly different between developed and developing countries, is now more similar. Table 1 depicts life expectancy at birth and at 65 in India (Biswas, 1994). In comparison, average life expectancy at birth in developed countries was 65.7 years in 1950 and grew to 74.5 years in 1990 (United Nations, 1991), indicating a rapid narrowing of the gap between the two types of nations. Life expectancy in the United States at age 65 in 1990, reported by Jarvik and Small (1995) as 15 years for males and 19.4 years for females, also indicates the gap is closing.

Unlike developed countries, demographic change in India has occurred in a relatively shorter time and without a full-fledged concomitant epidemiological transition. The change took place primarily due to dramatic reductions in mortality in infancy, childhood, and young adulthood, largely attributable to preventive medicine (immunization, mother-child care programs), antibiotics, and other curative drugs. Improvement in general standards of sanitation and nutrition, which played an important part in the long, drawn-out demographic transition in the West, played a modest role in India, at best. Nevertheless, variations in socioeconomic development seen in different regions in India largely determine their demographic status. There are areas that still lag considerably behind in reaching acceptable levels of health indicators. By contrast, the small state of Kerala in south India is demographically advanced, having achieved low birth and death rates and high rates of literacy and life expectancy. It is also the only state where the sex ratio is favorable to women. Otherwise, India is one of a few countries where males outnumber females. Among the elderly in Kerala, females outnumber males, except the very old. Surprisingly, the number of elderly females was much higher than elderly males in 1901, but the increase in

TABLE 1. Life Expectancy in India (In Years)

Year	At Birth		At Age 65	
	Male	Female	Male	Female
1901	22.5	23.3	7.3	7.6
1951	32.4	31.7	9.8	10.3
1991	60.1	59.8	14.6	16.9

the latter led to older males and females becoming equal in number in 1961; today, older males outnumber older females (Sharma & Xenos, 1992). Pervasive gender discrimination may be the cause.

Defining the Health of Older Persons

The World Health Organization (WHO) defines health as a state of complete physical, mental, and social well-being and not merely the absence of disease. One possible method to consider the importance of life's quality in old age is to combine survival with a concept of health to calculate healthy life expectancy (HLE) as an indicator of the population's health status. Disability-free life expectancy (DFLE) and life expectancy without chronic disease (LEWD) are two estimates of HLE. Application of this model allows epidemiologists to assess the evaluation of mortality, morbidity, and disability simultaneously and the discrepancies among these conditions. The model also offers a convenient target parameter towards which health policy actions can be aimed.

The concept of calculating HLE is, however, largely alien to India so far, due to the unavailability of data required for such health assessment. It is, however, obvious that HLE in India would be lower, as compared to Western countries. In the United States, although life expectancy at age 65 is greater, DFLE was only seven years for males and 10 years for females in 1990. At age 85, it was about two years for both sexes. Thus, in India, where life expectancy is lower, DFLE would be worse.

Determinants of Healthy Aging in India

Factors favorable to healthy aging operate over different stages during the individual life course. They are related not only to health, but also to financial, occupational, and educational attainment, as well as family circumstances and housing environment. Social factors operational in childhood and adulthood can exert a cumulative effect on the quality and health of later life. Medical factors, such as long-term sequelae of polio and rheumatic fever, along with poor hygiene and poverty, can lead to "premature aging" seen in poor countries. The direct correlation between organic impairment and socioeconomic status (SES) has been reported, with depression and visual, locomotor, and cognitive impairments being more common in older persons with low SES (Khetarpal et al., 1996). The percentage of negative health parameters in older persons, such as the presence of a physical handicap, health problem, or seeking medical help in the last month of life, is also inversely related to SES (Soneja et al., 1996). Positive lifestyles that include physical activity, healthy diets, absence of alcohol and tobacco abuse, promotion of self-care practices and sociocultural contacts are also important determinants of healthy aging. Genetics and gender-related factors also influence the onset of some chronic diseases, such as Alzheimer's and certain cancers.

Indian society is blessed with certain age-old traditional virtues such as good family support for elders, vegetarianism, non-sedentarism, spirituality, and practice of cost-effective alternative medical approaches, including yoga. Many practice fasting, a health-oriented custom common to many religions. It appears that many of these virtues promote healthy aging. A sizable proportion of the aged retains personal autonomy and enjoys physical and mental well-being well into their advanced age. The family care still prevalent in India almost guarantees their emotional health, and economic security. Older persons are usually well-respected in the family and society. There is a low rate of loneliness in old age in India.

Further, Indian elders often demonstrate a remarkable capacity for adaptation to changing goals; despite limitations, they tend to have satisfying lives. Many rural elderly live in sub-optimal conditions, yet they do not suffer from envy of prosperous members of society, do not see their situation as one of painful inequity, nor pine for reform. It would be hard to claim there is widespread dissatisfaction with age inequality or a fulminating desire for radical change among rural elders. Notwithstanding the need for uplift, they seem to be happy, expecting little, and perhaps even less scared of death.

Mortality, Morbidity, and Disability Profile in Older Persons

Age-related disorders include life-threatening diseases such as heart disease, stroke, cancer, diabetes, and infections, as well as certain chronic disabling conditions affecting vision, mobility, hearing, and cognition. Older persons also complain about various symptoms that may appear non-specific and unrelated to any classic disorder. These include general weakness, sleeplessness, constipation, flatulence, diminished appetite, decreased libido, and so forth.

Causes of death in old age. Causes of death are important indicators of health status in old age and reflect the load of diseases in the later years. In addition, data related to deaths can help in planning and the provision of health services for older persons. While infectious diseases continue to be a major cause of death in older Indians, mortality due to non-communicable degenerative disorders has become significant. According to Government of India (GOI) statistics (1991, 1995), the leading causes of geriatric mortality are respiratory diseases, followed by cardiovascular disorders, stroke, and neoplasms (see Table 2).

Geriatric morbidity and disability. The main sources of national data on geriatric morbidity are field surveys conducted by the NSSO in 1986-87 and repeated in 1995-96 (NSSO, 1991, 1998) and the multicentric collaborative studies supported by the Indian Council of Medical Research (ICMR) (Shah & Prabhkar, 1997). In addition, a number of segregated but useful studies have been carried out on health problems of the aged in different regions of the country, especially during the last decade (Purohit & Sharma, 1976; Rao, 1990; Sood et al., 1990). The earlier NSSO survey on the socioeconomic profile of older persons included an inquiry on physical mobility and seven chronic illnesses. It covered 50,000 households spread over 8,312 villages and 4,546 urban blocks. The data collected by lay investigators became available for all India, as well as for its different states (NSSO, 1991). Physical immobility was commoner in older females than older males: 5.4% of rural elders (male, 4.5%; female, 6.8%) and 5.5% of urban elders (4.6% male, 6.6% female). Those having chronic illnesses were evenly distributed among rural and urban elders (45% in each). Data with regard to individual illnesses are shown in Table 3.

These results indicate a higher rate of joint problems and cough among the rural elderly, while high blood pressure, heart disease, and diabetes were more common among urban elders. Only joint problems were more frequent in females, regardless of location. Chronic illnesses and physical immobility revealed increasing frequency with advancing age among older persons.

The second NSSO survey covered 72,883 households spread over 7,663 villages and 4,991 urban blocks. Trends over time indicate a similar pattern with regard to chronic diseases in rural versus urban areas.

TABLE 2. Distribution of Causes of Death in Older Persons in India (By Percentages)

Major cause of death	1991	1995
Bronchitis & Asthma	25.9	25.8
Heart	12.8	13.2
Paralysis	9.7	8.4
Cancer	6.0	7.1
TB/Lung	7.1	5.8
Anaemia	4.7	4.1
Diabetes	1.9	2.3
Acute Abdomen	1.7	1.6
Malaria	2.1	1.5
Typhoid	1.3	1.3
Old Age Deaths	21.95	28.19

However, collectively, the percentage of chronic diseases went up from 45% in rural elders (45.19% for males, 44.8% for females) to 52% (males, 52.7%; females, 51.4%) and from 44.8% in urban elders (males, 44.3%; females, 45.5%) to 54.5% (52.8% for males; 56% for females). Over time there was an overall increase in high blood pressure and diabetes, but a decrease in joint problems, coughs, and piles. The problem with such information collected via cross-sectional health interview surveys is that many persons are not aware of having health problems and therefore do not report them.

Several independent, multi-centric, ICMR-supported collaborative studies, however, have recorded with precision several conditions, namely: vision impairment (ICMR, 1997); hearing problems (ICMR, 1983); mental morbidity (ICMR, 1987); diabetes (Gupta et al., 1984); and cancer (ICMR, 1992). Also available are observations on hypertension (Chadha et al., 1989, 1990) and coronary disease (Chadha et al., 1989; Gupta et al., 1995).

It is reasonable to derive reliable statistics about the health problems of the aged from such studies. The estimation of load of selected chronic diseases in persons age 60+ for the year 1996 was carried out using population estimates of the Standing Committee on Population Projections (Registrar General of India, 1996). The weighted prevalence rate for each morbidity was first estimated by using the sample size covered at each center as the weight and then used for estimation of the number of persons with a specific morbidity in the year 1996 (Shah &

TABLE 3. Percentages of Aged Persons (60+ years) with Different Chronic Illnesses, 1986-87

	Rural		Urban	
	Male	Female	Male	Female
Joint Problems	44.5	50.5	35.1	44.1
Cough	35.5	32.6	26.0	22.4
Blood Pressure	6.3	6.5	16.8	18.5
Heart Disease	3.7	3.8	6.8	5.6
Urinary Problems	4.0	2.7	5.1	2.4
Piles	3.8	2.4	4.2	2.6
Diabetes	2.0	1.2	5.9	4.3

Prabhkar, 1997). The prevalence rates of chronic morbidity observed in the different studies and the estimated number of individuals with specific chronic morbidity for the year 1996 are shown in Tables 4 (urban) and 5 (rural). This information can be used to develop intervention strategies or to fix priorities for planning health services for the elderly.

The prevalence of blindness (mainly due to cataracts), hearing problems, and mental problems (70% due to depression) among the elderly was almost 10, eight, and two times higher, respectively, than the prevalence in the total population. In numbers, there were 11 million blind elders, 38 million with impaired hearing, and 1.2 million with mental problems in 1996. Furthermore, there were five million diabetics, one-third of a million cancer cases, and nine million cases each of hypertension and coronary heart disease among the elderly. The prevalence of diabetes in the elderly was about five times greater than that of the total population, and coronary disease about 20 times greater.

Significant gender differences are seen relative to prevalence of blindness (higher in females, both urban and rural), and coronary disease and hypertension (higher in rural females only). There was a greater prevalence of diabetes, hypertension, and coronary disease among urban elders compared to rural aged.

With regard to cerebrovascular diseases, data for hemiplegia (presumably of vascular origin) from community surveys from different regions of India indicate a crude prevalence rate in the range of 200 per 100,000 persons. In contrast, community-based surveys from the United States, Europe, and Japan have shown an annual stroke incidence of 110 to 180 and approximate stroke prevalence rate of 400 to 800 per

TABLE 4. Specific Morbidity Data on Persons Aged 60 Years and Above in India, 1996 (Urban)

Morbidity	No. of Persons (in Thousands)			Percentage Prevalence		
	Males	Females	Total	Males	Females	Total
Visual	788	1569	2357	9.8	19.2	14.5
Hearing	4909	5014	9923	NE	NE	61.3
Mental	NE	NE	NE	NE	NE	NE
Diabetes	1332	1254	2586	16.6	15.3	16.4
Cancer	203	152	355	0.6	0.5	0.5
Hypertension	2083	3504	5587	20.2	21.4	20.8
Coronary Heart Disease*	1825	1970	3795	22.8	24.1	23.3

NE: Not Estimated
* Prevalence rate for only 60-64 years of age group instead of 60 and above.

TABLE 5. Specific Morbidity Data on Persons Aged 60 Years and Above in India, 1996 (Rural)

Morbidity	No. of Persons (in Thousands)			Percentage Prevalence		
	Males	Females	Total	Males	Females	Total
Visual	3327	5301	8628	13.4	22.3	17.2
Hearing	10754	14152	24906	NE	NE	59.6
Mental	661	644	1305	2.0	2.0	2.0
Diabetes	1399	1254	2653	5.6	4.7	5.3
Cancer	NE	NE	NE	NE	NE	NE
Hypertension	1618	1750	3368	8.4	14.7	11.0
Coronary Heart Disease*	2545	2788	5333	10.3	14.3	11.7

NE: Not Estimated
* Prevalence rate for only 60-64 years of age group instead of 60 and above.

100,000 persons. Current trends suggest that the Indian population will survive through the peak years of stroke occurrence (ages 55-65) but these survivors with varying degrees of residual disability will present a major medical problem (Dalal, 1997).

An in-depth look at isolated reports on health problems of older persons brings out marked variations. In a rural study of 1,910 older persons in south India, Rao (1990) observed motor and visual impairments of 40% and 88%, respectively. Neurological and psychiatric symptoms were found in 19% and 9%, respectively, of those surveyed. In contrast, in an elderly sample of 612 subjects visiting a clinic at an urban tertiary teaching institution, only 117 cases of visual impairment were found, as well as 74 cases of impaired hearing and 32 of cognitive impairment (Kumar et al., 1996).

In common with many developing countries, older Indians have their share of morbidity related to infections, infestations, and malnutrition. Srivastava et al. (1996) observed that certain attitudes and practices are responsible for the inadequate diets of older persons, which are deficient in all major nutrients, fruits, and green leafy vegetables. Those who are poor are especially vulnerable. Lower respiratory and urinary tract infections, tuberculosis, and topical infections can be recurrent.

In most developing countries, including India, the scourge of tuberculosis continues unabated. Compared to the more classical upper lobe disease in younger patients, the elderly are more likely to have widespread, patchy infiltrates and in the lower lobes. Thus, the possibility of missing the diagnosis of pulmonary TB is significantly higher in elderly subjects (Khilnani & Kumar, 2001). Environmental pollution, overcrowding, mental stress, and urinary incontinence also add to geriatric morbidity. The last is not yet recognized as a priority problem. Instead, it may be perceived as a burden on the family (Melchior et al., 1998).

Because most geriatric morbidities are preventable, a focus is needed on strategies that address the determinants of health at a population, rather than an individual, level. Major preventable causes of morbidity and mortality take effect over extended time periods and thus, a life course perspective is very important for the health of older persons. Primary prevention strategies will be most useful when initiated as early as possible. Secondary strategies are applicable even at older ages where problems may already be apparent. Issues of health promotion and preventive geriatrics can be substantially addressed by primary health care measures, including self-care management (WHO, 1998).

HEALTH CARE SERVICES FOR THE ELDERLY IN INDIA

Standards and utilization of general health care services vary from country to country. India is a sub-continent of villages with deep-rooted cultural traditions. Several cheap and indigenous systems of medicine thrive and have their foundations in those traditions. Some are based on simple codes of lifestyle, namely, proper nutrition, exercise, and conduct (Wasir, 1996). In a way these codes continue to be relevant to health and quality aging in the modern era. Over the years, health care has become expensive, but it is not financial capability alone that determines the delivery of care. Attitudes and perceptions are also determining factors. Unlike the United States, where the health care system is largely entrepreneurial, the majority of people in India expect services for free or at a nominal expense. Economic constraints, coupled with illiteracy, political insensitivity, and lack of public awareness, are significant impediments to adequate health care for both young and old.

There are no separate health care services for the elderly in India. Rather, they are provided as services to the entire population. The national health policy envisages the need to provide primary health care, particularly to the rural population, with special emphasis on preventive, promotive, and rehabilitative aspects (Kumar, 1996). For this purpose, the GOI has established an extensive network of primary health centers and subcenters that are linked with secondary and tertiary care institutions. Over the years, maternal and child health, family planning, communicable disease control, and other national programs have been stressed as priority areas. Lately, the GOI has started supporting mobile medicare, day care, and old-age home services for older persons. Nevertheless, health care delivery, knowledge, and skills in rural geriatric care have not been accorded due attention so far. Urban health care is undergoing expansion, both in the public and private sectors, whereby older persons can also benefit. Unfortunately, this care is expensive, is almost completely devoid of primary care and takes the form of tertiary care. Only recently, geriatric clinics have been established in selected teaching institutions, but the concept of geriatric functional screening is still scarce. Separate wards for acute or chronic care of older persons and academic departments of geriatric medicine in Indian medical institutions are practically non-existent. Geriatric long-term care and rehabilitation have also not yet developed.

An important limiting factor in health care delivery to older persons is low utilization of available services. Compared to a developed country like Australia, illness among the elderly in the South East Asian Region (SEAR) is much higher, but as shown in Table 6, utilization of services is considerably lower (Yong, 1996).

Rao (1994) reported from a rural center in south India that of 603 older persons, only one-third utilized services from the primary health centers and subcenters. Of the remaining persons, 51.1% utilized services from hospitals and private practitioners, and 11.3% preferred indigenous methods of treatment, while the rest did not need services.

Health services utilization was also irregular and, despite the chronic nature of their illnesses, older persons were not able to visit these facilities on a regular basis.

Biswas (1994) observed that for major illnesses, about 70% of rural elderly obtained allopathic treatment, 10% homeopathic or folk medicines, and 20% received help from family, fellow villagers, or from themselves. The trend was quite different for minor illnesses: half of the elderly obtained treatment from family, villagers, or themselves, while only 40% used allopathy. Main reasons for non-utilization of formal health services include inaccessibility due to distance, the lack of escort, immobility, ignorance, and poverty (Vijaya Kumar, 1996). These can lead to dependence on non-specific home remedies.

Non-governmental organizations (NGOs) represent a significant resource for health care delivery for older persons in India. Some of these are quite active in providing outreach services and organizing medical camps in their local areas of operation. Eye camps have been very popular where large numbers of older persons get the benefit of cataract surgery within accessible distances and without much cost. (See "The Role of Non-Governmental Organizations for the Welfare of the Elderly: The Case of HelpAge India" by Maneeta Sawhney in this volume.) Many NGOs also extend assistance in procuring eyeglasses, hearing aids, and crutches for the needy elderly.

With the joint family being strained, many older persons lose family support. Here also, NGOs play a useful role by complementing Government efforts in erecting and maintaining old-age homes. The Jaycee, Rotary, and other clubs have established similar services (Barai, 1996). Currently, there are more than 750 homes (*HelpAge India*, 1995) capa-

TABLE 6. Percentage of Elderly Who Consulted a Health Professional

Study	Males	Females
AUSTRALIA		
Doctor	72.5	74.2
Nurse	0.1	8.2
Pharmacist	33.9	28.0
SEAR		
Doctor	29.2	32.4
Nurse	4.2	4.3
Pharmacist	2.2	2.3

ble of providing accommodation to 15,000 older persons. Of these, 63% are for destitute elders, 12% function on a "pay and stay" basis, and the remaining 25% are those where payment is not compulsory (Ara, 1997). (See "Old-Age Homes and Services: Old and New Approaches to Aged Care" by Dr. Phoebe S. Liebig in this volume.) Although family care is the best form of geriatric care and institutionalization of the elderly should be discouraged as much as possible, there is a need for more old-age homes in India. Moreover, greater efforts are needed to improve these facilities and the conditions of their residents.

FUTURE PROJECTIONS FOR GERIATRIC HEALTH SERVICES

Formulation of policies, program development, and implementation of health care for older persons must take into account the changing trends in the socioeconomic and cultural scenario. The increasing nuclearization of families highlights an urgent need for strengthening community-based services. Ongoing rapid urbanization calls for strategies to provide employment opportunities and income support for older persons, while the feminization of the older population requires setting up gender-sensitive programs. Above all, services should have a rural bias, operate through the primary health care system, help families in caring for the old, and encourage multigenerational living arrangements.

The existing primary health care (PHC) system, which is the backbone of rural health services, should play an increasingly central role in geriatric care. In the absence of preventive strategies, the medical profession will have to deal with greater dependence in the future, due to problems in mobility, speech and communication, severe visual decline, diseases causing terminal illness, severe incontinence, pressure sores, and a need for multiple and complex therapies. The PHC system should adopt vigorous methods of health promotion, disease prevention, and health education over a life-course perspective in order to provide a disability-free life expectancy. Self-care practices, including proper diet, must be actively encouraged at the primary health center level. The training of medical and paramedical health workers at those centers needs initiation and strengthening. The Panchayat Raj system of local self-governance at the village level and health insurance organizations are the new actors for geriatric care and should take on more activities.

AUTHOR NOTES

Dr. Vinod Kumar is Professor Emeritus, St. Stephen's Hospital, New Delhi, India. He is also a member of the World Health Organization, Expert Advisory Panel on Aging and Health.

Dr. Kumar can be contacted at 147 Charak Sadan, Vikas Puri, New Delhi, India 110018 (E-mail: vino_37@yahoo.com).

REFERENCES

Anklesaria, P. S., Pohujani, S. M., Ashar, V. J., Joshi, K. N., & Gupta, K. C. (1996). Demographic and clinical characteristics of urban elderly people. In V. Kumar (Ed.), *Aging–Indian perspective and global scenario* (pp. 26-31). New Delhi: All India Institute of Medical Sciences (AIIMS).

Ara, S. (1997). Old age homes and the profile of their residents. *Indian Journal of Medical Research, 106*, 409-412.

Barai, D. C. (1996). Integrated health care and allied services for the elderly: Some perspectives. In V. Kumar (Ed.), *Aging–Indian perspective and global scenario* (pp. 102-104). New Delhi: AIIMS.

Biswas, S. K. (1994). Implication of population and aging. In C. B. Ramachandra & B. Shah (Eds.), *Public health implications of aging in India* (pp. 22-35). New Delhi: Indian Council of Medical Research (ICMR).

Chadha, S. L., Radhakrishna, S., Ramachandran, K., & Gopinath, N. (1989). Epidemiological study of coronary heart diseases (CHD) in rural population of Gurgaon district (Haryana state). *Indian Journal of Community Medicine, 14*, 141-147.

Chadha, S. L., Radhakrishna, S., Ramachandran, K., & Gopinath, N. (1990). Epidemiological study of coronary heart disease (CHD) in urban population of Delhi. *Indian Journal of Medical Research, 92*, 424-430.

Dalal, P. M. (1997). Strokes in the elderly: Prevalence, risk factors and strategies for prevention. *Indian Journal of Medical Research, 106*, 325-332.

Dave, S. A. (2000). *Report of the project OASIS (Old age social and income security)*. Submitted to the Government of India. New Delhi: Project OASIS Expert Committee.

Government of India, Ministry of Health & Family Welfare (1991). *Annual Report*. New Delhi.

Government of India, Ministry of Health & Family Welfare (1995). *Annual Report*. New Delhi.

Government of India, Ministry of Social Justice and Empowerment (1999). *National policy on older persons*. New Delhi.

Gupta, O. P., Dave, S. K., & Jani, R. D. (1984). Prevalence of diabetes mellitus with special reference to role of undernutrition: An epidemiological and experimental study. In J. S. Bajaj, R. Madan, A. K. Shah, & V. Mohan (Eds.), *Diabetes mellitus in developing countries* (pp. 65-70). New Delhi: India Interprint.

Gupta, R., Prakash, H., Gupta, V. P., & Gupta, K. D. (1995). Prevalence of coronary risk factors in the population of Rajasthan. *Indian Heart Journal, 47*, 331-338.

HelpAge India (1995). *Directory of old age homes in India.* New Delhi.
Indian Council of Medical Research and Department of Science and Technology (1983). *Collaborative study on prevalence and etiology of hearing impairment* (pp. 30-31). New Delhi.
Indian Council of Medical Research and Department of Science and Technology (1997). *Collaborative study on blindness (1971-74): A report* (pp. 37-41). New Delhi.
Indian Council of Medical Research and Department of Science and Technology (1987). *Collaborative study on severe mental morbidity.* New Delhi.
Indian Council of Medical Research (1992). *National cancer registry programme, biennial report, 1988-89: An epidemiological study* (pp. 61-162). New Delhi.
Jarvik, L. F. & Small, G. W. (1995). Geriatric psychiatry: Introduction and overview. In H. I. Kaplan & B. F. Sadock (Eds.), *Comprehensive textbook of psychiatry* (6th ed.) (p. 2507). Baltimore: William and Wilkins.
Kalache, A. (1999). Active aging makes the difference. *Bulletin of the World Health Organization, 77,* 299.
Khetarpal, K., Soneja, S., & Kumar, V. (1996). Physical and neuropsychiatric impairments amongst the aged and their relationship to socioeconomic status. In V. Kumar (Ed.), *Aging–Indian perspective and global scenario* (pp. 134-136). New Delhi: AIIMS.
Khilnani, G. C. & Kumar, V. (2001). Tuberculosis in the elderly. In S. K. Sharma (Ed.), *Tuberculosis* (pp. 434-438). New Delhi: Jaypee Brothers Medical Publishers.
Kumar, V. (1996). *Care of the elderly* (SEARO/WHO/CSA No. SE ICP HEE 001 RB 94-95). New Delhi: World Health Organization SEARO.
Kumar, V. & Nagarkar, K. (1996). Mortality amongst elderly smokers: A north Indian perspective. *Bold, 7,* 18-21.
Kumar, V., Khetarpal, K., & Soneja, S. (1996). Geriatric assessment screening. Further observations on the AIIMS experience. In V. Kumar (Ed.), *Aging–Indian perspective and global scenario* (pp. 105-107). New Delhi: AIIMS.
Kumar, V. (1996). Care of the elderly. World Health Organisation, SEARO, New Delhi. (SEARO/WHO/CSA No. SE ICP HEE 001 RB 94-95).
Melchior, H., Kumar, V., Muller, N. et al. (1998). National public health policies for prevention and care in urinary incontinence in the elderly. *World Journal of Urology, 16* (Suppl. 1): S71-S73.
National Sample Survey Organization (NSSO) (1991). *Savekshana, 15* (49), Nos. 1-2. New Delhi.
National Sample Survey Organization (NSSO) (1998). *The aged in India: A socioeconomic profile.* Report No. 446. Ministry of Planning and Programme Implementation. Government of India, New Delhi.
Purohit, C. K., & Sharma, R. (1976). A study of general health status of persons aged 60 years and above in the rural training center area, Naila. *Indian Journal of Medical Research, 64,* 202-210.
Rajan, S. I., Mishra, U. S., & Sarma, P. S. (1999). *India's elderly: Burden or challenge.* New Delhi: Sage Publications.
Rao, A.V. (1990). *Health care of rural aged.* New Delhi: Indian Council of Medical Research.

Rao, A. V. (1994). Geriatric services at the rural level. In C. B. Ramachandra & B. Shah (Eds.), *Public health implications of aging in India* (pp. 166-175). New Delhi: Indian Council of Medical Research.

Registrar General of India (1996). *Population projections for India and states, 1996-2016.* New Delhi.

Shah, B., & Prabhkar, A. K. (1997). Chronic morbidity profile among elderly. *Indian Journal of Medical Research, 106,* 265-272.

Sharma, S. P. & Xenos, P. (1992). *Aging in India: Demographic background and analysis based on census materials.* Occasional Paper No. 2. New Delhi: Office of the Registrar General & Census Commissioner, India.

Soneja, S., Nagarkar, K. M., Dey, A. B., Khetarpal, K., & Kumar, V. (1996). Socioeconomic status and its relationship to parameters of social morbidity among elderly patients seeking outpatient medical care. In V. Kumar (Ed.), *Aging–Indian perspective and global scenario* (pp. 137-139). New Delhi: AIIMS.

Sood, R., Dey, A. B., Goel, K., & Kumar, V. (1990). Age-related factors in chronic obstructive disease. *Indian Practitioner, XVDLIII,* 207-211.

Srivastava, M., Kapil, U., & Kumar, V. (1996). Knowledge, attitude and practices regarding nutrition in patients attending geriatric clinic at AIIMS. In V. Kumar (Ed.), *Aging–Indian perspective and global scenario* (pp. 407-409). New Delhi: AIIMS.

Sureender, S., & Khan, A. G. (1996). Aging in India: Some emerging issues. In V. Kumar (Ed.), *Aging–Indian perspective and global scenario* (pp. 9-11). New Delhi: AIIMS.

United Nations (1991). *World population prospects 1988.* New York.

Vijaya Kumar, S. (1996). Rural elderly: Health status and available health services. *Research and Development Journal, 2,* 16-22.

Wasir, H. S. (1996). Life styles and longevity. In V. Kumar (Ed.), *Aging–Indian perspective and global scenario* (pp. 71-77). New Delhi: AIIMS.

World Health Organization, Aging and Health Programme (1998). Women, aging and health–Achieving health across the life span (WHO/HPR/AHE/HPD/96.1 Rev. I). Geneva.

Yong, L. B. (1996). Situation on health care of the elderly programme in WHO South East Asia. In V. Kumar (Ed.), *Aging–Indian perspective and global scenario* (pp. 3-8). New Delhi: AIIMS.

Aging, Disability, and Disabled Older People in India

Indira Jai Prakash, PhD

Bangalore University, Bangalore, India

SUMMARY. India is witnessing a demographic revolution, leading to a considerable increase in the proportion of older people in the population. Similarly, life expectancy of both the mentally and physically disabled has improved considerably. About 5% of Indian older people have problems with physical mobility. Aging has become a gender issue in India not only because more women are surviving into old age; they are also vulnerable and disadvantaged in many ways. In most cases they are the only caregivers available for the old and disabled. Older Indians are considered a high-risk group for multiple morbidity. It is estimated that nearly four million Indians suffer from mental problems. India has around 12 million people designated as "handicapped." However, little information is available about disabled people who grow older. The National Policy on Older Persons, which has been recently formulated, aims at providing an improved quality of life for millions of older Indians. However, the concerns of older disabled and of the disabled who grow old are still treated separately in both policy and practice. *[Article copies available for a fee from The Haworth Document Delivery Service: 1-800-HAWORTH. E-mail address: <docdelivery@haworthpress.com> Website: <http://www.HaworthPress.com> © 2003 by The Haworth Press, Inc. All rights reserved.]*

[Haworth co-indexing entry note]: "Aging, Disability, and Disabled Older People in India." Prakash, Indira Jai. Co-published simultaneously in *Journal of Aging & Social Policy* (The Haworth Press, Inc.) Vol. 15, No. 2/3, 2003, pp. 85-108; and: *An Aging India: Perspectives, Prospects, and Policies* (ed: Phoebe S. Liebig, and S. Irudaya Rajan) The Haworth Press, Inc., 2003, pp. 85-108. Single or multiple copies of this article are available for a fee from The Haworth Document Delivery Service [1-800-HAWORTH, 9:00 a.m. - 5:00 p.m. (EST). E-mail address: docdelivery@haworthpress.com].

© 2003 by The Haworth Press, Inc. All rights reserved.
http://www.haworthpress.com/store/product.asp?sku=J031
10.1300/J031v15n02_06

KEYWORDS. Mentally disabled elders, physically disabled elders, gender and aging, multiple disabilities

INTRODUCTION

Increased attention to aging issues has been necessitated by the demographic changes that the world has witnessed in recent years. In this new millennium, the world's population will have grown by 38%, while the over-age-60 segment will have increased at a more rapid rate of 57%. India is no exception to this phenomenon of the "graying of nations." A highly populous country, second only to China in sheer numbers, India is expected to have around 76 million people in the age 60+ category. One out of seven older persons in the world has been projected to be from India in the year 2001 (Sharma & Agarwal, 1996). Life expectancy at birth, which was as low as 22.5 years for males and 23.3 years for females in 1901, rose to 60.1 and 59.8 years, respectively, by 1991. Life expectancy at age 65 in India is also gradually rising and getting closer to that of the developed countries.

Such demographic trends pose multiple challenges that have not yet been fully understood by planners and policymakers. The rapid rise in the elderly population has not been met with an expansion in health-care service and the provision of socioeconomic coverage, although it is evident that age is often associated with disability, frailty, and demand for long-term care. There are two facets to the problem of aging and disability: First, older people develop disabilities and need long-term care; second, people who were disabled earlier in the life cycle grow old. In both instances, planning is required to meet the needs of such people adequately.

Older People and Disability

It is common to associate old age with disability. An important factor, however, needs to be kept in mind while examining the association between age and disability. First of all, older people are a heterogeneous lot. It is true that extreme losses of physical, mental, and social functions are often seen in old people. Yet, many may continue to maintain high levels of function. However, as "young-old" move into the "old-old" category, they tend to have more health complaints and diagnosed illnesses. Age and the presence and duration of chronic disease account for a portion of the variation in functional ability (Camacho et al., 1993). In the old-old group, there is likely to be a minority with no or mild disability in any domain of functioning. The majority, however, will have multiple disabilities, while a sizeable group will have difficulties with instrumental activities of daily living (IADLs) (Zarit, Johansson, & Berg, 1993).

Most researchers subscribe to the belief that an increased survival rate may lengthen the period of chronic illness and disability in old age. There is an opposing viewpoint that there may be a "compression of morbidity" with decline in incidence of chronic illness and restriction of disability to a brief period prior to death; thus, there will be a greater number of healthier people in the "old-old" group (Fries, 1983). Regardless of the outcome of these contrasting geriatric scenarios, there are problems in providing care for the old and support for the family members caring for frail and disabled elders (Venkoba Rao, 1996).

The impact of age and disability on well-being does not appear to be simple. Advancing age may symbolize the attainment of personal and institutional resources that contribute to a high sense of mastery and competence. On the other hand, age can also reflect loss and decline in health and status. As people age, sensory, motor, and cognitive capacities can decline. Associations among age, physical deterioration, chronic disease, impairment, and cognitive function are well-documented (Cockerham, 1997; Prakash, 1997).

Disabled People Growing Old

The other dimension to the question of age and disability concerns disabled people who grow old. Are there commonalties and differences between persons who become old and also disabled as opposed to those who are disabled at a young age and then grow old? The former have been able-bodied all their lives and later in life have disabilities. The latter have lived with a disability and now are aging. Does aging combine with disability and pose a "double disadvantage?" The pattern of adjustment and the nature of problems may not be the same for these two groups (Genskow, 1988). Health plays a significant role in aging, and the experience of chronic, ongoing disability is of particular importance to older persons. Long-term disabilities represent chronic sources of stress for older individuals; by their very nature, such disabilities are difficult to control.

Schieman and Turner (1998) argue that aging involves role losses that often imply a loss of social support. As age increases, age and disability jointly combine so that the disabled become more disadvantaged. But this relationship may be non-linear. There is a normative reference process–disabled compare themselves to non-disabled age peers along several dimensions of mastery that vary across the life span. The interactive effect of age and disability appears most dramatic during middle years. It is also argued that those who experience disability in earlier years may adjust to alternate life-styles (Lewis, 1989; Trieschmann, 1987). There may be a normative sense of impairment and physical decline that is age-specific such that the impact of physical disability on self-conception may differ, depending on when physical impairment occurs in the life course. For example, socializing agents like the media may reinforce the perception that aging is associated with physical decline and produce a general expectation that it is "normal" for older people to be physically impaired. Bultena and Powers (1978) note that it is ironical that the negative stereotypes about older persons may be functional in the sense of providing a sufficiently dreary picture of old age that many aged, by comparison, feel advantaged. Younger people may have more negative emotions associated with disability.

The concern about the disabled elderly is relatively new. Survival into adulthood of people with disabilities that once were often fatal poses new challenges. Traditionally, people who age and people with disabilities have been split into opposing camps in the eyes of both providers of services as well as their own self-perceptions (Zola, 1989). It is only recently that a need for more universal policies is being articulated, because the problem is not confined to any small fixed number of populations. The issues facing someone with disability are not essentially medical. They are not purely the result of physical or mental factors but rather the fit of such impairment with the social, attitudinal, architectural, medical, economical, and political environment.

The problems of disabled older people are hard to pin down. For example, problems of circulation and vision may be due to disease itself or due to the aging process, or even due to an original life-sustaining treatment. In the 1980s it was discovered that people who had been treated for polio were experiencing problems nearly 20 years later. The most common symptoms were fatigue, weakness in muscles previously affected or unaffected, muscle-joint pain, breathing problems, and intolerance to cold. Whether the new problems are merely concomitant of aging, the reemergence of a lingering virus, the long-term effect of early damage or of early rehabilitation programs, or something else is an issue still debated. Whatever the etiology, there are likely to be many more new manifestations of an existing disease as the disabled population survives beyond the acute onset of original disability. Still another source of challenge is the fit between any impairment and the larger social environment. Simply put, some disabilities become important only in certain social situations (e.g., impaired mobility in a sports-oriented society), at a certain time of life (e.g., sexual and reproductive issues were considered less important for very young and very old), and some only for one gender (Zola, 1986).

OLDER PEOPLE AND DISABILITY IN INDIA

It has repeatedly been pointed out that the progress India has made in extending the life span of its citizens has not been carried over to providing a healthy and disability-free old age (Satyanarayana & Medappa, 1997; Sharma & Agarwal, 1996). In the absence of reliable monitoring and reporting as well as poor coverage of health services, most of the vital health statistics are generalizations from limited samples (Kumar, 1997). Most researchers analyse the data released from the National Sample Survey Organization (NSSO) or depend on studies published by Indian Council of Medical Research (ICMR). Data from NSSO reveal chronic illness in 45% of elderly in rural and urban areas (Kohli, 1996). Further analysis by age shows that at the younger age of 60-64, more women than men have chronic illnesses.

Morbidity in Older People

Compiling data from several studies initiated by the Indian Council of Medical Researches, Shah and Prabhkar (1997) report considerable morbidity in the older population. Statistics from different studies quoted by them are summarized in Table 1.

The table shows the total number of persons from rural and urban areas covered in the studies and the prevalence rate of morbidity observed. However, the studies span nearly 25 years, from the 1970s to the 1990s.

Shah and Prabhkar (1997) further report visual impairments in 11 million Indians, while 38 million have hearing impairments. Hypertension among the urban elderly was twice as high as among the rural elderly. Older subjects had nearly 20 times higher prevalence of hypertension compared to total population. A study based in Delhi observed a prevalence rate of 229 and 210 per 1000 in old men and women. The prevalence rate of Coronary Heart Disease (CHD) was nearly three times higher in the urban than in the rural population. In

TABLE 1. Prevalence Rate per 1000 of Specific Morbidity in Persons Ages 60 and Above, in Urban and Rural Areas

Health Problem		Male	Female	Total
Visual Impairment	U	4611 (98.5)	3773 (191.9)	8384 (140.5)
	R	9217 (134.6)	6726 (223.6)	15943 (172.18)
Hearing Impairment	U	277 (NE)	284 (NE)	561 (613.2)
	R	367 (NE)	355 (NE)	722 (596.9)
Hypertension	U	267 (202.1)	327 (214.1)	614 (208.5)
	R	427 (84.3)	487 (147.8)	914 (110.1)
CHD (60-64 yr only)	U	145 (228.0)	116 (241.0)	261 (233.7)
	R	107 (103.0)	63 (143.0)	170 (117.6)
Diabetes	U	168 (166.4)	111 (241.0)	279 (164.7)
	R	183 (56.6)	132 (47.6)	415 (53.2)

U = Urban areas   R = Rural areas

1996, there were around 9 million CHD cases, with males outnumbering females. Urban areas also have larger numbers of diabetics than rural areas. Such differences could very well be due to poor diagnostic procedures and lack of access to health care in rural areas. The population-based cancer registries initiated in some large cities reported 0.35 million detected cases among elderly in 1996 alone. Tobacco-related cancer is common among males, while in females, cancers of uterine cervix and breast are more common (Shah & Prabhkar, 1997).

Because India is a vast country with wide interstate variations, generalizations may be difficult. Yet the trend is clear and unmistakable: The majority of the adult population is employed in unorganized and agrarian sectors. People work till they are no longer able to, since there is no comprehensive pension scheme or social security scheme to cover them in old age. Thus, work participation rate in old age is much higher in India than in developed countries (Dandekar, 1996). A sizeable portion of the population, nearly 273 million, is under the poverty line (Rao, 1990). Poverty and inadequacy of income leads to dependence on children in old age. The dependency ratio is high–around 67.6% in 2001. Given these factors, the health of older persons is bound to be poor.

According to Dandekar (1996), about 5% of old persons in rural and urban India were physically "immobile" (unable to move around without help). Women had more physical health problems, which is another offshoot of their generally lower status in society and a poor reproductive health-care system. Dandekar presents figures from the National Sample Survey regarding physical immobility, which are summarized in Table 2.

Nearly 60% of those who were immobile were from the age group 70+. In about 92% of cases, household members provided the necessary care; characteristically, the female members (spouse, daughter-in-law, or daughter) provided the care. Chronic illness increased with age. The percentage of those who were chronically ill rose from 39% in those age 60-64 to 45% in the 65-69 age group, to 55% in those age 70 and older. Regional variations in the nature of chronic illness are also evident. With the exception of rural Haryana, rural areas in other states had more women suffering from physical disability. Variations in blood pressure, heart disease, urinary problems or diabetes were apparently more common in urban areas (Dandekar, 1996). It is possible that rural areas lack basic facilities for diagnosis, and hence, there may be underreporting of illnesses.

A community-based study of health and functional competence (ability to carry on activities of living in spite of old age) on rural and urban elderly reports long-term illness in nearly 60% of people aged 65 and above (Prakash, 1998a). Thirty-nine percent of all the subjects rated their health as less than satisfactory than before, and 69% felt it was worse when compared to their own-age peers. While 75% preferred allopathic doctors, 23% were experimenting with alternative systems of medicine, especially Ayurveda.

Mobility and vision are two important factors affecting independence in old age. Nearly 55.5% of men and 50% of women in rural areas had problems with their sight. Their visual impairment was aggravated because they did not have access to corrective surgery or prosthetic

TABLE 2. Percentage of Physically Immobile Persons in Different Age Groups in Rural and Urban Areas

Age	Urban		Rural	
	Male	Female	Male	Female
60-64	2.236	3.297	2.404	3.251
65-69	4.111	4.723	3.332	4.871
70 & above	8.102	11.658	8.326	13.457

aids. About 45% of rural old complained of problems in walking. Yet, use of prosthetic devices was less common in rural areas.

Activities of daily living (ADL) measures were used as an index of functional competence in this study (Prakash, 1998a). Rural women had more problems with ADL, indicating the need for help in self-care. Also, rural people had less access to health facilities; most of them were illiterate and led marginal existences. These factors are likely to increase their dependence on others in old age. A more disturbing finding was while 26% of rural women required help with ADL, only 4.34% were getting such help. Urban men managed to get maximum care from multiple sources. Problems with ADLs were closely related to subjective well-being, sex, and social support apart from economic variables and age. Problems in sensory domain and mobility coupled with dependence on family did not augur well for this sample. Rural elderly and women are likely to be more vulnerable as they have more ADL problems, fewer social supports, and are economically dependent (Prakash, 1998a).

Mental Morbidity and Age-Related Disability

The elderly are considered a high-risk group for multiple morbidity: physical, mental, and social (Venkoba Rao, 1997). The prevalence rate of morbidity among those aged 60+ was estimated at 89/1000, which, when projected onto the population, yielded a figure of nearly 4 million, which is lower than the 263/1000 reported for the United Kingdom. It is possible that the lower prevalence rate is an artifact. Small-scale studies with small samples and underreporting of cases due to non-availability of mental health services could very well yield low rates of prevalence. Affective disorders, particularly depression, late paraphrenia, and dementias, form the bulk of mental morbidity in the Indian elderly. Neurotic disorders are relatively infrequent in this age group.

The risk for psychiatric illness in the elderly increases *pari passu* with age. The overall prevalence rate of psychiatric morbidity rises from 71.5% for those over 60 (but below 70) to 124% in the 70s to 155% in those over 80. In a study of psychiatric morbidity of an elderly population in a rural community in West Bengal (Nandi et al., 1997), the rate of mental morbidity was as high as 612/1000 population. Sixty-one percent of all the elderly contacted were diagnosed as mentally ill. Extrapolating this to the national aged population in 2000, the number of mentally ill comes to around 36 million, more than the total population of three metropolises–Mumbai, Calcutta, and Delhi–taken together.

Geriatric depression is the most common diagnosis with a prevalence rate of 60/1000 in the general population (Venkoba Rao & Madhavan, 1983). Nandi et al. (1997) also found depression to be most common in old age, with the rate of prevalence being 522/1000 population, with 101 cases out of 112 in their study being diagnosed as depression. Women had a higher rate of depression (704/1000). An analysis from an ICMR Task Force Geropsychiatric study revealed that 43% of psychiatric outpatients in the 60+ age group suffered depression. In the extended study of this task force involving 1910 rural elderly people, psychiatric morbidity was detected in 8.1% of them, with 133 cases of depression among the total 160 cases (Venkoba Rao, 1990). The clinical picture of geriatric depression generally conformed to those occurring at other ages. However, an increased agitation and restlessness rather than retardation, rarity of ideas of guilt and sin, and a higher frequency of somatic and paranoidal symptomatology were seen. Shah, Panchal, and Goswami (1995), in a study of geriatric medical inpatients, found depressive symptoms in 40% of the subjects. The majority were men who were widowed and belonged to joint families.

Not only is geriatric depression more common, but older patients also form a high-risk group for self-destructive behavior. The suicide rate rises sharply from the "young-old" to the "old-old" group, and the rate of completed suicide is around 12/100,000 (7/100,000 for general population). Underreporting of suicides to the extent of a third is also noted. The ratio of "completers" to "attempters" is 1:7 as compared to 1:15 in younger age groups (Venkoba Rao, 1985).

Physiological factors, particularly chronic disease, play an important part in mental illness among the aged. Poor hearing and eyesight, and reduced mobility affect the kinds of interactions one can have with others and thus affect inner experience of sensory stimulation. In addition, physical changes may make people less sure of themselves and more isolated from others. Such changes, when combined with losses that accompany old age and lowered social status, lead to psychopathology (Prakash, 1998b). Recent studies have found that depressive disorders can be caused by or aggravated by associated physical illness. In 67% of the elderly depressives, physical illness and disability were found to have an aggravating role (Satapathy et al., 1997). Multiple illnesses were seen in 90% of the patient population compared to only 20% of the control group.

A significant feature of late-life illness is that a psychiatric disorder is seldom an "isolated" event. A minimum of two or three clinical diagnoses is the rule. The number of symptoms older patients display may vary between six and 12. These are associated with disabilities and handicaps such as opthalmological (mainly cataract), degenerative arthritis, neurological, caradiovascular, respiratory, dermatological, hearing, urinary, nutritional, and neoplastic disorders in that order of frequency (Venkoba Rao, 1997). Delusional disorders increase with age, and hearing and visual problems often contribute to development of such symptoms. Sagar et al. (1995), in their investigation of psychogeriatric patients, found hypertension (28%), followed by problems with vision (22%) and deafness (14%), common in the patients registered in a psychiatric unit. The roles of factors such as widowhood (Nandi et al., 1997), low socioeconomic status (Khetrapal et al., 1996), and gender (Premarajan et al., 1993; Prakash, 1997; Nandi et al., 1997) in the etiology of depression in the elderly have been emphasized.

A World Health Organization (WHO)-coordinated multi-center study on estimating prevalence of dementia in those aged 65 and above has thrown some light on such disorders in India. The prevalence rate of dementia was reported to be 27/1000 in urban and 35/1000 in rural areas (Rajkumar, 1995). Around 35-40% of these were diagnosed as Alzheimer's disease (AD). As the number of elderly increases in the population, a concomitant rise in proportion of dementia is also expected. The prevalence may be more in the community but may not have been detected. The reasons for this include: families (traditional caretakers of the old) may consider the disturbances as part of normal aging; there is no confirmatory test to diagnose AD; associated illnesses like depression may mask cognitive impairment; and early death of patients due to co-morbid illnesses. In the majority of cases, dementia does not begin until after age 65. However, an estimated 5-10% develop the symptoms in middle age, which leads to financial and emotional problems. The level at which a person with dementia is able to function is affected by factors other than dementia, such as secondary psychiatric symptoms, presence of other illness, reactions to medication, sensory impairment, and external stressors.

Families are the most common caregivers. The burden of caregiving is considerable in the absence of a support system and respite services. Persons with dementia are at particular risk of receiving substandard care since they cannot communicate effectively and may have affective and behavioral problems that add to that burden. Though dementia is less common than depression in Indian elders, its impact on the individual and the family is much more serious and prolonged. Called the "disease of our century," it is likely to become a major problem in the next decades (Rajkumar, 1995). Many depressed patients present a clinical picture of cognitive impairment of pseudodementia. Such dementia is reversible and disappears with the treatment of depression.

Efforts have been made to diagnose elderly subjects for possible dementing disorder using screening devices. Krishnamurthy et al. (1998) report the Mini Mental State Examination (MMSE) to be useful with Indian geriatric patients. Out of 21 patients tested, 11 cases were diagnosed as dementia-based on MMSE. With further examination and a CT scan, only three patients were confirmed later as dementia cases. However, none who had been screened out was later identified as a dementia case. Khandelwal et al. (1992) found that behavioral symptoms, because of their disturbing nature, are the major causes of anxiety and concern for caregivers and, frequently, the causes of hospitalization of old people. Behavioral changes are present from the beginning of the disease process or may appear at a later stage.

Using a Global deterioration scale, Khandelwal and associates found 12 patients among 30 individuals with symptoms that would classify them as low-severity dementia. In 14 of the cases, severity was rated as high and four belong to the stage of mild cognitive decline. Patients with mild cognitive decline tended to have symptoms of anxiety and depression. Patients with moderate intensity of dementia had depressive and paranoid symptoms. In severe cases, paranoid and motor symptoms were predominant. Different types of behavioral problems such as stealing, delusions of infidelity, suspicion, wandering, and aggression were noticed.

Very little has been done so far in India either in identifying people with cognitive impairment in the community or in providing long-term care for such cases. In the West, behavioral gerontologists have honed a number of techniques to manage cases of dementia and other types of cognitive impairment in the family or in the community itself. Wisocki (1991) reports several successful attempts to train geriatric patients in self-care and in reducing behavioral problems in demented patients. In India, only recently behavior therapists have started paying attention to geriatric cases. A study was undertaken at Bangalore University (Nagendra, 1998) to identify cognitive impairment in older people living in the community and to train family members in behavioral management of such cases. Many families burdened with caregiving suffer from lack of information about the illness, lack of information about management issues, lack of support systems, and lack of respite services. Since deeply entrenched traditional values make parent care obligatory, many families suffer from stress and guilt due to their inability to provide quality care.

DISABLED OLDER PEOPLE IN INDIA

From the very beginning, the Indian census included information on physical "infirmities." In 1872, questions about blind, deaf, dumb, insane, idiot, and lepers were included in the census (Sen, 1995). However, from 1931 to 1981, such information was not elicited. When the practice was resumed in 1981, the disabled population was found to be around 1.709 per 1000. Estimates of the disabled in the population vary as different definitions are used to identify them. Many surveys include five categories:

1. Orthopaedically handicapped,
2. Visually handicapped,
3. Deaf and dumb,
4. Mentally handicapped, and
5. Leprosy afflicted.

Different statistics have been published by various agencies at various times regarding prevalence of disability. In 1981, the census of India reported the proportion of handicapped as a mere 1.8% of the population; that figure amounted to 12.27 million. This figure did not include about 3.20 million people afflicted with leprosy. Leprosy is a major public health problem in India; worldwide, the total number of leprosy patients is highest in India (Dalawari, 1988). A cluster sampling study of a rural area in Uttar Pradesh (Joshi et al., 1988) found 703 handicapped persons in a population of 25,743 people. Orthopedic handicap was the most prevalent (69.7%), followed by visual (45%). Multiple handicaps were reported in 6%, and mental handicap was seen in 2.99%.

Several studies were conducted in the 1980s. Some reported findings on samples that include psychiatric patients, epileptics, and mentally retarded individuals (Verghese, 1984) and indicate that one-third of the disability is due to mental illness. Problems related to schizophrenia are higher than other illnesses. In another survey of a village in Maharashtra, Mathur (1985) found disability to be high in the 31-60 age group and higher in males, in low-income groups, and in those living in poor environments and crowded conditions. Interestingly, this study included three types of "handicaps": physical, which included accidents, polio, tuberculosis, blindness, deafness; mental, including retardation, epilepsy, neurosis, psychosis, and alcoholism; and social, which included juvenile delinquency, behavior problems, drug addiction, marital problems, and illegitimacy. In another survey, the prevalence of physical handicap was reported to be 1.69% (Yelurkar & Mazumdar, 1985) overall, but highest (7.75%) in those age 51 and above. Among the neurologically disabled, the majority were found to be in the 20-35 age group (Rajaram & Gourie-Devi, 1988). There are suggestions that with an ever-growing HIV-positive population, HIV and AIDS should be considered as chronic illnesses and rehabilitative services should be planned accordingly (All & Fried, 1994).

A sample survey conducted by NSSO in 1991 covered four types of disabilities: Visual, Hearing, Speech, and Locomotor. About 16.15 million people were estimated to have one or other of the four types of disabilities. This constituted 1.9% of the estimated total population of the country. For the country as a whole, the prevalence rate was 20 per thousand in rural areas and 16 in urban areas. Between the two sexes, the prevalence was marginally more among males than females. About 3% of the estimated child population were said to have delayed development. Random sample surveys report 2-2.5% of the population of the country as mentally retarded; 28.56 million are said to have visual impairments; 4 million are affected by leprosy; and 3.636 million are orthopedically handicapped. One report from an NGO states that while 9.6 million people in India are affected by locomotor disabilities, only 5% have access to some kind of mobility aid (Mobility India, 1997). Accidents involving farming implements are considered to be a significant factor in causing disability in the rural Indian adult population (Mittal, Bedi, & Gulati, 1987; Mittal & Singla, 1987).

The Invisible Disabled

The most striking aspect of the disabled population is its invisibility (Thudipara, 1998). Until recently, disability was not an "issue" of great concern with thinkers, politicians, or human rights groups. This persisted in spite of the fact that disabled persons, along with their families, are not a minority group. If a WHO estimate is correct, 10% of the population is disabled. This, along with another 40% who are the families of disabled, constitutes a major group (Thudipara, 1998). The most tragic aspect of all these statistics is that over 70% of disabilities are preventable. While 80% of the disabled live in rural areas, most of the rehabilitative services are located in urban areas. Only 2% of the rural and 5% of the urban disabled population have access to rehabilitative services. Until the late 1970s, rehabilitation involved either institutionalization or physical management. The staggering number of handicapped–as numerous as the populations of Sweden and Denmark put together–has not been targeted as a priority group and provided with comprehensive service. The majority of the handicapped are found in nearly destitute conditions (Rao, 1990).

Statistics are not available regarding the older disabled in India. With increased life expectancy, many handicapped are surviving into middle and old age. Most agencies that work with the disabled serve them only up to age 18 or to a maximum of age 25. Institutions, however, have more flexible policies. Once institutionalized, the disabled (who are usually destitute) continue to live in facilities throughout their lives. Published information about adjustment or life-style of such older disabled is not available. The Persons with Disabilities Bill of 1994, drafted by the Ministry of Welfare, Government of India, alludes to the establishment of educational, vocational, and other training of disabled, in an obvious reference to young disabled. But nowhere is a mention made of disabled who survive to be old. A thorough search of rehabilitation literature in Indian journals yields poor results. Except for some sporadic reports on disabled workers (Agrawal & Dhar, 1984; Ittyerah & Rani, 1990; Karbanda, 1988; Daftuar, 1993), there is hardly any substantial information about issues relevant to older disabled persons. Such reports usually deal with one or two social/psychological variables and are not studies dealing with the issue of aging as such. The complexities of interaction between age and disability or the aging process in disabled persons are not the theme of any such efforts.

This trend may be largely due to two factors. Lack of attention to the problems of disabled has already been mentioned. Focusing on the older persons as a special group meriting special attention is also new to India. For a very long time planners and policymakers assumed that the traditional family structure would take care of its old and found it difficult to imagine that aging was an issue to be taken seriously. Until the demographic truth hit them hard and problems became too serious to be ignored, there was complacency that all was well with Indian elderly. Only when these demographic changes result in a large body of disabled adults who can act as a pressure group will the government take notice of them. The curious absence of research interest in older disabled persons stems from the fact that gerontology is only recently emerging as a field of study in the academic world. Currently, there is no national database on the older population, and data are trickling in at a slow pace.

A study of burden experienced by aging parents caring for their adult disabled children was carried out at Bangalore University (Sitther, 1999). Sixty parents (30 each of mentally and physically disabled adult children) were interviewed and assessed on various measures. The ages of the mentally retarded adults ranged from 20 years to 47 years; ages of physically handicapped ranged from 20 to 36 years; and the ages of the caregiving parents ranged from 50 to 74 years. Feminization of caring was evident with mothers being the major caregivers, regardless of the type of disability (mental or physical) and the sex of the child (34/50). Women depended on their spouses (if care recipient is a son), and on daughters-in-law (if it is a daughter), as helpers in caregiving. Men had larger networks of helpers in caregiving compared to women. More women were the sole caregivers and did not have any helpers in this task. Inability of the children to care for themselves, not having facilities for alternate care, and sentimental reasons were cited as prompting caregiving.

Research shows that the use of formal services by older caregivers is low (Krout, 1985) even in the West where fairly-well-organized formal systems are available. Since most institutions provide service to younger disabled and many do not maintain contact with "discharged" clients, identification of adult disabled is difficult. Special employment exchanges cater to the needs of the "employable" disabled. There are a few rehabilitation homes where the residents are mostly psychiatrically disabled or destitute. Hence, data collection is slow and tedious. The trend, however, confirms the general findings in other countries regarding feminization of caring. Most families accept the disability, especially mental, as "karma," fate, or "god's will." There is little planning for transfer of care if the disabled out-survive their families. Even in the developed countries, there is a trend for most developmentally disabled people to live with their families, unknown to formal service providers. Wood (1993) found, for example, that caregivers, whose mean age was 69.4 years, had not made adequate plans for transfer of care of their adult children (mean age 46 years). This was mainly because they did not expect their children to out-survive them and because information about appropriate alternatives was not available. Sometimes mutual dependence develops between elderly caregivers and dependent adults, and sometimes caregiving may be beneficial to the elderly family member (Heller, 1993).

THE GENDER ISSUE

Aging is a universal phenomenon, but gender makes a difference to the aging experience. Gender is a very important variable that influences quality of life at all ages, especially in old age (Prakash, 1997). Aging has become a gender issue in India, as in other countries. India is one of the very few countries where the sex ratio is biased in favor of men (974 female/1000 male). The effect that the low status of women has on mortality is expected to decline in future. The biological advantage that women have over men is seen in India in the 70+ age group, with the percentage of women being 50.9% as compared to 49.1% for men (Dandekar, 1996). Thus, in spite of relatively higher mortality, the percentage of women in older age groups will be higher.

The main social effect of the extension of life in later years for women is the extended periods of widowhood. The percentage of widows in India is disproportionately larger than that of widowers. At 60, 65, and 70 years, the percentage of widowers is 14.13, 17.06, and 27.12, respectively. By contrast, the percentages are 55.98, 58.41, and 77.57 respectively for widows. Most older women are likely to be illiterate or poorly educated, unlikely to have held a remunerative job, and are likely to be dependent totally on others for economic needs (Prakash, 1995). Older women have more problems of health, have higher ADL difficulties, and are psychologically distressed and more depressed. Older women form a vulnerable group, usually ignored by planners and policymakers as well as by the health-care delivery system, which is largely preoccupied with reproductive health and birth control (Prakash, 1997).

Published information on the disabled hardly makes any reference to gender differences or comments about aging disabled women. This is to be expected, because only recently has there been any gender-based analysis of data in any of the fields, including psychology. Given the patriarchal structure of Indian society, it would be highly interesting to examine the social response to disability in women. Women occupy a disadvantaged position as a consequence of traditional sex-role socialization. Although men may also be victimized due to their disabilities, cultural expectations and traditional socialization patterns send oppressive messages to women about power, economic independence, occupational aspirations, attractiveness, sexuality, and family roles (Alston & McCowan, 1994). Britt (1988) asserts that being female and possessing a disability compounds the effect of stigmatization. The negative impact of this double stigma may be illustrated in numerous ways, but none so clearly as a cursory examination of employment statistics for women with disabilities (in the West). Bowe (1984) reports that nearly 60% of non-disabled women are employed, compared to less than 20% of disabled. More disheartening is the fact that disabled women earn only 74% of the income earned by the employed non-disabled.

Bartholomew (1982) outlines the myths that surround disability and sexuality: (1) Women with disabilities can never be considered sexually attractive. (2) They cannot engage in sexual activity. (3) They should not consider becoming mothers. (4) They should consider themselves fortunate if they ever find a partner. Internalizing such negative beliefs may make a woman question her own sexuality. It is common knowledge in India that marriage prospects for a disabled woman are very poor. In a country where the auspiciousness of the star under which a girl is born still decides her marital prospects, this is hardly surprising. There are special provisions for free education for the disabled, which may help the female disabled. Special employment exchanges set up by the government help provide jobs for all disabled. It has been reported that most people, unless they have a handicapped person in their own family, do not know how to respond to, or interact, with a handicapped person, which makes social integration of the disabled problematic (Rao, 1990).

Reproductive Rights of Disabled Women

In 1994, a controversy was created when a state-run institution for mentally disabled women in Maharashtra permitted hysterectomies on the residents. This created an explosive public debate about human rights, medical ethics, the right to survival and reproduction, dignity and decency, and the responsibility of the family and state. The primary argument for conducting the hysterectomy was first of all to maintain menstrual hygiene of the mentally retarded women and secondarily to avoid unwanted pregnancy and sexual abuse (Britto & Simon, 1994). There were very vocal confrontations among women's groups, families, and institutional staff on this issue. This was the only time the problem of disabled adults came into public view.

Many of the families involved felt that a hysterectomy would protect their mentally disabled womenfolk from sexual abuse, but women's groups called this irresponsible. They pointed out that the state had the responsibility to ensure dignified life to all citizens. If primary care in terms of bathing, cleaning, and feeding is being provided for dependent inmates year round, managing them for a few days of each month should not be really difficult. Similarly, fear of unwanted pregnancy may deter potential abusers. Hysterectomy may remove this deterrent and make the women more vulnerable. It was also pointed out that the idea of sexual abuse in protective custodial care itself goes against the very philosophy of such a care facility. Women's groups considered the state's intervention an offensive technical assault on women.

It is interesting that an Association of Parents of Mentally Retarded and those afflicted with cerebral palsy strongly supported the decision to conduct hysterectomies. But most of the institutionalized women did not have parents, and the question of parental permission for the surgery was irrelevant. A local branch of the Indian Medical Association criticized the public outcry against the operations and denied the allegation that medical ethics had been violated. Another expert questioned whether it was not a gross invasion of privacy of a woman to have someone else take care of her menstrual hygiene. Some chose to dismiss the whole debate as the "antics of dumb-witted busy bodies" (*SNDT News Letter*, 1994). This debate is certainly of interest to social psychologists regarding analysis of social attitudes and practices, as related to women and especially to disabled women.

POLICIES AND PROGRAMS FOR OLDER PEOPLE

The problems of older persons who are disabled are truly multidimensional and call for a multisectorial approach involving health, social, economic, and psychological disciplines. The government-supported health programs targeted for the elderly are quite inadequate due to economic constraints. Geriatric health care has risen on the Nation's health agenda only recently. Schemes such as the National Social Assistance Programme launched in 1995 that costs the exchequer over 4000 million rupees annually to provide economic assistance have not covered the entire section of needy "destitutes." The Constitution of India urges the state to shield older people from undeserved want in their old age. An Old Age Pension (OAP) scheme has been introduced to meet the needs of people who have no means to support themselves. But many states accord OAP a low priority, and the monthly amount given is low. The Ministry of Welfare makes some financial assistance available to voluntary agencies to run day-care centers.

The Indian government formulated the long-awaited National Policy on Older Persons in 1999. The national policy seeks to assure older persons that their concerns are national concerns and that they will not live unprotected, ignored, or marginalized (Government of India, 1999). The policy recognizes the need for affirmative action in favor of the elderly. It does not view age 60 as the cut-off point for beginning a life of dependency, but rather as an active and productive phase of life. The policy values an integrated society and endeavors to strengthen integration between generations. It recognizes older persons as resources and believes in their empowerment.

Principal areas of intervention outlined in the policy include a provision for financial security by expanding the pension cover for all. Taxation policies are to be revised to favor older people, and long-term savings will be promoted. Health-care needs will be given high priority, and heavily subsidized health services are planned. Training of medical and paramedical personnel is also envisioned to provide health care for elderly. Ten percent of houses/house sites are to be allotted to older persons to provide shelter for them. The layouts of housing colonies will be more older-friendly. There is also emphasis on meeting educational and training needs of older persons and removing discriminations in availing such opportunities.

The main thrust of welfare will be to identify the more vulnerable among older persons. Apart from setting up a welfare fund, voluntary organizations will be encouraged and assisted to organize services such as day care. Protection of property and life as well as the rights of the older persons will be given special emphasis. Both family and nongovernmental organizations will be involved at every level of providing for the elderly. The policy recognizes the importance of research and training of manpower and the role of media in promoting the concept of active aging. The Ministry of Social Justice and Empowerment will be the lead Ministry to coordinate all matters relating to the implementation of the policy. Planning, coordination between different sectors, supervision, and review of the implementation of the policy are spelled out in the policy statement.

With regard to the disabled, the Ministry of Welfare has several schemes for their assistance. This includes assistance to voluntary organizations for education, training, and rehabilitation of disabled, and assistance for aids and appliances, and to establish special schools. A National Trust for the welfare of persons with Mental Retardation and Cerebral Palsy has been proposed. The National Programme for Rehabilitation of the disabled provides assistance for guidance and vocational placement, attempts to rehabilitate persons in their own environments, and mobilizes community support.

Four National Institutes have been established for mentally handicapped, orthopaedically handicapped, visually handicapped, and hearing handicapped. An Artificial Limbs Manufacturing Corporation has also been established. In 1995, the government of India established the Rehabilitation Council of India to enforce uniform standards in training professionals in the field of rehabilitation. Twenty-three special employment exchanges, 55 special cells in regular employment exchanges, and 17 vocational rehabilitation centers are also functioning. Efforts are being made to create media awareness and a barrier-free environment.

Since so many schemes exist already, perhaps what is needed is coordination among different agencies and programs to help disabled elders. By incorporating the care and rehabilitation of older people who face disability within the broader rehabilitation schemes, much of the distress of that group could be reduced. Already, recommendations have been made that caring for disabled older people should be brought under the Integrated Child Development Scheme (ICDS). Although it appears incongruous at the outset, it makes practical sense (Prakash, 1991). The ICDS scheme covers the entire country, and ICDS workers reach every nook and corner of India in an effort to educate people about child and maternal health, to provide basic nutritional and hygiene information, and to provide basic health care to infants, expectant mothers, children, and adolescents. By adding another component of elder care to this network, India could avoid creating another vertical structure that it cannot afford. There are also proposals to start a National Institute on Aging that may supervise and guide research, issue guidelines for training, monitor work of agencies, evaluate programs, and influence government policies.

The problem of aging and disability in India is not just a medical problem. It is basically an economic problem. The lack of social security and a comprehensive Medicare system renders health care highly expensive. Modern health facilities are all concentrated in urban areas, depriving 75% of the population that is rural. The country is still struggling to control epidemics and infections and introduce immunization programs for children, and to attend to the older segment of its population. Meanwhile, the threat of HIV and AIDS has introduced a new dimension to health care. Around 11% of the HIV-infected are supposed to be in the age 50+ group in India. But the public perception of HIV and AIDS is as a disorder of the young. However, a conference was organized in 1999 at a prominent Social Science Institute on HIV/AIDS to focus on the older population. This marks a beginning of a shift in attitudes.

It is disappointing that the new national policy on aging does not anywhere mention the condition of the disabled who are likely to survive to old age. They will soon be a recognizable part of the population. The policy, however, takes cognizance of the increased health-care needs of old persons due to disability and consequent loss of autonomy. Health education, nutrition, and mental health are given due emphasis. As before, the old disabled and disabled old are perceived as two separate groups, though their needs and the services they require are similar.

On the positive side, the government has taken the step in the right direction by formulating a national policy that is more or less comprehensive. A long-standing demand of gerontologists, NGOs, and older persons themselves for governmental action has been fulfilled. How well it will be implemented is left to the future to reveal.

AUTHOR NOTES

Dr. Indira Jai Prakash is Professor of Psychology, Bangalore University, Bangalore, India. Her doctoral work and post-doctoral work were in the field of aging, especially aging women in India. As a Commonwealth Fellow, she studied at the International Institute on Aging, Malta, and was visiting Professor at the Institute for Gerontology in Heidelberg, Germany. Dr. Prakesh was appointed advisor for the expert committee on Aging and Health of the World Health Organization in Geneva from 1996-2000. She has over one-hundred research papers and ten books/monographs to her credit.

Dr. Prakash can be contacted at Bangalore University, Bangalore 560 056, India (E-mail: jprak@bgl.vsnl.net.in).

REFERENCES

Agrawal, K. G., & Dhar, V. (1984). Disabled and attributional theory: A factorial study. *Psychological Studies, 29*(1), 88-92.
All, A. C., & Fried, J. H. (1994). Psychosocial issues surrounding HIV infection that affect rehabilitation. *The Journal of Rehabilitation, 60*(2), 8-12.
Alston, R. J., & McCowan, C. J. (1994). African American women with disabilities. Rehabilitation issues and concerns. *The Journal of Rehabilitation, 60*(1), 36-40.
Bartholomew, J. J. (1982). A word about the issue (Editorial). *Rehabilitation Literature, 43*(7-8), 194.
Bowe, F. (1984). *Disabled women in America.* Washington, DC: President's committee on Employment of the Handicapped.
Britt, J. (1988). Psychosocial aspects of being female and disabled. *Journal of Applied Rehabilitation Counseling, 19*(3), 19-23.
Britto, G., & Simon, E. I. (1994). Hysterectomy and mentally retarded women. Issues and debate. *Perspectives in Social Work, 9*(1), 17-20.
Bultena, G., & Powers, E. (1978). Denial of aging: Age identification and reference group orientations. *Journal of Gerontology, 33*, 748-54.
Camacho, T. C., Strawbridge, W. J., Cohen, R. D., & Kaplan, G. A. (1993). Functional ability in the oldest old. *Journal of Aging and Health, 5*(4), 439-454.
Cockerham, W. C. (1997). *This aging society.* Upper Saddle River, NJ: Prentice Hall.

Daftuar, C. N. (1993). Power distance and other work values among handicapped and normal employees. *Disabilities and Impairment*, 7(1), 7-15.
Dalawari, B. S. (1988). Employment of cured leprosy patients. *Social Welfare*, 35(2), 38-39.
Dandekar, K. (1996). *The elderly in India*. New Delhi: Sage.
Fries, J. F. (1983). The compression of morbidity. *The Milbank Quarterly*, 61, 397-398.
Genskow, J. K. (1988). Independent living programs and services for older persons with disabilities. *The Journal of Rehabilitation*, 54(4), 43-47.
Government of India (1999). *National policy on older persons*. New Delhi: Ministry of Social Justice and Empowerment.
Heller, T. (1993). Aging caregiver of persons with developmental disabilities. In Roberto, K. A. (Ed.), *The elderly care giver*. Newbury Park: Sage. 21-38.
Ittyerah, M., & Rani, V. (1990). Manual dexterity, job satisfaction and job involvement in the visually handicapped. *Journal of Indian Academy of Applied Psychology*, 16(2) 1-5.
Joshi, P. C., Bhattacharya, M., Rastogi, A. K., Dwedi, S., Raj, B., & Verma, J. (1988). Handicapped persons–A demographic profile in a rural area of U.P. *Disabilities and Impairment*, 2(2), 135-141.
Karbanda, S. (1988). The disabled crane operator. *Social Welfare*, 35(2), 16, 29.
Khetrapal, K, Soneja, S., & Kumar, V. (1996). Physical and neuropsychiatric impairment amongst the aged and their relationship to socio-economic status. In Kumar, V. (Ed.), *Aging: Indian perspective and global scenario*. New Delhi: All India Institute of Medical Sciences, 134-136.
Kohli, A. S. (1996). *Social situation of the aged in India*. New Delhi: Anmol Publications.
Krishnamurthy, K., Joseph, E., James, P. J., Kishore, N. R. A., Shaji, K. S., Harish, M. T., & Praveenlal, K. (1998). Experiences with MMSE as a screen test in hospitalized geriatric patients. *Indian Journal of Psychiatry*, 40(Supplement), 32.
Krout, J. (1985). Relationship between informal and formal organizational networks. In Sauer, N. & Coward, R. (Eds.), *Social support networks and the care of the elderly*. New York: Springer, 178-195.
Kumar, V. (1997). Ageing in India–An overview. *Indian Journal of Medical Research*, 106, 257-264.
Lewis, K. P. (1989). Persons with disabilities and the aging factor. *The Journal of Rehabilitation*, 55(4), 12-13.
Mathur, S. (1985). Socioeconomic profile of handicapped population of Parel village, Bombay. *The Journal of Rehabilitation in Asia*, 26(3), 1-10.
Mittal, R. L., Bedi, G. P. S., & Gulati, A. (1987). A follow-up study of above-knee prosthesis manufactured in Artificial Limb Centre, Rajendra Hospital, Patiala. *The Journal of Rehabilitation in Asia*, 28(1), 5-9.
Mittal, R. L., & Singla, V. K. (1987). Firearm amputees of rural Punjab and their rehabilitation. *The Journal of Rehabilitation in Asia*, 28(2), 1-5.
Mobility India (1997). *Newsletter of Mobility India*. Bangalore: Mobility India.
Nagendra, K. S. (1998). *Memory and behavioral problems in older people living in community: Assessment and intervention*. Unpublished doctoral dissertation submitted to Bangalore University, Bangalore.

Nandi, P. S., Banerjee, G., Mukherjee., S. P., Nandi, S., & Nandi, D. N. (1997). A study of psychiatric morbidity of elderly population of rural community in West Bengal. *Indian Journal of Psychiatry, 39*(2). 122-129.
Prakash, I. J. (1991). Caring for the disabled elderly in India: Some suggestions. *BOLD, 1*(4), 11-12.
Prakash, I. J. (1995). Psychosocial situation of older women's lives and potential for empowerment. In Formasa, S. (Ed.), *AgeVault: An anthology on aging of INDIA*. Malta: International Institute on Aging, 69-94.
Prakash, I. J. (1997). Women and Ageing. *Indian Journal of Medical Research, 106*, 396-408.
Prakash, I. J. (1998a). Maintenance of competence in daily living and well-being of the elderly. *Research & Development Journal, 4*(2-3), 26-34.
Prakash, I. J. (1998b). Issues in mental health and psychological well being of older persons. In Desai, M. & Raju, S. (Eds.), *Gerontological social work in India*. Delhi: B. R. Publishing Corp., 185-203.
Premarajan, K. C., Danabalan, D., Chandrashekar, R., & Srinivasa, D. K. (1993). Prevalence of psychiatry morbidity in an urban community in Pondicherry. *Indian Journal of Psychiatry, 35*(2), 99-102.
Rajaram, S., & Gourie-Devi, M. (1988). Rehabilitation of neurologically disabled persons: Implications for community participation. *The Journal of Rehabilitation in Asia, 29*(1), 8-10.
Rajkumar, S. (1995). The tragedy of Alzheimer's Disease. *Research and Development Journal, 1*(3), 32-38.
Rao, M. N. (1990). Integrating the disabled–A reality? *The Indian Journal of Social Work, 51*(1), 149-156.
Sagar, R., Mahajan, R., Agnihotri, B. R., & Munjal, G. C. (1995). Medical problems in psychogeriatric consultation. *Indian Journal of Psychiatry, 37*(2) (Supplement), 59.
Satapathy, R., Kar, N., Das, I., Kar, G. C., & Pati, T. (1997). A study of major physical disorders among the elderly depressives. *Indian Journal of Psychiatry, 39*(4), 278-281.
Satyanarayana, K., & Medappa, N. (1997). Care of the aged–A long haul ahead (Editorial). *Indian Journal of Medical Research, 106*, i-ii.
Schieman, S., & Turner, H. A. (1998). Age, disability, and the sense of mastery. *Journal of Health and Social Behavior, 39*, 169-186.
Sen, A. (1995). Disability counseling. *Disabilities and Impairment, 9*(1), 3-14.
Shah, B., & Prabhkar, A. K. (1997). Chronic morbidity profile among elderly. *Indian Journal of Medical Research, 106*, 265-272.
Shah, V. H., Panchal, B. N., & Goswami, U. A. (1995). Depression in geriatric medical inpatients. *Indian Journal of Psychiatry, 35*(Supplement), 60.
Sharma, S. D., & Agarwal, S. (1996). Ageing: The Indian perspective. In Kumar, V. (Ed.), *Aging: Indian perspective and global scenario*. New Delhi: All India Institute of Medical Sciences, 12-19.
Sitther, B. (1999). *Caring burden and well being of elderly parents with disabled adult children*. Unpublished M. Phil thesis submitted to Bangalore University, Bangalore.
SNDT News Letter (1994). *The rights of the mentally retarded women*. Research Centre for Women's Studies, SNDT University, Bombay, *15*(1).

Thudipara, J. Z. (1998). Integration of the disabled in society. *Social Welfare, 45*(2), 3-5.
Trieschmann, R. B. (1987). *Aging with a disability.* New York: Demos Publications.
Venkoba Rao, A. (1985). Suicide in the elderly. *Indian Journal of Social Psychiatry, 1,* 3-10.
Venkoba Rao, A. (1990). *Health care of the rural aged.* New Delhi: Indian Council of Medical Research.
Venkoba Rao, A. (1996). The frail elderlies, coping with their needs. In Kumar, V. (Ed.), *Aging: Indian perspective and global scenario.* New Delhi: All India Institute of Medical Sciences, 45-46.
Venkoba Rao, A. (1997). Psychiatric morbidity in the aged. *Indian Journal of Medical Research, 106,* 361-369.
Venkoba Rao, A., & Madhavan, T. (1983). Depression and suicide behaviour in the aged. *Indian Journal of Psychiatry, 25,* 251-259.
Verghese, A. (1988). Problems encountered in rehabilitating the mentally disabled. *The Journal of Rehabilitation in Asia, 25*(2), 25-30.
Wisocki, P. A. (Ed.)(1993). *Handbook of clinical behavior therapy with the elderly client.* New York: Plenum.
Wood, J. B. (1993). Planning for the transfer of care. In Roberto, K.A. (Ed), *The elderly care giver.* Newbury Park: Sage, 95-107.
Yelurkar, S. K., & Mazumdar, R. D. (1985). Prevalence of physical handicapped in a village and its relation to some of the host factors. *The Journal of Rehabilitation in Asia, 26*(1), 23-30.
Zarit, S. H., Johansson, B., & Berg, S. (1993). Functional impairment and co-disability in the oldest old. *Journal of Aging and Health, 5*(3), 291-305.
Zola, I. K. (1986). Depictions of disability. Metaphor, message and medium in the media. *Social Science Journal, 22,* 5-17.
Zola, I. K. (1989). Aging and disability. Toward a unified agenda. *The Journal of Rehabilitation, 55*(4), 6-8.

SOCIAL AND FAMILIAL RELATIONS

Social Networks of Old People in India: Research and Policy

John van Willigen, PhD
University of Kentucky

N. K. Chadha, PhD
University of Delhi, India

SUMMARY. This article presents a comparative analysis of the available research on the social networks of older persons in India. Most of this research has been done in North Indian cities. The research foci of the available studies include network size, core networks and beyond, life course changes in networks, impacts of residency in old-age homes, gender differences, and joint and nuclear family residence. This research is discussed in terms of its policy implications. Because the research demonstrates that social networks are important for the welfare of older Indians, one can conclude that social policy that encourages the maintenance of robust networks throughout the life course may be worth pursuing. One aspect of policy is discussed. The analysis of the relationship

---

[Haworth co-indexing entry note]: "Social Networks of Old People in India: Research and Policy." van Willigen, John, and N. K. Chadha. Co-published simultaneously in *Journal of Aging & Social Policy* (The Haworth Press, Inc.) Vol. 15, No. 2/3, 2003, pp. 109-124; and: *An Aging India: Perspectives, Prospects, and Policies* (ed: Phoebe S. Liebig and S. Irudaya Rajan) The Haworth Press, Inc., 2003, pp. 109-124. Single or multiple copies of this article are available for a fee from The Haworth Document Delivery Service [1-800-HAWORTH, 9:00 a.m. - 5:00 p.m. (EST). E-mail address: docdelivery@haworthpress.com].

© 2003 by The Haworth Press, Inc. All rights reserved.
http://www.haworthpress.com/store/product.asp?sku=J031
10.1300/J031v15n02_07

between social network and gender suggests that current policies that can be seen as supporting gender inequality in terms of property may have a negative impact on the networks of older women. *[Article copies available for a fee from The Haworth Document Delivery Service: 1-800-HAWORTH. E-mail address: <docdelivery@haworthpress.com> Website: <http://www.HaworthPress.com> © 2003 by The Haworth Press, Inc. All rights reserved.]*

KEYWORDS. Social networks, support networks, joint families, nuclear families

INTRODUCTION

Comparative social network analysis is useful for understanding aspects of the social aging process. Comparisons can be made to understand better the conditions of life of different population segments within countries and transnationally. Studying social networks of older people in India is important because research has focused primarily on the role of the family. Some argue that the study of older people in family settings has been a kind of preoccupation in Indian aging studies (Cohen, 1998). At the same time, family structure is rapidly changing. These changes have increased concern about the capacity of families to meet the needs of older men or women. Coupled with this is the relative absence of special government programming for older people. These factors taken together increase concern for the aspects of older persons' social worlds that are neither family nor social programs. It is likely that social support from the world beyond the family will come to be more important in the future. Network analysis provides a perspective to the entire social world of individuals. This is important from a policy perspective because, like many economically poor countries, India's national policy dealing with aging is not very well-developed.

We begin by discussing some of the advantages of a network approach, what we mean by social network, and how social networks can be measured. From there, we review the available research on social networks of older people in India and conclude with a focus on, and an interpretation of, one aspect of policy affecting social aging.

SOCIAL NETWORKS:
APPROACH, DEFINITION, MEASUREMENT

One can use the network concept in a very wide variety of settings to understand important aspects of a person's social world. The reason for this is that one can reduce networks to very simple structural elements, the interaction of dyads. With this as a starting point, it is possible to observe and record fundamental aspects of the social life of virtually anybody on roughly equal terms. Think of the problem of comparing the social world of a rural older American living in a household alone with that of an urban older Indian resident in a complex joint family household with its three-generation composition. These are very different social settings; yet, with a network approach, one can see similarities in the underlying structures of the person's social world while we observe differences in cultural meaning of the flow of social behavior. Seeing network structures and their correlates is as useful as seeing the rich complexity of the lived life.

While there are many ways to conceptualize social networks, it is important to recognize that networks are abstracted from human life rather than being highly constructed theoretically. Although collecting network data is not easy, the operationalizations available are quite naturalistic and therefore can be used in a variety of settings.

The social network concept is more direct than the various network proxies such as social supports (Ramamurti & Jamuna, 1991). We think it is important to realize that social network analysis is an approach to studying social organization rather than as a kind of psychological variable.

The substance of all social networks is persons and their relations with others. Relations are observable, and therefore a person's social networks are easily observed in reality. We can see two persons speaking with each other. We can ask a person whom he or she interacts with using very natural questions, like "whom do you talk to every day?" or "who are the people you see when you go to the market?" It is even possible to tag along to get some idea of the content of the person's life in a network or ask a person to keep a diary of his or her daily interactions.

Analytical use of social networks appears first in work done by the British anthropologist, J. A. Barnes, with Norwegian fishermen. His innovation grew from his dissatisfaction with the constructs, often based on kinship analysis, available to him as a social anthropologist. He started with a visual metaphor. "The image I have," he wrote, "is of a set of points, some of which are joined by lines. The points of the image are people, or sometimes groups, and the lines indicate which people interact with each other. We can, of course, think of the whole of social life as generating a network of this kind" (Barnes, 1954).

There are a variety of ways of measuring a person's social networks. We have discussed these alternatives in other settings (van Willigen,

1989, pp. 62-70; van Willigen & Chadha, 1990). Most techniques rely on self-reports and consist of either a single question or a closely related set of questions that results in a list of names. We have used a set of questions that starts with "Tell us the names of the people you see every day." The questions are framed to include a few times a week, weekly, and monthly. Other approaches use subjective importance (Pattison, n.d.), specific time periods (Sanjek, 1978), or places (Sokolovsky, 1985) as the reference for the basic question or question set. The list of names produced through the questions is the operationalized network. After the list is constructed, then one can ask questions about the persons on the list. Variables include gender; status as kin, friend, neighbor, co-worker, fellow association member; importance, content of interaction; duration; residence (e.g., from the neighborhood or not). Most of these questions are straightforward.

In our work we have linked the idea of social network with the concept of the process of social aging. We define social aging as the life-span process of change in the amount, content, and meaning of a person's social behavior, produced by his or her adaptive decisions carried out in the structural context of the communities within which the person lives. We are interested in understanding how this process operates when looked at from a network perspective. How are networks of people of different ages different? We have usually interpreted our results in terms of exchange theory at a micro-level and political economy at a macro-level (Dowd, 1975).

If we define social network in the typical egocentric mode, we see that networks include both the person's fellow coresidents as well as persons from beyond the household. Gangrade has referred to networks as a "multiple linkage group" (Gangrade, 1988, p. 54) including coworkers, friends, neighbors, other kin, and persons linked through joint association membership. The importance, emotional intensity, and frequency of the relationship may be highly variable, possibly even quite limited.

Gangrade argues that, because of the difference in family relationships in India in comparison to the "West," the household/kin group core of the network will be more important in India than in the West. As he says it, "In social networks the family, and especially the joint family, is considered a more significant entity than the individual" (Gangrade, 1988, p. 54). As a corollary to this, one would expect that links with non-kinship groups would be more limited in India.

Networks are important for welfare. Speaking of the Indian setting, Gangrade says, "Social networks in Indian situations provide vitality to social work in managing crisis situations in Indian families. This should be properly used and strengthened to solve many problems faced by the aged, rather than advocating the development of institutionalized programs" (Gangrade, 1988, p. 56). If the joint family's role in the social life of older people declines as much as social commentary indicates, one can imagine that social networks will become even more important for the welfare of older people. We then can ask the question, "What government policies encourage the creation and maintenance of robust social networks of older people?"

While the social network concept has been used in the Indian setting in a formal analytic sense, it is more frequently used metaphorically. It is our view that while references to network appear often in the Indian social gerontology literature, the empirical research on social networks of older people in India is limited and unevenly distributed.

The core of this article is a review of literature available to us that is based on empirical network data. The literature and, presumably, the research on social networks of older people in India are quite limited. Studies that have made use of the network concept in an analytical rather than metaphorical sense include Arora, 1995; van Willigen & Chadha, 1995, 1999; van Willigen, Chadha, & Kedia 1996a, 1996b, and 1996c; Shankardass & Kumar, 1996; Chadha, 1996; Chadha & Singh, 1996; Chadha & Mangla, 1991; Nagpal & Chadha, 1991; Chadha, Easwaramoorthy, & Kanwara, 1990; and Malhotra, 1996.

Almost all studies of social networks of older people in India have made use of the same technique, which was described early in our work together (van Willigen & Chadha, 1990). A study carried out among older men and women visiting the Geriatric Clinic of the All India Institute of Medical Science, New Delhi, focused on what the researchers called "support network." They did not specify how they measured support network (Shankardass & Kumar, 1996). The focus was not on general social interaction but on "all those from whom support can be sought," which is seen as a smaller subset of the person's larger social network (Shankardass & Kumar, 1996, p. 195).

The studies that appear in the research literature are almost all based on Delhi populations. The studies of the networks of non-institutionalized elderly appear to be entirely from the middle class. For more than a decade, we have attempted to obtain copies of articles, conference papers, and the like, which use social network as an analytical variable. We feel that the studies reported in this article represent a comprehensive selection of the available empirical studies. It is useful to reiterate that there is bias caused by where the studies were done. They are almost entirely urban, North Indian, and middle-class (unless institutionalized). It would be very useful to have more studies done in villages, where the majority of the population resides, with poor people, and in South India. Further, the studies make use of a limited range of measurement strategies. The literature review is organized around topics rather than as a study-by-study inventory.

Network Size

Network size has been an important variable in our work. We get comments from other researchers who indicate that they regard network size as unimportant. They argue that quality of ties can compensate for quantity of ties. Some are quite dismissive of findings focused on differences in size of networks. However, we believe network size has an important relationship to people's welfare. There are many reasons for this. You and your caregivers can draw upon networks in times of need; this is the basic social support argument. If you have a larger network linking you into the community, there is no doubt a greater likelihood that you will be treated well by those close to you because of their fear of social sanction. Speaking subjectively, it seems that fear of social sanction in this regard is very intense in the Indian neighborhoods in which we have worked or lived. Old people with large networks are known, and being known has protective effects. This relates to the "old person as loathsome stranger" argument that has been expressed in the literature (De Beauvoir, 1972). Further, to state the obvious, most people like to socialize.

We made use of a measure of life satisfaction developed for our study (Chadha & van Willigen, 1995) to show that persons with larger networks report higher life satisfaction than those with smaller networks (van Willigen & Chadha, 1999). Similarly, Shankardass and Kumar found that an "active support network strongly influenced the social well-being of the elderly. The elderly who had more contact with their family members, neighbors, and friends, and also those who had someone in whom to confide, had a more positive attitude toward living" (Shankardass & Kumar, 1996, p. 196).

In addition, we examined the relationship between network size and two other measures, subjective health and a measure we termed "power" (van Willigen & Chadha, 1999). This last measure focused on the person's participation in decisions about the allocation of household assets. We found that women had much lower power scores than men. Power was highly correlated with gender, life satisfaction, and subjective health. While power was clearly related to life satisfaction, the factor most strongly related to life satisfaction was subjective health. All the relationships cited here were very robust, however. This research outcome helps link property resources with social aging outcomes. There are no other studies that make this link with direct empirical evidence.

Supportive Core

Discussions of network size tend to de-emphasize the qualitative differences between relationships. Networks, however large, have a more intimate, supportive core. Shankardass and Kumar found in their analysis of support networks that the active support network consisted of two to four people from a much larger social network. The larger network was used "for reaching to members of the active network in case of their absence from home" (Shankardass & Kumar, 1996, p. 197). The presence of a more stable core of more intimate network links is also found in studies of networks of older people in America (van Willigen, 1989). Shankardass and Kumar (1996) also found some gender differences: Women received much less help from their husbands than men received from their wives. Women were much more engaged in self-help.

Networks Beyond the Core

The supportive core is extended in important ways with neighbors, coworkers, friends, and other household members. Feelings about neighbors are complex. In their study, Chadha, Aggarwal, and Mangla found that a neighbor was an important source of practical support, yet "the relationship is characterised by [a] certain reserve" (Chadha, Aggarwal, & Mangla, 1990, p. 27). One of their respondents said, "A good neighbor is interested in things that affect you but still they are not intrusive" (Chadha, Aggarwal, & Mangla, 1990, p. 27). They also found that relations with good neighbors, according to the people they interviewed, could be characterized by lack of envy and by trust and pleasurable interaction.

Life Course

There are almost no discussions in this literature of the relationship between age and network size beyond the fact that the studies are of older people. One study compared network size of persons in various age strata (van Willigen, Chadha, & Kedia 1995). The study indicated that network size is more or less stable until late life [old-old]. The network size of persons age 80 and over is quite small. There is apparently a tendency for networks to be maintained until a certain threshold of decrepitude is passed. The pattern follows often-used categories "young-old" and "old-old." Above 75 years of age, there is a decline in size; at 80 and above there is a substantial reduction in network size. These findings appear to be virtually identical with those found in an earlier study done in the United States (van Willigen, 1989).

The relationship between the life course and networks can be seen in other findings. Research done by Chadha and Easwaramoorthy indicates that retired people have smaller social networks than pre-retired people (Chadha & Easwaramoorthy, 1992). The social network size of married persons is greater than that of widowed persons (Chadha, Aggarwal, & Mangla, 1990).

Residency in Old-Age Homes

There are very large differences between the social involvement of persons residing in old-age homes and those staying at home (Chadha & Mangla, 1991; Chadha & Arora, 1995). The mean network size reported for people living at home ranges from 12 to 26, while the institutionalized persons have networks consisting of five to six people. Using similar measurement strategies, McDonald (1993) found in her study of an American nursing home that residents had very small social networks, reflecting a pattern more or less identical to the relationships found in the Indian studies.

Based on his observations while interviewing people in old-age homes, Chadha reported that you could see the limited social interaction of people, especially males. In another study, Arora and Chadha report, "During the interview with institutionalized elderlies it was observed that they hardly talk to each other in spite of living in the same room. According to them they can manage on their own and there is not need to talk to others except the helpers working there" (Arora & Chadha, 1995, p. 77).

The social networks of persons living in old-age homes, as well as those who were not, varied in other ways. Malhotra reports a comparison of Delhi men and women living in both old-age homes and at home. The comparison in terms of residence revealed a similar pattern for both men and women. In the case of both men and women, those living in old-age homes showed smaller networks and less interaction with both consanguineal and affinal relatives (Malhotra, 1996, p. 86). The networks of men living in old age homes were about one-third the size of those living at home (Malhotra, 1996, p. 90); the differences for women were not so pronounced.

Studies indicate that institutionalized elderly have lower life satisfaction (Nagpal & Chadha, 1991). This finding is consistent with research results of other cultural settings.

Gender

Most of the studies indicate that women tend to be more socially isolated than men in the sense that women have smaller networks. At least two studies of social networks of the aged in Delhi reported that men had larger networks than women (Chadha, Aggarwal, & Mangla, 1990; van Willigen & Chadha, 1999). The social world of women also tended to be "inside," while that of men was "outside." Similarly, men and women varied considerably in the number of coworkers present in the network. This is attributed to rigid "cultural roles of males working outside the home and females working inside the home" (van Willigen & Chadha, 1999). Shankardass and Kumar (1996) developed a similar result and interpretation. In a rural American study, the networks of men and women were more or less the same size (van Willigen 1989), although the same "inside-outside" difference was noted.

Chadha and Singh (1996) found an interesting split in their study of Delhi men and women residing in joint and nuclear families. They found males living in joint families had networks about 13% larger than joint-family resident females. The men and women living in nuclear families had more or less identically sized networks.

Renu Malhotra's study of institutionalized and non-institutionalized men and women in Delhi indicated that women had significantly larger networks than men (1996). It is worth noting that she used the same method as that used in the other studies mentioned in this section.

Network composition for males and females shows similarities and differences. Two studies, Malhotra (1996) and Chadha (1996), found that networks of males had relatively fewer cross-sex relationships than did the networks of females. They also showed that networks of females had higher numbers of "blood relatives" than did males. These differences were not statistically significant. However, there was a significant difference between men and women in the number of non-relatives in their network. Men have more non-relatives in their networks. Chadha et al. (1990, p. 30) found that two-thirds of their sample of men and women consisted of family members, with the percentage of family members being higher in women's networks. Cross-sex relationships tended to be among kin. Friends tended to be of the same sex. Males and females differed significantly in the number of coworkers present.

Joint and Nuclear Family Residence

Research that compares the social networks of persons residing in joint and nuclear families has produced interesting, although mixed, results. Chadha and Singh (1996) have shown that persons living in joint families have larger social networks than those living in nuclear families. They did a gender-based comparison of the two family types. The significant differences in network size determined through a t-test were all between joint family males and nuclear family males and females. There were no significant differences between nuclear family males and females, joint family males and females, and joint family females and nuclear family males. Clearly, the situation of the patriarchal joint family has an impact on social aging in terms of gender. Being an older male in a joint family results in high social involvement.

Van Willigen and Chadha (1999) found that there was no significant difference in the sizes of networks of people living in nuclear and joint family settings. They speculated that persons living in nuclear family settings might tend to compensate for having fewer household members in their networks by developing relationships with persons like neighbors, friends, and coworkers. This view is complicated by the fact that the persons living in nuclear households were significantly younger than those living in joint family settings.

It is worth noting that Chadha and Singh did not find significant differences in the "components of the wider social network" of persons living in nuclear and joint families. Networks of both included similar numbers of friends and neighbors. They found on average that male networks included more friends and that "contact with friends does not decrease with age" (Chadha & Singh, 1996, p. 204).

POLICY

While there is a large gap between research on social network and the world of policy, we think that policy provides a useful interpretive framework for considering the results of these research efforts. There are basically three elements to our argument, all supported in the research literature. First, network size is important. Research on social network indicates that the size of a person's social network relates to an important measure of his or her welfare: life satisfaction. We take life satisfaction as a reasonable indicator of a positive aging outcome. There are similar relationships between social network and subjective health. It is clear that maintenance of robust social relationships as a person ages is very important. This relates to the question we asked earlier about how government policy encourages the creation and maintenance of robust social networks for older people.

The second point is that gender has a significant impact on social aging outcomes as depicted in this body of social network research. Women have smaller networks, and they are linked less with the community outside the family. Coupled with this is lower life satisfaction. The stresses that older women face, which result in negative aging outcomes like lower life satisfaction, are products of many things. The patriarchal pattern of the traditional joint family in which power resources are unequally distributed in terms of gender is implicated in this. While this pattern is supported by cultural institutions–the idealized seclusion of women or purdah (Minturn, 1993); idealization of the obedient, sacrificing, and faithful wife as personified in the Goddess Sita (Kakar, 1981); the patrilineal kinship structure (Mandelbaum, 1970); and the dowry and arranged marriage system (van Willigen & Channa, 1991)–it also has a basis in policy. It is very difficult to separate causes in this framework. There is a very clearly expressed cultural pattern of male dominance. It is both caused by and is a cause of policy.

At the nexus of social aging, gender, and policy, one finds the laws that relate to family structure. One of the most important of these is the Hindu Succession Act of 1956 (Kesari & Kesari, 1998) that defined the legal framework for inheritance while it reformed customary law. Important in its own right because it serves as the legal basis for succession in Hindu, Sikh, and Jain families, the Act also represents the array of cultural, economic, and legal aspects of Indian society that are both a cause and expression of the weakened position of women.

It is beyond the scope of this article to review all laws that may have an impact on social aspects of aging (see van Willigen & Channa, 1991, for a discussion of the Dowry Prohibition Act). These effects are enhanced among older women because they are old and they were raised when the effects of these institutions, laws, and policies were greater. Our argument is that the property allocation system, associated with the patrilineal joint family, results in women having fewer resources than men. Hypothetically, this puts them in a weaker position socially, resulting in a reduction in the likelihood that their needs will be met. This problem is at the core of exchange theory (Bengston & Dowd, 1980), which would predict that the social involvement of women in India would be curtailed because they have few power resources. This situation is seen in both culture and policy. The Hindu Succession Act is one, albeit important, policy manifestation of these gender conditions of Indian life. It can be thought of as a projection of the underlying economic and cultural conditions, as well as one of the causes.

In looking at the Hindu Succession Act, readers will grasp the irony, given our argument, that this law has been legitimately described as providing a revolutionary *improvement* in the property rights of women. It is important to recognize the circumstances prior to the passage of the Hindu Succession Act. The legally recognized customary law that controlled property and inheritance was derived from a religious text called the *Mitakshara*. These texts created the idea of what legal scholars called *Mitakshara* coparcenary property, which contemporary legal scholars such as Kesari and Kesari sometimes treat as synonymous with "joint family property" or "ancestral property" (1998). By definition, coparceners are the male members of a joint family, up to three generations. Neither daughters nor wives are part of the mix. To be clear, under this regime, women did not own joint family property. There was a provision of women's property, usually jewelry and clothes and other things they may have been given from their parents, but they did not have a birthright to either the property of their natal families nor did they participate in community property along with their husbands in their conjugal families.

Under this regime, at death, property went to other members of the coparcenary through survivorship. When a man died, joint family property went to his brothers and sons, to the exclusion of his sisters and daughters. A male also participated in ownership of joint family property as a birthright. This type of ownership is constituted more as belonging to the group of owners rather than as controlling the deposition of title or allocation of a stream of income or other benefits (Derret, 1962).

The Hindu Succession Act of 1956 radically improved the way women were treated in the inheritance of property by providing them with a right to inheritance of "joint family property." The law states that when a Hindu male dies intestate, his property is distributed according to a list of prioritized heirs. On this list, sons and daughters and husbands and wives are treated equally.

Nevertheless, there remains a legal bias toward continued male inheritance of property. The gender bias is expressed in a subtle way. First, the *Mitakshara* principle of ancestral property and related male succession is still legally recognized in the Act while, at the same time, inheritance by females is provided.

Second, the Act did not make a provision for conjugal community property or a survivorship succession between husband and wife. Widows inherit an equal share with their children instead of having property devolve to them. Women, in the framework of the Hindu Succession Act, are treated as the equivalent of children. The right of children diminishes the property rights of women. In America, at death, in the absence of a will, a man's property devolves to his wife without probate or taxes. By contrast, in India, older women get a share along with children. The property, which they may inherit, may be hard to partition, and therefore, it may be difficult for a woman to take possession of her share of a house, for example.

Third, the provisions of the Act are limited in the case of agricultural land in order to reduce fragmentation of ownership. This, in effect, means that the principles of *Mitakshara* inheritance based on survivorship in the male-only coparcenaries are retained in what might be the most important economic arena in an agricultural society: land ownership.

Fourth, in the lower-priority classes, there is a male bias. The category that contains the most peripheral heirs is prioritized in terms of those linked through males and those linked through females. Those linked through males have higher priority than persons linked through females.

It is important to remember that these provisions apply in cases where a person dies intestate. It is also possible for males to use testamentary succession to preserve male interests. In addition, women also may not claim a share of an estate to avoid being "disruptive."

CONCLUSION

Our argument is that gender inequality in wealth and power is created by the cultural and legal system associated with the joint family. This inequality is manifested in a manifold way in the life course of women. Looking at the entire life course in this framework, it is possible to demonstrate a succession of negative outcomes for females from the pre-natal period to old age. These negative outcomes include female-specific abortion (Bumiller, 1990), lower survival of girl babies (Miller, 1981), violence toward women in marriage (van Willigen & Channa, 1991) and lower-life satisfaction of older women (van Willigen & Chadha, 1999).

Whether policy change would have much effect on these life course prospects is another question since the position of women in Indian society is the product of a wide range of cultural institutions and the historical nature of the political economy. Further, we need to consider the positive contribution that the joint family makes to the welfare of old people, both men and women. Policymakers face the difficult task of protecting women while they are pro-family. The paradoxical nature of the Hindu Succession Act is a product of the need to achieve two outcomes that are, in part, contradictory. While the policy is pro-female, at its core it leaves the male-biased property system largely intact.

We think that laws that are gender-biased are one of the mechanisms that produce negative impacts on the outcome of social aging processes for women in India throughout the life course. Interestingly, the frequency of at least some of these negative outcomes varies from state to state in significant ways. Females are, in many ways, better off in South India. They have far more access to education, for example. This is why a comprehensive study of social aging from the perspectives of states (e.g., Kerala) with higher levels of gender equity would be so interesting. In turn, this research might lead to some insights as to why state-level social policies for the aged have been more proactive in the South India region.

AUTHOR NOTES

John van Willigen is on the faculty of the University of Kentucky, Department of Anthropology and Gerontology and Health PhD Program. He has done aging research in Kentucky and India. He is co-author of *Social Aging in a Delhi Neighborhood* and author of *Getting Some Age on Me: A Study of Social Organizations of Older People in a Rural American Community*. Other publications include articles in the *Indian Journal of Social Work*.

Dr. van Willigen can be contacted at the Department of Anthropology, University of Kentucky, Lexington, KY 40506 (E-mail: ant101@pop.uky.edu).

N. K. Chadha is on the faculty of Psychology at the University of Delhi. He has conducted a number of research projects on aging persons, primarily in North India, and has focused on life satisfaction and social networks among other topics. He is co-author of *Social Aging in a Delhi Neighborhood* and *Aging and the Aged: Challenges Before Indian Gerontology*, and he is author of numerous articles in several journals, such as the *Indian Journal of Gerontology*.

Dr. Chadha can be contacted at the Department of Psychology, University of Delhi, Delhi, India 110007.

REFERENCES

Arora, M. (1995). Social support and life satisfaction of institutionalized elderlies. *Indian Journal of Gerontology*, 9(3&4), 74-82.

Barnes, J. A. (1954). Class and committees in a Norwegian Parish Island. *Human Relations*, 7, 39-58.

Bengston, V. L., & Dowd, J. J. (1980). Sociological functionalism, exchange theory and life cycle analysis: A call for more explicit theoretical bridges. *International Journal of Aging and Human Development, 12*(1), 55-73.

Bumiller, E. (1990). *May You Be the Mother of a Hundred Sons: A Journey Among the Women of India.* New York: Fawcett Columbine.

Chadha, N. K. (1996). Life satisfaction of aged: Psychological and social network analysis. In *Aging: Indian Perspective and Global Scenario,* Vinod Kumar (Ed.), Proceedings on the International Symposium on Gerontology and Seventh Conference of the Association of Gerontology (India).

Chadha, N. K., & Arora, M. (1995). Social support and life satisfaction of institutionalized elderlies. *Indian Journal of Gerontology, 9,* 74-82.

Chadha, N. K., & Easwaramoorthy, M. (1992). A study on some psychosocial aspects of elderly in relation to their pre-retirement, retirement, and post-retirement years. *Seminar on Aging and Its Associated Problems.* Coimbatore.

Chadha, N. K., & Easwaramoorthy, M. (1993). Aging: Issues and rehabilitation strategies. In *Issues and Trends in Rehabilitation Research,* N. K. Chadha & Surinder Nath (Eds.). Delhi: Friends Publications.

Chadha, N. K., Easwaramoorthy, M., & Kanwara, P. (1990). Quality of life among aged. *Indian Journal of Psychology, 68*(1&2), 15-21.

Chadha, N. K., & Mangla, A. P. (1991). Social network approach to old age. *Eastern Anthropologist, 44*(4), 355-365.

Chadha, N. K., Aggarwal, V., & Mangla, A. P. (1990). Social network and aging. *Spectra of Anthropological Progress, 12,* 15-32.

Chadha, N. K., & Singh, S. (1996). Intergenerational gap and psychosocial health. In *Aging: Indian Perspective and Global Scenario,* Vinod Kumar (Ed.), Proceedings on the International Symposium on Gerontology and Seventh Conference of the Association of Gerontology (India).

Chadha, N. K., & van Willigen, J. (1995). The Life Scale: The development of a measure of successful aging. *Indian Journal of Gerontology, 9*(3&4), 83-90.

Cohen, L. (1998). *No Aging in India: Alzheimer's, the Bad Family, and Other Modern Things.* Berkeley, CA: University of California Press.

De Beauvoir, S. (1972). *The Coming of Age.* New York: Putnam and Sons.

Derret, J. D. M. (1962). The development of property in India c. ad 800-1800. *Zeitschrift fuer Vergleichende Rechtswissenschaft, 64.*

Dowd, J. J. (1975). Aging as exchange: A preface to theory. *Journal of Gerontology, 30*(5), 584-94.

Gangrade, K. D. (1988). Social networks and the aged in India. In *The Aging in India: Problems and Potentialities.* New Delhi: Abhinav Publications.

Kakar, S. (1981). *The Inner World: A Psycho-analytic Study of Childhood and Society in India.* Second Edition. Delhi: Oxford University Press.

Kesari, U. P. D., & Kesari, A. (1998). *Modern Hindu Law.* Second Edition. Allahabad: Central Law Publications.

Killworth, P., & Bernard, H. R. (1974). Catij: A new sociometric and its application to a prison living unit. *Human Organization, 33*(4), 335-50.

Malhotra, R. (1996). *Institutionalization and the Aged: A Study in Social Support and Psychological Well-Being.* Unpublished PhD. Thesis, University of Delhi.

Mandelbaum, D. G. (1990). *Society in India: Continuity and Change.* Berkeley, CA: University of California Press.
McDonald, J. (1993). *Social Networks of Nursing Home Residents.* Unpublished M.A. Thesis, University of Kentucky.
Miller, B. D. (1981). *The Endangered Sex.* Ithaca, NY: Cornell University Press.
Minturn, L. (1993). *Sita's Daughters: Coming Out of Purdah.* New York: Oxford University Press.
Nagpal, N., & Chadha, N. K. (1991). Social support and life satisfaction among aged. *Indian Journal of Psychometry and Education, 22*(2), 91-100.
Pattison, E. M. (n.d.) *The Psychosocial Network Inventory.* Santa Ana, CA: Department of Mental Health, County of Orange.
Ramamurti, P. V., & Jamuna, D. (1991). Social supports inventory for the elderly. *Journal of Psychological Researches, 35*(2), 132-136.
Sanjek, R. (1978). A network method and its use in urban ethnography. *Human Organization, 37*(3), 257-69.
Shankardass, M. K., & Kumar, V. (1996). A sociological analysis of support networks in old age in India. In *Aging: Indian Perspective and Global Scenario,* Vinod Kumar (Ed.), Proceedings on the International Symposium on Gerontology and Seventh Conference of the Association of Gerontology (India).
Sokolovsky, J. (1985). Network methodologies in the study of aging. In *New Methods for Old Age Research: Anthropological Alternatives,* C. L. Fry & J. Keith (Eds.). South Hadley, MA: Bergin and Garvey.
van Willigen, J. (1989). *Getting Some Age on Me: A Study of Social Organization of Older People in a Rural American Community.* Lexington, KY: University Press of Kentucky.
van Willigen, J., & Chadha, N. K. (1990). Techniques for collecting social network data for studies of social aging. *Indian Journal of Social Work, LI*(4), 615-621.
van Willigen, J., Chadha, N. K., & Kedia, S. (1995). Personal networks and sacred texts: Social aging in Delhi, India. *Journal of Cross-Cultural Gerontology, 10*(3), 175-198.
van Willigen, J., & Chadha, N. K. (1999). *Social Aging in a Delhi Neighborhood.* Westport, CT: Bergin and Garvey.
van Willigen, J., Chadha, N. K., & Kedia, S. (1996a). Personal networks of older people in a Delhi neighbourhood: Power and the process of disengagement. *Indian Journal of Social Work, 57*(3), 414-428.
van Willigen, J., Chadha, N. K., & Kedia, S. (1996b). Power and social engagement: A study of social aging in a Delhi neighborhood. *Ageing and Society, VI*(I&II), 33-47.
van Willigen, J., Chadha, N. K., & Kedia, S. (1996c). Late life changes in social networks and disengagement: Perspectives from a Delhi neighbourhood. *Research and Development Journal of HelpAge India, 2*(3).
van Willigen, J., & Channa, V. C. (1991). Law, custom, and crimes against women: The problem of dowry death in India. *Human Organization, 50*(4), 369-377.

Issues of Elder Care and Elder Abuse in the Indian Context

D. Jamuna, PhD

*Centre for Research on Ageing, Department of Psychology,
S. V. University, Tirupati, India*

SUMMARY. With 7% of the population of India being elderly, two-thirds of whom live in villages and nearly a half of them in poor conditions, the care of the elderly is a difficult problem to be tackled. The dwindling of the joint family, the rise of dual-career families, a possible shift in filial piety values, the increasing life expectancy with greater chances of a prolonged old age characterized by poverty, degeneration, more empty-nest years, and dependency, have all added to the seriousness of the problem and made the elderly more susceptible than ever to abusive treatment. This paper examines these issues as well as the issue of elder abuse in light of available data and suggests some strategies to meet the problem. Also discussed are the problems, stresses, and strains of caregivers of the elderly. A greater role is envisaged for Non-Governmental Organizations (NGOs) than the state in the care of the elderly, particularly in providing support services to family caregivers. *[Article copies available for a fee from The Haworth Document Delivery Service: 1-800-HAWORTH. E-mail address: <docdelivery@haworthpress.com> Website: <http://www.HaworthPress.com> © 2003 by The Haworth Press, Inc. All rights reserved.]*

KEYWORDS. Old-age homes, destitute elderly, elder abuse, family caregivers, caregivers' stress

INTRODUCTION

As human beings, everyone wishes for a healthy old age without prolonged suffering, but not many really achieve it. In old age, as a result of frailty and/or sickness, if disability becomes inevitable, caregiving of some sort becomes essential. Thus, it may be relevant to consider the sorts of constraints that hamper quality caregiving and how best to overcome them. This article is devoted to two key issues of caregiving: (1) descriptive issues of caregiving and the role of the family, the state, and the community in the care of the elderly, and (2) elder abuse.

BACKGROUND

Caregiving issues must be examined against the background of the unique sociocultural and demographic context of India. As a result of demographic and epidemiological transitions, it is estimated that in the coming decades, developing countries like India will carry the bulk of the burden of caring for the elderly. According to the United Nations Population reports, about two-thirds of the world's elderly live in developing countries. In India, the elderly population–about 7%–is growing at a faster rate than the general population. Life expectancy at age 60 has now increased to 18 years from 11 years in 1941 (Registrar General of India, 1991). Among the old-old, women will continue to outnumber men, with a majority of them being widowed. Most of the elderly live in rural areas, and agriculture is their main occupation (Sarvekshana, 1991). The demographic transition in India is characterized by a sandwich generation who have to care for their aged parents on the one hand and their own children on the other (Jamuna, 1999a).

The rural-urban distribution of the elderly in India reveals that about two-thirds of the elderly hail from rural areas. A majority of the rural elderly depend on agriculture for their source of income. Agricultural labor requires physical capability but does not provide old-age income security. Earnings hardly meet their needs of daily living. Thus, the elderly have to depend on their children. Those who live with their adult children often have less financial and psychological stress compared to those who live alone or with their spouses in the villages and belong to the lower rungs of the social or economic ladder.

Medical and health services are not available in most villages, and a person must travel some distance to reach a Primary Health Centre (PHC) or other medical facility. With transport facilities being poor, the elderly have to contend with local country medication or resign themselves to their condition until other help becomes available. Compared to these elderly, their urban counterparts have better health care and transportation facilities, but appropriate services are costly and often beyond the reach of the economically poor. While the urban elderly have better medical services, not all can afford them; in the case of rural elderly, the services are not only difficult but also costly (Ramamurti & Jamuna, 1997).

The rural-urban scenario also indicates that 12.4% and 9.5% of men live alone in rural and urban areas, respectively. On the other hand, only 1.4% and 0.8% of elderly women live alone in rural and urban areas, respectively. Only 20% of men are willing to move to old-age homes. The majority of the elderly men living alone prefer to move any place outside their village or town or state if proper care is available (Dandekar, 1996). The National Sample Survey Organisation (NSSO) report of 1991 indicates that there is no significant difference in the living arrangements; in both rural and urban areas, elderly mostly stay with their adult children (NSSO, 1991). It is customary for the aged parents to move and stay with their children, particularly with their eldest son and daughter-in-law. This is because the elderly feel that it is the duty or obligation of the eldest son to take care of them in their old age (Jamuna, 1997; Ramamurti & Jamuna, 1994).

Disability of some kind is common for many of those who have achieved 65 years. Arthritis, osteoporosis, circulatory disorders, arteriosclerosis, malignancies, and fractures due to falls are some of the common causes of disability in old age in India (Kumar, 1996; Roy, 1994). The prevalence rates of disability have been higher for males than for females in both rural and urban areas. Although women have slightly lower life expectancies than men, disability-free life expectancy was greater for women than men. Also, life expectancy is longer in developed urban areas than in the less developed rural areas (Roy, 1995). Thus, increasing longevity with attendant disability in late life is contributing to a higher burden experienced by the caring family.

TYPES OF CARE AND PRIMARY CAREGIVERS

Elder care in India consists of three broad types: care by adult married children and their families, care by the spouse, and institutional care. Mostly, elderly parents are cared for by their adult children (usually sons) and their families. This is particularly so when the elderly parents become disabled.

According to the NSSO Report (Sarvekshana, 1991), about 7% of men and 11% of women were supported by their spouses. Approximately three-fourths were supported by their own children, and about 8% and 12% of elderly men and women, respectively, were supported by others. This latter group needs government, private, or community support.

When parents stay with their married offspring, the primary caregiver is the daughter-in-law. Otherwise, it is the wife of the elderly man and/or his daughter. It is only infrequently that an elderly man (husband) acts as the primary caregiver to his aged wife, or the married son acts as the primary caregiver to his aged mother or father (Jamuna, 1999a, 1999b).

It is clear from this arrangement that it is mostly women (daughter-in-law, wife, or daughter) who take on the responsibility of being the primary caregivers of the elderly. The caring role of the woman is part of the cultural conditioning from childhood. Girls, as they grow, imbibe caregiving as their role. On the other hand, boys are conditioned, at best, to be helpful to the elderly and extend instrumental support (e.g., escorting them out, helping with financial assistance, or running errands outside the house, etc). Women caregivers, in view of their diverse obligations–particularly when they are employed–such as housekeeping, food preparation and service, child rearing, employment obligations, and care of the elderly, often suffer from role overload and consequent stress (Jamuna, 1992).

In the Indian cultural scene, when a women gets married, she leaves her parent's family and joins the family of the husband's parents. When the parents of her husband get old, it becomes her duty as the daughter-in-law of the house to care for her aged parents-in-law. She becomes their primary caregiver. Even if the parents-in-law are healthy, it is her obligation to serve not only her husband but also her parents-in-law.

Role of Family and State in Elder Care

The agricultural economy, the patriarchal joint family system, and traditional values such as reverence for age that bound parents and their adult children are the distinguishing characteristics of the ancient Indian culture. In the patriarchal joint family system, the oldest male member of the joint family is the head of the family. Property inheritance is patrilineal (from father to son to grandson). In a joint family, all members of the family live, cook, and eat together and share the responsibility of managing common land holdings or business. The oldest male member may also live with his siblings, his and their children and grandchildren under the same roof. In such a joint family, its elderly members, even if disabled, are easily taken care of by the other members. Elder care was not a problem (Suryanarayana, 1998).

A series of developments, such as urbanization, industrialization, and migration, and a growing sense of materialism and individualistic orientations have threatened the culture of yesteryear. Strong filial obligations and mutual ties, the hallmarks of the traditional family, are becoming weakened (Bose, 1995; Jamuna, 1987, 1998; Singh, 1997; Nayar, 1999; Ramamurti et al., 1992a, 1992b). As a result of these developments, care of the aged by the family is becoming problematic (Jamuna, 1987, 1990, 1997a, 1998).

There are no different opinions regarding the impact of urbanization, industrialization, and modernization on elder care. Traditionally, it is expected that parent care is the duty and obligation of adult children. The elderly, too, expect that their children are their old-age security. Interestingly, the surveys on elder care issues show that there are winds of change in the perceptions of different generations towards various issues of elder care (Jamuna, 1991, 1999a).

In a study of attitudes towards elder care issues and living arrangements carried out in 1984, 91% of adult children surveyed said it was their duty to care for their elderly parents. But a repeat survey in 1994 showed that only 77% of adult children held the same view, suggesting a shift in attitudes. Also, in the 1984 study the younger age groups *enbloc* stated that it is not proper to send the elderly to old-age homes. But, in the 1994 study, a substantial number of the younger persons (23%) felt that more homes for the elderly might be needed in future, as many are unable to keep their elderly at home, for various reasons. Only those elderly persons whose spouses were alive and/or who had moderate means, fair health, and functional competence in self-help skills preferred to live by themselves (Jamuna, 1997a, 1998).

The Mechanics of Caregiving

In either a formal or informal setting, caregiving must be understood as a delicate dyadic relationship between the caregiver and care receiver. In the Indian cultural context, the dyadic relationship for the most part is either between the elderly spouses (husband and wife) or between the elderly and their daughters-in-law (Jamuna, 1997a, 1997b). A host of factors seem to affect the caregiving relationship, such as health status of dyad members, time spent in caring, effort and human resource costs, economic costs, health maintenance and disability management measures, institutional care facilities, caregiver-care receiver interperception, and the type of interaction between them, as caregiving proceeds (Jamuna, 1995, 1997b).

Studies on the mechanics of caregiving show that the most significant determinant of good care is a favorable interperception between the caregiver and care receiver. Favorable interperceptions refer to likability of each other's personal qualities, compatibility of interests, and the degree of emotional attachment between the dyad members (Jamuna, 1992, 1995).

In the Indian culture, legends, folklores, and episodes abound wherein the mother-in-law is pictured as an authority figure in her family, wielding power over her daughters-in-law–a behavior not taken kindly by the daughter-in-law. Also, the daughter-in-law is viewed by the mother-in-law as responsible for influencing her son to develop a prejudicial attitude towards her (Jamuna & Reddy, 1992). Studies have shown that there is a strained relationship between the mother-in-law and daughter-in-law in their day-to-day interactions. This sort of strained interaction is so common that it has become stereotyped. The severity of the prejudicial interperception between the daughter-in-law and the mother-in-law vitiates the caregiving relationship between them. In fact, a congenial mother-in-law/daughter-in-law interperception is an infrequent occurrence (Jamuna & Reddy, 1992; Ramamurti & Jamuna, 1994).

The difficulty in caregiving, among other things, depends on the nature of the disability of the care receiver, for example, people suffering from mental disabilities like severe dementia, psychoses like schizophrenia, and manic conditions. In all these disabilities, the care receiver has severe difficulties in communication. There can be no doubt that this type of caregiving is strenuous and stressful (Abraham et al., 1997; Rajkumar et al., 1996). However, except for hospital records and a couple of regionally-based community studies (Rajkumar, 1995; Rao, 1999), there are no other sources of information about the prevalence of these conditions in the community.

The characteristics of good caring in the family may also be affected by several mediating factors: lack of accommodation, strained caregiver (CG)-care receiver (CR) relationships in the past or during the caring, health of the CG, lack of support from the family, severity of CR disability, role overload, economic costs of care, and multiple responsibilities of CG. The extent of stress experienced by the CG is dependent on the interplay of these mediating factors. Also, the presence of certain idiosyncratic psychological factors like generosity, altruism, sympathy, and other behavior in the rubric of pro-social behavior in the personality of caregivers are some of the ingredients of good caring (Jamuna, 1996, 1997a, 1997b).

Institutional Care Services

According to a regional survey, 71% of the elderly are living with their children (family care), 26.3% are living by themselves, including spousal care or self-care, and only 2.73% are in institutions (Jamuna & Ramamurti, 2000). Residential institutions for the elderly may be considered under two broad heads: free homes and "pay and stay" homes. The free homes are generally run by voluntary bodies, with or without government assistance. A few are run by quasi-governmental organizations. The free homes usually provide shared accommodation (e.g., dormitory type) and food, free of cost. Governmental assistance is in the form of a subsidy or grant to meet the cost of rented accommodation, furnishings, and food to the inmates (i.e., residents) on a per capita basis. Often, the aid from the government is inadequate and the organization must find additional resources to meet the costs. Mostly, destitute elderly–those who state that they do not have their kith and kin to care for them–are admitted into these homes. Sometimes, other elderly are also admitted. They must furnish the name and address of a person to be contacted in case of an emergency. Many of these institutions prefer to enroll people who have a fairly high ability to perform activities of daily living (ADLs) and can take care of themselves for the most part. If individuals become sick, they are admitted into a "free" government hospital, and the next of kin are informed (Ramamurti & Jamuna, 1997).

The "pay and stay" homes charge the elderly who live in the homes. The charges vary depending on the quantity and quality of services provided. Generally, these institutions provide accommodation, food, and a few other amenities. Most of these institutions also prefer to admit persons who are in fair health and have a fair ADL capability, at least at the time of admission. Very few institutions provide for admission of sick and disabled individuals. If an individual becomes sick, he or she is usually admitted to a hospital and if treatment is charged, the individual will have to defray the expenses. In case of death of the inmate living in either type of home, the next of kin or the reference person whose name was registered at the time of admission is informed, so he or she may take charge. Some institutions do arrange a funeral, provided the incumbent authorized the home to do so.

Traditionally, most elderly persons live with their children or live by themselves. Because of these supports or arrangements, there has been no need of reasonable magnitude for the community to step in and organize homes for the elderly. Only in recent times, has there been a growing tendency, however small, for elderly people to seek institutional support. In the coming years, as the demand increases, it is expected that more voluntary organizations will be starting homes for the needy elderly. It should not be forgotten that even today the proportion of elderly seeking institutional support is well under 5% of the elderly population. The Census of 1991 reported that only 2.73% of persons were staying in homes for the elderly (Sarvekshana, 1991).

According to a survey carried out to evaluate old-age homes (Ramamurti & Jamuna, 1997), the elderly who are destitute, childless, uneducated, and who have less desire to live with their children opt for institutional care in the free homes. The most common reasons for institutionalization of residents at "pay and stay" homes are desertion by the family members, abuse by adult children, childlessness, and elders' own preferences to live away from children (Ara, 1995; Jamuna, 1997; Nalini, 1997).

Based on the Central Government Welfare Department's survey (Ramamurti & Jamuna, 1997) and the HelpAge India study (Ara, 1995), the persons who seek institutional care may be classified in the following manner:

1. The first category includes the aged who live alone; a widow or widower; and couples who are financially sound and have regular income, are either childless, or their children have migrated to other places. Also, feelings of loneliness and frustration, longing for company, health problems, and lack of security in their living environments cause some elderly to seek institutional care. For example, Mr. Raghunathan is a 71-year-old retired railway employee who was living with his wife (age 63) in a "pay and stay" home. The couple stated that, prior to joining the home, they were feeling lonely and apprehensive about their future, particularly if their health were to deteriorate. They depended on a home-helper, since their two sons were in the United States. However, their servant was exploitive and threatening. They realized that living in an old-age home would be the best solution for their problems, and they moved into that setting.

2. Elderly couples without children who are not in a position to live by themselves due to insufficient income make up the second category. Take the case of Mr. Yerraiah (age 69) and Mrs. Reddamma (age 62) who had no one to fall back on. They were not receiving any income from their small piece of land, and they were incapable of working. Harinath, their nephew, was willing to support them on condition that their property be transferred to his name. Thus, they had no alternative except to seek refuge in an old-age home.
3. The third category includes persons who are unable to bear the mistreatment in the family of their children. Mr. Reddy (age 63) is a typical case in this category. He retired as a teacher and stayed with his eldest son since his wife's death two years ago. He feels that he is unwanted most of the time. His two daughters and two sons who are all married state that each can support him only for three months at a time. Mr. Reddy said that he was humiliated by his sons and daughters-in-law and was feeling ill-treated. He even attempted once to end his life. One of his friends brought him to the old-age home.

The survey conducted by HelpAge India (1995) indicates that out of 258 homes surveyed, 63% were destitute homes, and the others were "pay and stay" homes run by NGOs or religious organizations. They admit the elderly regardless of their caste, gender, and religion. There are also homes that provide care only for specific communities (e.g., homes for Parsis, Brahmins, Christians, etc.). The majority of these institutions are run by voluntary organizations with or without government assistance.

The homes that received assistance from the Ministry of Welfare increased from 62 in 1992-93 to 209 in 1994-95, while the day-care centers increased from 157 in 1992-93 to 236 in 1994-95. Services such as Mobile Medicare Units are just developing. The total expenditure of the Ministry for the welfare services of the aged increased from 1.06 crores of rupees in 1992-93 to 5.28 crores of rupees in 1994-95. Most old-age homes are in Kerala, followed by Karnataka and Andhra Pradesh. There are homes that are exclusively for elderly women in Kerala, Maharashtra, Tamil Nadu, and one or two homes in other states. These data suggest that institutionalization is very high in Kerala, followed by Maharashtra and Karnataka (Ara, 1995).

The existing elder care institutions house less than 1% of the elderly, covering 0.68% of the old as recorded in the data from the NSSO. Community care institutions are very few. There are very few geriatric nursing homes to care for the chronically disabled and terminally ill elderly. Since family care is preferred over institutional care, services such as day-care centers, home help services, meals on wheels, and home healthcare units need to be encouraged. Voluntary service, through community-care institutions, will be a good alternative to family care in rural areas. But community-managed institutions have not developed in any significant way.

There are several legal and constitutional provisions with regard to care of the elderly. The care of the aged is mentioned in the Indian Constitution along with the care of disabled persons, the infirm, and women (Directive Principles of State Policy in Article-4). Article 41 of the Indian Constitution recognizes the needs of the elderly and enjoins upon the state the responsibility of making effective provisions for public assistance in cases of unemployment, old age, sickness, disablement, and in other cases of undeserved want. The welfare of the aged is a government concern, with the lead responsibility at the national level assigned to the Ministry of Social Justice and Empowerment. Section 20 (1) of the Hindu Adoption and Maintenance Act (1956) states that an aged infirm parent, if unable to maintain himself or herself, is entitled to maintenance. Muslim law also imposes an obligation to maintain needy parents, subject to certain circumstances. Independent of the above personal laws, the code of criminal procedure 1973 [Section 125 (1) (d)] makes it incumbent for a person having sufficient means to maintain his father or mother who is unable to maintain himself or herself. On getting proof of neglect or refusal, a first class Magistrate may order such a person to make a monthly allowance not exceeding Rs.500/- (EAGLE, 1995; Mohanpuria, 1996; Pandit, 1999). But this requires that parents lodge a complaint that their children are not caring for them. Due to social issues and emotional attachment towards their children, many elderly do not seek legal redress.

Stress Among Caregivers

Elder care is a stressful job that gets compounded when the elder is disabled and when the caregiver has multiple roles. The caring role, which is normative for women, is not generally appreciated by others and often becomes socially invisible. Literature on elder care indicates that long-term care with commitment and continued responsibility carries frustrations that affect the quality of life and well-being of the caregiver. In the absence of systematic efforts to help these caring families in India, the care of the elderly with severe disability increases the physical and psychological burden on the primary caregiver. When caring becomes complex and taxing, it has the potential to affect the physical and mental health of the caregiver. Stress generation in a caring situation is not due only to external conditions of a carer's life; it is also due to the interplay of subjective and external conditions (Jamuna, 1997b, 1999b; Ramamurti et al., 1992b).

Some attempts have been made to ensure the mental health of the caregivers of elderly by reducing the stress among the carers through pilot interventions (Jamuna, 1996, 1997b, 1999b). The intensity of stress in caring is directly related to self-perceptions of caregiving, amount of time spent in caring, and the health status of the caregiver. Group counseling, support group interventions, and behavior modification procedures to manage the disabled have been found to be effective strategies for reducing carers' stress. The pre- and post-evaluations of interventions indicate that the extent of gain through interventions varies among carers (Jamuna, 1997b, 1999b; Ramamurti et al., 1992a). The need for supplementary care services like home help services, hospice, and other domiciliary services should be recognized as adjuncts to family care in India.

ELDER ABUSE IN THE INDIAN CONTEXT

Abuse or mistreatment of the elderly is not a new phenomenon. However, it came into focus only during the 1970s. Between then and now, a host of books and articles on the subject have appeared in the Western literature. However, articles based on empirical observation on the elderly in India are few. Consequently, it is difficult to write on elder abuse in India, adequately supported by empirical evidence, despite the fact that many can observe its existence in their day-to-day interactions. The material presented here is based on the author's own study and a few other writings on the elderly in India (Bambawale, 1996; Jamuna & Padmasree, 2000; Kapoor, 1997; Padmasree, 1991; Ramamurti & Jamuna, 1999).

According to Decalmer and Glendenning (1997), elder abuse refers to a willful mistreatment and neglect. Glendenning (1997) states that elder abuse/mistreatment is an act of commission, while neglect is an act of omission. The mistreatment can be physical, psychological, social, or of miscellaneous types. Willful neglect, deprivation of the elderly's normal privileges, and exploitation also constitute mistreatment.

A study by Padmasree (1991) revealed that elder abuse may be patent (as is seen in blatant forms of mistreatment) or latent (as evident in veiled threats, exploitation of their weak position in the family, giving them a low priority in family matters, etc.). The studies show that abuse is more often focused on the elderly who are physically and economically dependent (Jamuna & Padmasree, 2000; Kapoor, 1997; Padmasree, 1991).

A few relevant cases are presented here:

Case 1

Mr. Vasudeva (age 80) and Mrs. Sitamma (age 76) lived in a multi-storeyed flat in an affluent residential area with their son and daughter-in-law. They owned the house and had some bank balance, too. As they became frail, they needed care. In an interview they stated that often they felt they were unwanted and their daughter-in-law and son harassed them because they refused to part with their property at the moment. Mrs. Sita said, "Everyday, me and my husband have to wait until the grandchildren left for schools and my son left for office before getting our breakfast. Facilities for bathing and washing our clothes were meagre. We had to keep watch over the house and care for the grandchildren when my son and daughter-in-law went out, or when our daughter-in-law went on social visits. When we got sick, they simply said, 'it's all due to old age, it will be like that.' Our pleas for medication were often ignored. We were not allowed to live independently, taking a flat. This, they said, would invite criticism from neighbors and relatives, stating that my son and daughter-in-law drove us out." The couple was vexed by this daily "harassment." A follow-up visit after several months revealed that both of them jumped from the 4th floor and died. A suicide note mentioned that they were vexed with their lives and wanted to die and that nobody was responsible for their deaths, which were of their own choice.

Case 2

Jayaram is an artisan of small means, a widower, and 75 years old. He is frail and suffers from arthritis and mild incontinence. He used to live with his eldest son and daughter-in-law in a flat. He had sold his lands and house in the village to help his son to buy a flat in the city and, hence, he now had no independent income.

Earlier he used to be very helpful to the family, doing housekeeping jobs and helping the family in many other ways. Now he is not able to do most of those things and has become somewhat dependent. He had complained that his son and daughter-in-law were not treating him properly, despite giving them all his assets. As the old man was a liability, his son and daughter-in-law used to state openly that it is not possible to maintain him at home. Also, they said that he was becoming unhygienic and dirtying the place due to his urine incontinence. He was often humiliated and harassed because he had not cared to secure a pensionable job in his younger years. Unable to bear the humiliation, he decided to leave the home, took the advice of a friend to join a home for destitutes by stating in writing that he had nobody to care.

Case 3

Das (age 70) is also a widower, living with his elder son and daughter-in-law. He was a shepherd earlier in his life and did not put by any money for his old age, thinking that his son would take care of him. He had given his hut to his son to live in. His son was tending pigs while his daughter-in-law was an agricultural laborer, getting jobs only in season. Das used to keep watch over the house when his son and daughter-in-law were away at work. Das stated that every day there was an altercation between him and his son on something or other. The son was given to alcohol and in a drunken state used to beat him. One day when his son was away, a dog entered the hut and ate up all the food kept in the hut when Das was sleeping. In the evening, the son, knowing what had happened, beat his father so badly that he was physically hurt. The son drove him out of the house saying that he would never again entertain him. Das was living by begging alms in the streets.

The aforementioned cases of abuse within three different economic groups are only representative cases. The incidence of these cases appears to be on the increase. One can observe that a host of factors, including the economic conditions of carers, lack of space, frailty and dependency of the elderly, and the feeling of "burden," are associated with abuse (Padmasree, 1991).

The adult children whose parents have been allegedly abused have a different story to relate. They point out that these elderly were authoritarian, rigid, inflexible in their ways, and highly demanding of attention.

They often disturbed the peace at home by making teasing comments, interfering in home affairs, and making a nuisance of themselves. Hence, the caregivers had no alternative than to ask the aged parents to leave the home and/or care for themselves. Some said they could not keep them at home because they have neither the resources nor the time to care for the aged parents (Padmasree, 1991).

It is difficult to eliminate elder abuse altogether from the family. What can perhaps be done is to mellow and temper it by a series of measures. Family counseling services need to be established to educate both the elders and their family members. Hotline services could be started by NGOs to register, monitor, and redress the situation of elder abuse. Inculcation of "humane" feelings and human touch through spiritual or value-oriented education from the younger years is necessary to develop a positive outlook towards the family's elderly.

Monitoring the contextual factors related to elder abuse and neglect is necessary to overcome abuse conditions in the family. Elders, too, should accept the reality that their interests are different from those of young people and adjust to the changed life situation. Keeping oneself occupied through familial and socially useful activities may help the elders avoid a negative disposition.

The foregoing brief discussion of elder abuse illustrates that in the first instance, we need more documented information of cases of various types of elder abuse. We require "in-depth" studies on the antecedent and contextual factors influencing various forms of elder abuse. This will enable appropriate interventions to be planned and executed, at least to reduce their severity, if not prevent them altogether.

CONCLUSION

This paper is a bird's eye view of the issues and problems of elder care in India. There appears to be a steady slide in caregiving from the traditionally secure joint family care of the elderly towards extended family care in which care by adult children forms a major part. If the present trends continue, there will likely be a decrease in elder care by adult children in the future, which will create more demand for old-age homes. Old-age homes could be utilized more as supplements rather than easily available alternative care arrangements. Inasmuch as the national policy on the elderly emphasizes the support and strengthening of family care for the elderly, what India badly needs is a series of measures and the provision of care facilities that would not only encourage family care; such measures and provision would also provide respite for over-burdened female carers in the family.

The Western model of care provides certain useful ideas in the care of the elderly: home help services, respite care, volunteer services, acute care, infirmary care, and hospice care. Such services help the family overcome the crises situations of elder care at home. At the moment, the medical model of care or physician-driven care models cannot be emphasized in India. Nevertheless, geriatric nursing homes tied to a National Medicare Program need to be envisaged to care for the sick and the severely disabled. At the same time, family care needs to be strengthened with incentives like tax remission, medical and food subsidies for the elderly, priority housing, and other supplementary attractions to encourage family care. Because India has been wedded traditionally to family care of the elderly, community care has not developed as an alternative. Institutional care is still viewed as a last resort. Yet, we need old-age homes for those who need them and for those who do not want to live with their children.

At present, India is at a crossroads and has to decide whether to go the family care way or the institutional/community care way. For a country like India, the state cannot enter as a major player in elder care in view of its high (prohibitive) cost to the exchequer and the low national priority given to elder care. Nevertheless, the country could plan for short-span experimentation with different care models to test their suitability as supplementary solutions, keeping the dignity of an elder person uppermost. Whatever it turns out to be, our cultural traditions do not favor the adoption of the complete medical model or professional care that would probably take away the homelike, humane element. What we really need is an integrated system of care that would provide options for different types of supplemental care within the reach of an average Indian family.

We need to develop models of home or family care that may be supplemented by a variety of respite services by suitably adapting them to Indian conditions. Only such arrangements can act as a safety valve to the overburdened family caregiver. What the future will hold is difficult to say, but it is the hope of all that elder care will *not* be *sans love and dignity* for the elder.

AUTHOR NOTES

As a distinguished scholar, Dr. Jamuna was awarded a Research Associateship from the University Grants Commission, New Delhi, to work on gender aging for a period of five years. She secured the prestigious "Tilak Award" of the Association of

Gerontology, India (AGI), for the best paper in social gerontology in 1983. As a UNDPF Fellow she underwent training in social gerontology at the International Institute of Aging, Malta. She has to her credit sixty-two research publications in the area of Aging and secured grants for three National and two International Projects on Aging. She is on the Editorial Board of the *Journal of Health Care and Later Life* published from New Castle, U.K. She was awarded the Sandoz International Training Fellowship to work at the Gerontology Center, Pennsylvania State University (USA) during 1996-97. She has reviewed (periodically) the research on aging in India with Professor P. V. Ramamurti, Director, Center for Research on Ageing. She has been continuously teaching Gerontology courses at the Masters and P.G. Diploma levels since 1985.

Dr. Jamuna can be contacted at the Centre for Research on Aging, Department of Psychology, S. V. University, Tirupati-517502, India (E-mail: jumunad123@rediffmail.com).

REFERENCES

Abraham, S. T., Shaji, S., Verghese, A., George, B., & Shibu, V. P. (1997). The care of the demented elderly–Issues and implications. In Indrani Chakravarty (Ed.), *Life in Twilight Years*. Calcutta: Kwality Book Co., 351-363.

Ara, S. (1995). Old age homes: The last resort. *R & D Journal*, 2(1), 3-10.

Bambawale, U. (1996). Abuse of the aged. In Vinodh Kumar (Ed.), *Aging: Indian Perspective and Global Scenario*. New Delhi, 298-302.

Bose, A. (1995). Care of the elderly in the unorganized sector. *R & D Journal*, 1(3), 3-14.

Dandekar, K. (1996). *The Elderly In India*. New Delhi: Sage Publications.

Decalmer, P., & Glendenning, F. (1997). *The Mistreatment of Elderly People*. New Delhi: Sage Publications.

EAGLE (1995). A study of legislation affecting older people in India. International Exchange on Ageing, Law and Ethics and International Federation on Ageing. *R & D Journal*, 1(3), 39-55.

Glendenning, F. (1997). What is elder abuse and neglect? In P. Decalmer & F. Glendenning (1997). *The Mistreatment of Elderly People*. New Delhi: Sage Publications.

HelpAge India (1995). *Directory of Old Age Homes in India*. New Delhi: HelpAge India, R & D Division.

Jamuna, D. (1987). Self and caregivers' perceptions of needs and problems of elderly women–A case for guidance and counselling. *Journal of Counselling and Community Guidance*, 4(3), 25-32.

Jamuna, D. (1990). Caring for elderly women: Perspectives at the turn of the century. *Journal of Indian Academy of Applied Psychology*, 16, 17-22.

Jamuna, D. (1991). Perceptions of the problems of the elderly in three generational households. *Journal of Psychological Researches*, 35, 99-103.

Jamuna, D. (1992). Caring for the disabled elderly: Problems and perspectives. In S. K. Chowdary (Ed.), *Problems of the Aged and of Old Age Homes*. Bombay: Akshar Pratiroop Pvt. Ltd., Wadala, 111-116.

Jamuna, D. (1995). Contributors to good caregiving: A study of the dyadic relationship in the India scenario. Paper presented at the 5th Asia/Oceania Congress of Gerontology. Hong Kong, 19-23, November.

Jamuna, D. (1996). Psychological dimensions of caregiver's stress. In Vinodh Kumar (Ed.), *Aging: Indian Perspective and Global Scenario*. New Delhi: Vinodh Kumar, 253-255.

Jamuna, D. (1997a). Public perceptions on caregiving–Then (1984) and now (1994): An evaluation. In Indrani Chakravarty (Ed.), *Life in Twilight Years*. Calcutta: Kwality Book Co., 365-374.

Jamuna, D. (1997b). Stress dimensions among caregivers of the elderly. *The Indian Journal of Medical Research–Special Issue: Ageing In India, 106*, 381-387.

Jamuna, D. (1998). Challenges of changing socioeconomic and psychological status of the aged. *R & D Journal, 5*(1), 5-13.

Jamuna, D. (1999a). Elder care in India. Conflicting tradition and modernization. Proceedings of 3rd International Conference of IAHSA: *Aging Societies in a New Millennium*, Honolulu, Hawaii, 33-35.

Jamuna, D. (1999b). Stress among caregivers. Do interventions help? *Indian Journal of Gerontology*.

Jamuna, D., & Padmasree, V. (2000). Psycho-social profiles of abused elderly. *Indian Journal of Gerontology*.

Jamuna, D., & Ramamurti, P. V. (2000). *Psychological Correlates of Long Lived Individuals*. Major Research Project Report, University Grants commission, New Delhi (unpublished).

Jamuna, D., & Reddy, L. K. (1992). Elder care in India: The dynamics of in-law equation. *Aging & Society: Indian Journal of Gerontology, 11*(4), 40-43.

Kapoor, P. (1997). Elderly abuse: Some counseling tips. *R & D Journal, 3*(3), 13-23.

Kumar, Vinodh (1996). *Aging: Indian Perspective and Global Scenario*. New Delhi: Vinodh Kumar.

Mohanpuria (1996). Constitutional and legal aspects of elderly welfare. In Vinodh Kumar (Ed.), *Aging: Indian Perspective and Global Scenario*. New Delhi: Vinodh Kumar, Bombay, 97-98.

Nalini, B. (1997). Institutional care for the aged: The issues and implications. In Indrani Chakravarty (Ed.), *Life in Twilight Years*. Calcutta: Kwality Book Co., 63-79.

National Sample Survey Organization (1991). Socioeconomic profile of the aged persons: NSSO 42nd Round (July 1986-June 1987). *Sarveh Shana, 15*(2). New Delhi: Author.

Nayar, P. K. B. (1999). Changing role of the family in the care of the elderly. In S. D. Gokhale, P. V. Ramamurti, N. Pandey, & B. J. Pendse (Eds.), *Ageing in India*. Bombay: Somaiya Pubs. Pvt. Ltd., 168-178.

Padmasree, V. (1991). *A Study of Incidence of Elder Abuse and Some Factors Related to Abuse*. Unpublished Masters Thesis, S.V. University, Tirupati.

Pandit, N. (1999). Laws relating to elderly. In S. D. Gokhale, P. V. Ramamurti, Nirmala Pandey, & B. J. Pendse (Eds.), *Ageing in India*, Bombay: Somaiya Pubs. Pvt. Ltd., 181-198.

Rajkumar, S. (1995). The tragedy of Alzheimer's Disease. *R & D Journal 1*(3), 32-38.

Rajkumar, S., Ravi, S., & Sahabdeen, M. (1996). Burden in caregivers of Alzheimer's disease patients. In Vinodh Kumar (Eds.), *Aging: Indian Perspective and Global Scenario*. New Delhi: Vinodh Kumar, 249-252.

Ramamurti, P. V., & Jamuna, D. (1994). Self-others perceptions of issues and problems of aged women in Andhra Pradesh. *Indian Journal of Gerontology*, 8(1&2), 29-36.

Ramamurti, P. V., & Jamuna, D. (1997). *Evaluation of Old Age Homes, Day Care Centers and Mobile Medical Units in Andhra Pradesh.* Report submitted to Ministry of Welfare, Govt. of India, New Delhi (mimeo).

Ramamurti, P. V., & Jamuna, D. (1999). Elder abuse in the Indian context. *Indian Journal of Gerontology.*

Ramamurti, P. V., Jamuna, D., & Reddy, L. K. (1992a). Improving human resources among the elderly–Effect of an intervention. *Journal of Personality & Clinical Studies*, 8(1&2), 77-79.

Ramamurti, P. V., Jamuna, D., & Reddy, L. K. (1992b). Psycho-social aspects of caregiving and disability among the elderly in India. In K. Mahadevan & P. Krishnan (Eds.), *The Elderly Population, Policies, Problems and Perspectives*, New Delhi: D.K. Publishers, 471-482.

Rao,V. (1999). *Current perspectives on clinical profile and management and diagnostics.* Paper presented at ICMR - WHO workshop on geriatrics, New Delhi, 16-18 March.

Registrar General of India (1991). *Census Reports.* Government of India, New Delhi.

Roy, S. G. (1994). Morbidity-related epidemiological determinants in Indian aged–an overview. In C. R. Ramachandran & Bela Shah (Eds.), *Public Health Implications of Ageing in India.* New Delhi: ICMR, 114-125.

Roy, S. G. (1995). *Sub National Comparisons of Disability Indicators: The Indian Example.* Proceedings of the 50th Session of the International Statistical Institute, Beizing.

Sarvekshana (1991). *Journal of the National Sample Survey Organisation*, XV(49) Oct.-Dec.

Singh, Y. (1997). Changing trends in the Indian family and the adjustment of the aged. *R&D Journal*, 3(2), 31-42.

Suryanarayana, M. (1998). *Changing status in the family life of the rural and tribal aged.* Paper presented at the Regional Conference of HelpAge India, Madras.

CURRENT INTERVENTIONS

Geriatric Hospitals in India, Today and in the Future

K. R. Gangadharan, Dip. SSA
Association of Gerontology India

SUMMARY. In a country that shuns hospitalization of the elderly, regarding it as disrespect of those who helped youngsters evolve, Heritage Hospital (HH) is a welcome change, a model and pioneer stand-alone geriatric hospital. With its non-ambulatory services looking after sick elderly, HH is like an extended family of seniors. HH's love and fresh air complement its Meals-on-Wheels program, guided by the nutritionist's healthy food. HH's Volunteer Guild; its Diabetes Club, ever growing with India's dramatic rise in the number of diabetics; its Senior Net Club's *Click@50*, making elders computer savvy; and Grandparent-Grandchild and Golden and Silver Couple contests celebrated on October 1st, are all widely appreciated, enforcing strong values Indians still share on marriage and family. Heritage brings together 10,000 seniors in Hyderabad, strengthening its motto of Eastern philosophy with its strong emphasis on care for the elderly. *[Article copies available for a fee from The Haworth Document Delivery Service: 1-800-HAWORTH. E-mail address: <docdelivery@haworthpress.com> Website: <http://www.HaworthPress.com> © 2003 by The Haworth Press, Inc. All rights reserved.]*

[Haworth co-indexing entry note]: "Geriatric Hospitals in India, Today and in the Future." Gangadharan, K. R. Co-published simultaneously in *Journal of Aging & Social Policy* (The Haworth Press, Inc.) Vol. 15, No. 2/3, 2003, pp. 143-158; and: *An Aging India: Perspectives, Prospects, and Policies* (ed: Phoebe S. Liebig, and S. Irudaya Rajan) The Haworth Press, Inc., 2003, pp. 143-158. Single or multiple copies of this article are available for a fee from The Haworth Document Delivery Service [1-800-HAWORTH, 9:00 a.m. - 5:00 p.m. (EST). E-mail address: docdelivery@haworthpress.com].

© 2003 by The Haworth Press, Inc. All rights reserved.
http://www.haworthpress.com/store/product.asp?sku=J031
10.1300/J031v15n02_09

KEYWORDS. Community outreach/resource, service clubs, geriatric care, nutritional care, intergenerational programs

AGING IN INDIA AND GERIATRICS

The population of India has already crossed the one billion mark and is expected to grow substantially in the 21st century. Demographic projections indicate that the 70 million persons age 60+ today will increase to 100 million by 2016. By the year 2021, it is anticipated that nearly 10% of India's population will be age 65 and over (Rajan, Mishra, & Sarma, 1999). According to the Indian census, it is expected that India's elders age 60+ may number 323 million by 2050–more than the entire U. S. population. Gains in longevity have been occurring steadily since 1900, when the average life expectancy at birth was less than age 25. In 1996, life expectancy at birth for Indian males was age 61.6 and age 62.2 for females. By the year 2021, it is projected that male life expectancy will be age 69.6 for males and age 70.2 for females (Rajan, Mishra, & Sarma, 1999). In that same year, 52 million Indian elders will be "old-old" or age 75+ (Rajan, Mishra, & Sarma, 1999).

Old age, unfortunately, is often accompanied by sickness and immobility, due to chronic diseases. Appropriate acute and chronic care of elderly patients has not kept pace with demographic shifts. The subjects of gerontology and aging are relatively new in India, and the practice of geriatrics as a specialized branch of medicine has not yet received its due. Unlike the geriatric societies of the United States and the United Kingdom, India's counterpart, established in 1979, has only a few hundred members.

The lack of academic geriatric medicine is yet another factor. Geriatric clerkships created at schools of medicine in the United Kingdom and the United States (see Goodman, 1985), do not exist in India. Most practicing physicians have little or no knowledge about aging and often view their elderly patients in a negative and mechanistic fashion. Subject to availability, they attend a handful of continuing medical education programs to gain adequate knowledge about aging. One outcome is that the few geriatricians in India with any formal training in aging have generally been educated in the developed world. This is not always compatible with Ayurveda and other traditional Indian approaches to health care (Cohen, 1998). Besides this lack of physician training, only very small numbers of other health-care personnel, such as nurses, have had any training in geriatrics.

Furthermore, care centers for older persons are few and largely found in big cities. In rural areas, where nearly 80% of Indian elders reside, these specialized facilities are virtually non-existent. In fact, it is difficult to find general hospitals with medical doctors in non-urban areas. Villagers tend to visit city centers for specialized medical care, and as is true in many developing nations, family members often provide many care functions, such as bathing, to their hospitalized relatives.

In addition, unlike most industrialized nations where government plays an important role in aged care, health care for the elderly is not provided by the Government of India beyond primary health care centers that serve all ages. Nor is there any system of health insurance, either private or public, so familiar to citizens in industrialized nations. While there has recently been some limited development of the former, it is not likely to be an important source of payment for geriatric care for some time.

The general lack of geriatric care facilities is also heavily influenced by the continuing tradition of Indian families taking care of their elders in multi-generational households. This time-honored pattern has been strained by a decades-long trend in migration to India's urban areas and other parts of the globe in pursuit of career opportunities, often due to a lack of non-agricultural jobs in rural areas. Other factors, such as the growth of nuclear families, the high costs of housing in urban centers that make it problematic to maintain traditions of familial co-residence, and more women working outside the home, have also strained family caregiving capacities. Additionally, families find it difficult to render care for their chronically ill older family members, for want of adequate nearby facilities. Still, India does not have large numbers of old-age homes, thanks to the willingness of families to provide their elders with care at home.

Typically, general hospitals and nursing homes in India are unable and often unwilling to provide geriatric care because they lack the capacity to provide needed psycho-social care for the aged beyond standard medical and nursing services. The typical small nursing home provides medical care but, due to a lack of trained personnel, problems in maintaining a multidisciplinary team of professionals, and a wide range of often costly services, is unable to deliver elder-specific care.

For these reasons, the demand for specialized care for elders has not been paramount; health care for the non-elderly, especially women and children, is often a greater problem and therefore a higher priority. Thus, the pattern of developed countries establishing specialized geriatric hospitals, while developing countries are still at the stage of trying to provide hospital care for the majority of their citizens (Little, 1979; Apt, 1995), is evident in India today.

The Development of Geriatric Facilities

Thus far, only a few clinics or hospitals with any focus on geriatrics have been established in India, often by individuals or non-governmental organizations (NGOs) that perceive a growing need for specialized health care for the aged. Some receive minor state or Central Government assistance, but characteristically, such hospitals are privately funded. It is difficult to track them down, due to the vastness of the Indian subcontinent and the lack of any reliable directory or listing. These hospitals can be divided into three categories:

1. hospitals combined or co-located with other geriatric services;
2. existing hospitals to which a geriatric program has been added; and
3. free-standing geriatric hospitals.

In the first group, small numbers of hospitals are combined with old-age homes (senior housing). For example, near Pune, a city southeast of Mumbai (Bombay), a rehabilitation hospital with an old-age home has a geriatrics focus, but it also serves as a general-purpose hospital for the nearby rural population of all ages. This development has largely been the effort of a single physician without formal geriatric training. Similarly, in Bangalore, a hospital offers geriatric-oriented services to a population of retirees that lives in an old-age home located in the same complex. Another program of adding senior housing to a multifaceted complex that includes a hospital providing geriatric services and a senior day-care center (similar to senior centers in the United States) has been in operation in Mumbai for more than three years. Another old-age home also found in the greater Mumbai area has a hospital with a substantial geriatric ward and independent apartments for elders, some of which are available on a respite care basis. This senior housing-hospital combination is somewhat similar to continuing care retirement communities (CCRCs) in the United States; however, CCRCs characteristically have nursing home beds as part of their care continuum, rather than a general hospital.

In other parts of India, geriatric programs have been created in general hospitals, but without the senior housing component. A research aspect often is included, similar to the Geriatric Research, Education, and Clinical Care Centers administered by the U. S. Veterans Administration. For example, a research and clinical care center on osteoporosis is being developed in one of the major hospitals in Pune. This program will undoubtedly be strengthened by the creation of an academic program in gerontology currently underway. In New Delhi, geriatric research and clinical care have been conducted by a small cadre of physicians at the All India Institute of Medical Sciences.

Another, more recent development is the establishment of stand-alone geriatric clinics and, to a far lesser extent, geriatric hospitals. These clinics have begun to appear in several cities, most notably in the south, in Madurai, Chennai (Madras), and Bangalore (Cohen, 1998). One such clinic in Dehradun in the north was started by a doctor who had become proficient in geriatric medicine during his more than 20 years of practice in the United States (Cohen, 1998).

The handful of geriatric hospitals established in India are centered around the principles of restoring and maintaining functionality, in keeping with the tenets of Western geriatric medicine. However, they must also take into account aspects of care that are based on Indian customs and culture. For example, a unique aspect of care in India is the existence of several religions and castes. Thus, geriatric centers must provide facilities and services to meet the varied spiritual needs and traditional preferences of their patients, such as having a prayer room.

As indicated by the foregoing, the development of geriatric care centers in India is barely in its infancy. However, one comprehensive program that has been in operation less than a decade is worth noting as a model for the development of similar programs elsewhere in India. But it also can serve as a model for geriatric hospitals in other parts of the world.

THE EXAMPLE OF HERITAGE HOSPITAL

Heritage Hospital (hereafter, HH) was established in Hyderabad in the state of Andhra Pradesh in November, 1994, to fulfill the needs of families of older patients searching for a facility that would provide convalescent care after a major illness or due to increasing frailty. The parent company was Swathi Health Care, established in 1994. HH was created with the help of a consultant group, Sishrusha Management Consultants, specialists in hospital management designed to raise small and middle-sized hospitals to levels of professionalism exhibited by larger corporate hospitals. A two-year feasibility study was first conducted; then, media cultivation and aggressive marketing were focused on capturing the attention of medical practitioners and the public.

The acquisition of venture capital for this undertaking was problematic, due to the perception that a health-care facility exclusively serving the elderly would not be financially viable. However, partial financing was secured via a term loan from the Bank of Baroda, and within three years, HH broke even in its operations; the five-year loan of 2.4 million rupees was paid off before it was due. Despite various problems including a severe water shortage, loan repayments, raising the initial equity of the promoters, coping with inadequate revenue in the initial stages and countering physician apathy towards the innovative idea of geriatric medicine, HH has steadily grown since its first year. From a gross income of .7 million rupees and .9 million rupees in operating costs in 1994-95, in its first year, HH's gross income grew to 72 million rupees with operating expenses of 71.8 million in 1997-98.

In 1995-96, HH gained tax-exempt status to allow it to receive domestic contributions. In 1998, it acquired tax-exempt status that permits it to receive foreign contributions. HH now operates under the auspices of Dr. Reddy's Heritage Foundation, with a five-member governing council, three of whom reside abroad, and two trustees, one of whom is the managing trustee.

Patients. In its first seven years of operation, HH treated more than 5,000 inpatients and nearly 59,000 outpatients from various parts of India (see Table 1). The hospital attracts patients from neighboring districts within a 200-kilometer radius of its location; 90% of HH's patients are from Hyderabad City. Due to the development of large-size industry and infrastructure, more people are migrating to Hyderabad, now a city of approximately five million. Assuming that 8% of that population is aged 60 and over, HH could serve a population of 400,000 patients from the local area alone. However, patients also come from several Indian states and major cities such as Mumbai, Chennai (Madras), Calcutta, and Delhi.

The patient population has not shown a marked increase in more recent years, due to home-care services having been launched in 1999. Thus, the number of beds in the ambulatory ward was reduced from 16 to 10. Because the number of patients who are provided 24-hour care at home ranges from between 50 to 60 persons daily, essentially another 750 patients have been added to HH's caregiving efforts.

The primary problem of patients is diabetes (38%), followed by anemia including bed sores (15%), and musculoskeletal disorders including stroke (15%). Other problems include mental health (10%) and falls and orthopedic problems (10%), followed by cardiovascular diseases

(7%) and respiratory disorders (5%). Patients with hypertension are included in the pool of those with diabetes and cardiovascular diseases.

To meet the needs of these patients, HH has developed a wide-ranging series of services and activities, including geriatric hospital care focused on rehabilitation; a non-ambulatory long-term care unit; an extended home-care service and other home- and community-based care programs; several community outreach and training activities, including national conferences; and consultation. All of these efforts are guided by the belief that health care does not stop at treating patients and declaring them medically fit; instead, the care is focused on their overall well-being (social, emotional, psychological, and physical).

For the terminally ill, the emphasis is on palliative care. There is no attempt to cure the illness or use heroic attempts to extend life. The focus is on relief of pain and providing emotional support, not only for the ill individual, but for the family as well. Thus, HH's philosophy is to respond to the specific needs for attention and care of the elderly that go beyond medical intervention, with a commitment to promote dignity, respect, and self-esteem of elders.

Medical Facilities and Services. HH occupies a building of 10,000 square feet. It is the only geriatric hospital in India with 30 beds. It has a well-equipped operation theater and an intensive care unit to handle acute and emergency cases and to treat patients with cancer, diabetes, hypertension, chronic liver problems, heart and cerebrovascular disorders, and pneumonia and other respiratory diseases. Basic diagnostic services include x-ray, ultrasonography; treadmill, electrocardiography, echocardiography; and semi-automated biochemistry, clinical pathology, and microbiology. CT scans, MRIs, EMGs, and similar investigations are provided through other agencies nearby. HH's equipment is

TABLE 1. Inpatient and Outpatient Census, 1995-2001

Year	Outpatient	Inpatient
1995	6,000	450
1996	7,000	540
1997	9,500	830
1998	7,600	900
1999	8,600	972
2000	9,600	1,021
2001	10,300	967

similar to that of non-geriatric hospitals and nursing homes in Hyderabad; however, other similar-size hospitals do not offer physiotherapy, audiology, ophthalmology, or dietary and dental services, largely because these services are not considered to be lucrative. A one-stop approach to patient care of the kind offered by HH remains the prerogative of large-size hospitals; HH persists in doing so, due to its philosophy and non-profit status. Total investment in the facility is 225 million rupees. The hospital is able to generate an adequate surplus to meet future development, maintenance, new and upgraded equipment, and staff compensation.

In addition to the services named above, other services include counseling for family and patients; geriatric psychiatry; hospice; comprehensive therapies (audiology, physical, respiratory, and speech); recreation services including a gymnasium; diagnostic services; outpatient clinics; a day hospital; and a diet kitchen. The diet kitchen is not a common aspect of either nursing homes or medium-sized hospitals in India, but it is of great importance to HH physicians, who look to that facility to recommend nutritional care for their patients.

All HH care and services are offered at a reasonable cost that is within the reach of middle income salary earners. Bed charges covering 24-hour nursing care, medical attention and food are 300 rupees per day (at an exchange rate of Rs. 49 for $1). Charges for medicines and consultations by specialists are charged on a use basis. Families are informed about all charges before admission.

On a limited basis, HH also offers the equivalent of nursing home care in a non-ambulatory 10-bed unit for elders who, due to medical conditions and advanced frailty, are no longer able to care for themselves and/or may have no family or no family nearby. Medical and food services are provided, as they are to any hospital patient, but daily services of a personal attendant or companion also are available. While relatives or friends of patients may stay with the patient if they choose, the basic purpose of this unit is to reduce the burden of caregivers and provide respite care, but not to isolate older persons from their families.

As part of its comprehensive program, HH also tried to develop an old-age home some distance from the city center, but it dropped those plans when prospective residents indicated they did not wish to be so far away from the center of town. However, HH has added a small 10-unit, three-story apartment complex for singles and couples who prefer to live independently, but with the knowledge that care and services are readily available, if needed.

The hospital also has adopted a village of 60,000 people located about 30 kilometers from Hyderabad. In collaboration with the local government, HH has been conducting regular health camps at the primary health center once a month since the end of 1998. A team of doctors and nurses offer basic medical attention to all inhabitants, not just the elderly. In this regard it is somewhat different from the medical mobile units sponsored by the Government of India and various NGOs that specialize in geriatric care.

The HH Volunteer Guild is composed of individuals, such as registered patients at HH, members of the Senior Forum (see below), or general volunteers. They render patient service on a weekly or fortnightly basis, depending on their schedules. Services include reading books to and chatting with patients and helping with intergenerational programs.

Service Clubs. HH has organized a range of services under the label, "clubs," as a means of offering needed and reliable services to its older middle-class patients. These include the Privilege, Heritage Senior Net, Heritage Caregivers, and Heritage Diabetes Clubs. They were established to promote networking among people with similar interests. The Privilege Club provides several benefits like care and maintenance services, at-home quarterly health check-ups by a multi-disciplinary team, housekeeping, meals, and companion services. But home maintenance services of an electrician, plumber, and carpenter also are available, as are courier and ticketing services. The last service is particularly important for obtaining intercity bus, train, and airplane transportation, as these transactions in India often require several trips and waiting in line. While the National Policy on Older Persons has recommended special queues for the elderly that may eventually help alleviate long waits, this kind of service now provided by HH is extremely popular. Members, who can be of any age, also get automatic memberships in other Heritage Clubs.

The Senior Net Club–Click@50–is aimed at creating computer literacy, avoiding the problems of surface and air mail delivery, and narrowing the intergenerational gap. Since December, 2000, over 500 seniors have been trained in computer classes, enabling them to stay in touch via e-mail with their family members who live abroad or elsewhere in India. Discounted fees are offered to couples to encourage their pursuing a course together. Members of the Net Club remain in touch with their fellow students and attend monthly courses.

The Caregivers Club, similar to caregiver support groups in the United States, finds innovative methods and solutions to problems faced by individuals who need to manage sick patients at home. It was first designed for caregivers to share their knowledge and experiences and to provide advice to caregivers about managing sick and bedridden older persons. The club has since become the place for identifying and addressing issues and problems faced by typical caregivers.

The Diabetes Club was created when it was found that nearly 40% of patients admitted to the hospital were diabetic. This club helps these patients and their family members cope with the challenges posed by the disease, facilitating a "team approach" by physicians, dietitians, and physiotherapists. Monthly meetings include a medical examination and a review of blood sugar levels.

Other Services. Other services include Meals on Wheels, Dial-a-Driver, Call-a-Car, Heritage Pharmacy Services, and the Heritage Home Care Services Program. The Meals program was launched in January 2000. Over 60 persons use this service that delivers hot breakfasts, lunches, and dinners; only special diet food is served. Members of various Heritage clubs also can order therapeutic meals to be delivered at home. In a similar fashion, the pharmacy service provides for home delivery of medicines so elders or their families do not have to come to the hospital to pick them up.

The Dial-a-Driver (DAD) and Call-a-Car (CAC) programs were created to overcome transportation problems. Initiated in August 2000, DAD provides a driver for elders who own their own cars but no longer want to drive. This program consists of 10 drivers who have been trained to be reliable chauffeurs, providing them with needed employment. CAC offers elders the services of a car and a driver, on an on-call basis. Both of these programs are membership-based. Also offered on a membership basis, Heritage Home Care Services was initiated in November 1999, to strengthen the hospital's capacity to remain a community resource. This program offers an array of services that enable older persons to leave the hospital when they no longer need 24-hour medical care, and to remain at home, their clear preference. The program serves two purposes: employing young girls and boys who are unable to attend high school due to economic reasons and who otherwise would only be employed in menial jobs; and assisting families who do not have anyone to look after their older family member when they are not at home. Services include bedside assistance, diagnostics by a home health team, home medical equipment supply and drug distribution, and physiotherapy. Payment of bills (e.g., utilities) for bedridden patients, and food services, often catering to the special diets required, are also provided. This combination of services allows HH clients not only to maintain their health but also to age in place and to maintain ties with friends and family.

Community Outreach. HH has consistently sought to be a community resource since it was created. The Senior Forum is one of HH's major community outreach programs. Started in early 1995, the Forum's objective is to facilitate fellowship and regular interaction among healthy elders age 50 and older. It offers support and advice to its members on issues related to health-care, legal, and family concerns through monthly meetings. It organizes dinners and discussions on issues of common interest and publishes a monthly newsletter. Guest lectures are presented by eminent geriatric speakers. Members are engaged in various social activities, such as the telephone club and the annual celebration of World Elders' Day. They also are entitled to special health checkups and other benefits offered by HH. Through Dial-a-Doctor, life members are eligible for home visits from physicians, nurses, lab technicians, and social workers.

The Forum is similar to senior clubs found in many major cities elsewhere in India, but is unique in its ties to a hospital. It is designed to create a positive outlook toward life and promote senior citizen self-respect, independence, and health through cultural activities, tours, picnics, games, and visits to old-age homes. Recent events include a cricket match for people over age 65 and a January 2001, South Asian 10-day tour enjoyed by 13 elders.

HH also has been conducting the Heritage Senior Citizens' Festival since 1995. A three-month long program, the Festival comprises various activities, events, and contests aimed at celebrating the golden years. It also helps to sensitize the community to the specific needs of the elderly. Activities include a Golden Couple and a Silver Couple contest that has drawn participation from more than 150 couples who have been married 50 and 25 years, respectively. The contest includes an assessment of their compatibility, understanding, and team work, with a focus on leading a successful and happy married life and on fostering family bonds. Other Festival activities include a fashion show performed by elders age 50 and over, depicting Indian traditions. An evening of music and dance features the diverse cultures that make up India, including special folk dances and textiles and jewelry from different regions of the country.

Intergenerational programs, aimed at promoting lasting family values and fostering bonds of mutual love, understanding and respect, also are major Festival events. The Grandparent-Grandchild Bridge Program invokes the participation of children by visiting various schools and by conducting activities like skits, painting and poster competitions, poetry and essay writing, and a Grandparent-Grandchild quiz competition. The "War of the Ages" also focuses on intergenerational issues, such as love, romance and courtship, as viewed by the younger and older generations, featuring music and dance. The Festival ends with the celebration of World Elders' Day, an annual event on October 1st that also is hosted by other senior groups and organizations across India.

Training Activities. India, like many Asian-Pacific nations, lacks the necessary trained personnel to support families in their caregiving roles (HelpAge International, 2001). To overcome this lack of geriatric care training, HH has developed several programs. While most of these are focused in their local areas, the hospital is beginning to expand its efforts elsewhere in India. HH collaborates with various public and private entities to develop and present quality training in aging.

HH, in cooperation with the Municipality of Hyderabad and UNICEF, created a three-month "Dust Busters" training program for more than 120 hospital housekeepers. In cooperation with the national Ministry of Social Justice and Empowerment, the lead agency in implementing India's National Policy on Older Persons, the hospital has already conducted two training programs on the care of older persons for employees of old-age homes in Andhra Pradesh, with others planned. HH recently created a one-day training program on management issues for administrators of these homes. This program may be expanded in the future.

In cooperation with Dr. Reddy's Foundation for Human and Social Development, a local Hyderabad foundation, HH developed the first training program in India for bedside assistants. This has involved training slum children, primarily girls, about geriatric bedside care, creating much-needed employment for them while also creating a pool of trained home care personnel. Several hundred trainees between ages 16 and 18 have gained employment in various facilities; 20 persons have been engaged in home nursing. This program was expanded in 2002 to train 120 bedside assistants in Chennai in a year's time and also to start similar programs in Mumbai, Pune, and Bangalore.

It should be noted that a similarly hospital-based, but more formal, home care training program has been developed at the Vidyasagar Institute of Mental Health and Neuroscience (VIMHANS), a nonprofit hospital in New Delhi. Initiated in 1995 with funding from HelpAge India and the Alzheimer's Society of India, this 18-month program has trained 75 students between the ages of 18 and 35, with basic knowledge of spoken and written English. After a careful screening for admission and paying a fee for the first six months of the course, students are assigned to a six-month hospital rotation and then to a family for 12 months on a residential basis. The students receive a stipend and the family supplies meals and bus fare during the training. Families also pay for extra work shifts. At the end of the training, students must pass an exam. Many end up being hired permanently by the families with which they were placed (HelpAge International, 2001).

However, unlike the HH program, this Delhi-based program does not have securing employment for its trainees as one of its major purposes. HH recruits its trainees through road shows in slums and then conducts aptitude and psychological tests before selection. It counsels the trainees and, in the majority of cases, their parents as well. A stipend is paid to the trainees; those who are poor are not expected to pay for their training. To guard against the likelihood that these trained assistants are not used as servants by the families where they are placed, permanent placements are avoided. Rather, the assistants are rotated.

Another training program, initiated in 2001-2002 by HH, is based on collaboration with the University of South Australia. This program is focused on research and training in geriatrics and diabetes. Undergraduate students in their final year undergo training at HH for three to seven weeks in these important areas.

Over the past several years, HH also has held several national conferences to highlight particular issues in gerontology and geriatrics. They have included a focus on housing, on Alzheimer's disease, the challenges of caregiving, celebrating aging by designing the future, and most recently, on emerging trends and challenges in aging in India. Major themes and principles of these conferences are published in HH's *Senior Heritage Selections*, a bimonthly publication.

Consultation. Staff of HH are currently engaged in providing technical assistance to organizations in other parts of India seeking to create geriatric centers. HH also has served as a technical management consultant to several small and large hospitals in different parts of India, such as Bangalore, Delhi, and Mumbai, and Baroda in Gujarat, and Udaipur in Rajasthan. These efforts are likely to grow in the future, due to demand.

New Programs. HH, as part of its mission to serve as a community resource, is establishing an adopt a foster-/grandchild program. Similar to Foster Grandparent and Foster Child programs in the United States, this program will offer economic support to older adults looking after children whose own parents have died or who have gone away. This program is another link in the intergenerational programming conducted by the hospital.

HH is embarking on new ventures through a series of partnerships. Within the next year, it anticipates establishing a Diabetic Hospital and Research Center in association with an international organization. Additional plans include the development of a Hyderabad Institute of Gerontology to conduct research and train researchers in a hospital-based setting. HH also plans on establishing more geriatric centers in India through joint partnerships.

Heritage Hospital as a Model of Geriatric Care

There are at least two ways to look at HH as a model of geriatric care: one, in terms of its relevance for the developed world, the other as a model for India and other developing nations. In the first instance, the HH program can be assessed by its ability to meet standards for quality geriatric hospital care. In the *Journal of the American Geriatrics Society*, Brymer and Ellett (1997) noted that a 1996 article in *U.S. News & World Report* ranked quality of geriatric care in America's best hospitals, based on reputational score, hospital-wide mortality rate, membership in the Council of Teaching Hospitals, breadth of community services offered, availability of technology in geriatrics, ratio of full-time RNs to beds, number of post-discharge services, and number of geriatric services. However, given the lack of this kind of sophisticated medical infrastructure (e.g., a council of teaching hospitals, hospital-based research programs) in India (as well as other developing nations), HH would appear not to fall into the best geriatric hospital category. It does, however, get high marks for the breadth of community services offered and the number of post-discharge and geriatric services provided.

However, Brymer and Ellett (1997) raise specific concerns about the various criteria used (e.g., bias towards tertiary care centers with extensive clinical research); the minimal relationship between hospital-wide mortality and extensive use of cutting-edge technology to quality care of the elderly; and the likelihood that a high full-time RN-bed ratio is associated with procedurally-oriented hospitals with large intensive care units. They also criticize the "more is better" emphasis on the number of distinct community, discharge, and geriatric services offered. Instead, they suggest that, based on their own experience in a regional geriatric program in Canada, a move toward "one-stop shopping" for all these services improves continuity of care; and that quality of care is better achieved in multi-disciplinary care programs. Based on this kind of appraisal, it appears that the HH, with its regional multi-disciplinary program of well-integrated services, especially those that are community-based, is an approach worthy of study and emulation by geriatric hospitals in developed nations.

In many ways, however, HH may be an even better model for developing nations, where traditional family ties are still important. India's national policy on aging, similar to that of other developing or newly industrialized nations (especially in the Asia-Pacific area), focuses on supporting families in their caregiving roles. In that context, the main purpose of geriatric hospitals is not to make geriatric care centers dumping grounds or to isolate the elderly from their families, but to help the families carry the burden of care. Thus, good geriatric care involves providing elders *and* their families with psychological and emotional support, as HH is doing. In the United States, the importance of this has gradually been recognized as evidenced by recent passage of the National Family Caregivers Initiative.

Furthermore, all developing nations look to nonprofit NGOs as one of the key solutions to meeting the needs of their aging citizens. Again, India's national policy on older persons identifies a key role for such entities. HH provides an excellent example of how a well-managed hospital, guided by a well-articulated philosophy of care, can overcome the reluctance of the medical profession to become engaged in geriatrics and become a regional geriatric care center, serving both urban and rural needs. Through strategic development, community outreach and public relations, partnerships with both public and private entities, and positioning itself to be eligible for both international and domestic funding, HH has shown that over a short time such an enterprise can be successful and exemplary.

However, the HH program is not without its limitations. Due to financial realities and the lack of any government program of geriatric health care, it has chosen to serve middle- and upper-income Indians. It is clear, however, that geriatric care is needed by low-income elders as well, a need that is only barely addressed by other NGOs and a very limited number of Government of India grants. It is unlikely that HH can fill this gap, even within its own region. However, it has expanded its outreach to the less fortunate through the provision of health care in the village it has adopted and through its activities that include the employment of poor younger adults, a matter of great importance in India, where officially 30% of the population lives below the poverty level. By "exporting" its model elsewhere in India through the mechanism of joint partnerships and technical assistance, HH is in a good position to show that quality geriatric care can be provided in nations that are still struggling with the development of widespread hospital care for their citizens.

AUTHOR NOTES

K. R. Gangadharan is a postgraduate in Social Service Administration and a qualified trainer, having completed a certificate course by the Indian Society for Training & Development (ISTD). Having worked for large, major hospitals in India, he established India's first ever Geriatric Hospital in Hyderabad in 1994. He is Managing Committee Member of Association of Gerontology India (AGI); Joint Secretary General, Alzheimer's and Related Disorders Society of India (ARDSI); Secretary of the Indian local Office, International Federation of India (IFA); and Membership Ambassador, International Association of Homes & Services for Ageing (IAHSA). He was Chairman of the National Committee on HRD in Health Sector of the ISTD. Mr. Gangadharan organizes several national seminars and conferences on Aging and Hospital Management. He has presented papers at several international conferences and participated in United Nations meetings, at both the global and Asia-Pacific regional levels.

Mr. Gangadharan can be contacted at Heritage Hospital, 6-3-655/12 Somajiguda, Hyderabad-500 082, India (E-mail: krganga@hotmail.com).

REFERENCES

Apt, N. A. (1995). Health care of the elderly in Africa: Focus on Ghana. *Caring, 14*(1), 42-45.

Brymer, C. & Ellett, F. (1997). America's best geriatric hospitals? *Journal of the American Geriatric Society, 45*(4), 531-540.

Cohen, L. (1998). *No aging in India: Alzheimer's, the bad family, and other modern things.* Berkeley, CA: University of California Press.

Goodman, G. (1985). Geriatric medicine: A requirement for fourth-year medical students. *Nursing Homes, 34*(2), 43-45.

HelpAge International (2001). *Ageing in my own place: Home care for older people in the Asia-Pacific region.* Chiang Mai, Thailand: Author.

Little, V. C. (1979). For the elderly: An overview of services in industrially developed and developing countries. In M. Teicher, D. Thursz & J. Vigilante (Eds.), *Reaching the aged: Social services in forty-four countries.* Beverly Hills, CA: Sage.

Rajan, S. I., Mishra, U. S., & Sarma, P. S. (1999). *India's elderly: Burden or challenge?* New Delhi: Sage Publications.

Old-Age Homes and Services: Old and New Approaches to Aged Care

Phoebe S. Liebig, PhD

University of Southern California

SUMMARY. Although generational co-residence continues to be the dominant form of housing and care for Indian elders and only 1% live in old-age homes, the numbers and types of these homes are growing. This article describes a recent study of 48 old-age homes in different parts of India, approximately 12%-15% of all homes. They included the more traditional free homes for the aged poor who have no family to care for them and the more recent for-pay homes for the middle-class. A small number of day-care centers, also a new phenomenon, were investigated. Two- to three-hour structured interviews were conducted with managers, supervisors, and trustees, augmented by a checklist of environmental and neighborhood features. Most homes house small numbers of residents, have common spaces for dining, TV and prayer, have access to medical care and transportation, provide meals and some assistance with activities of daily living, and are open to all castes. All are run by non-governmental organizations (NGOs), only one-third with any government assistance. Free homes tend to be bigger and older, serve non-aged clients, have less privacy and emphasize occupational therapy and income-generating activities, and are more like board-and-care homes.

[Haworth co-indexing entry note]: "Old-Age Homes and Services: Old and New Approaches to Aged Care." Liebig, Phoebe S. Co-published simultaneously in *Journal of Aging & Social Policy* (The Haworth Press, Inc.) Vol. 15, No. 2/3, 2003, pp. 159-178; and: *An Aging India: Perspectives, Prospects, and Policies* (ed: Phoebe S. Liebig, and S. Irudaya Rajan) The Haworth Press, Inc., 2003, pp. 159-178. Single or multiple copies of this article are available for a fee from The Haworth Document Delivery Service [1-800-HAWORTH, 9:00 a.m. - 5:00 p.m. (EST). E-mail address: docdelivery@haworthpress.com].

© 2003 by The Haworth Press, Inc. All rights reserved.
http://www.haworthpress.com/store/product.asp?sku=J031
10.1300/J031v15n02_10

For-pay homes have more privacy and western-style amenities, focus on local community outreach and provide fewer meals. The gradual increase of all old-age homes has given rise to debates about their appropriate roles in Indian society and about their quality. Government grants to NGOs for homes and day-care centers (often considered more appropriate support for elders) are limited. With the National Policy on Older Persons looking to NGOs and village councils to be the primary sources of non-familial aged care, several ways to build their capacity are suggested. *[Article copies available for a fee from The Haworth Document Delivery Service: 1-800-HAWORTH. E-mail address: <docdelivery@haworthpress.com> Website: <http://www.HaworthPress.com> © 2003 by The Haworth Press, Inc. All rights reserved.]*

KEYWORDS. Free and for-pay homes, generational co-residence, non-governmental organizations, day-care centers, National Policy on Older Persons

OVERVIEW

Old-age homes are not a new phenomenon in India; institutions for care of the elderly, such as the Venkatagiri Chaultries, have been in operation at least since the early 18th century (Nair, 1995). Traditionally, these homes served destitute people, that is, persons who were poor and had no family to care for them. Such homes were free and often run by various Christian orders, predominantly in south India. This pattern persists today, with heaviest concentrations in the states of Andhra Pradesh, Karnataka, Kerala, and Tamil Nadu (Rajan, Mishra, & Sarma, 1999).

Recent developments in eldercare include for-pay homes (known as "pay-and-stay" homes) and community-based services. This new type of home, similar to retirement communities in the United Sates, is a response to the growing demands of middle-class and upper-income families whose younger members are not available to care for their elders. Due to growing affluence, higher rates of migration and job mobility within and outside of India, multiple income earners (especially women in urban areas), and increased choices for asset-building, multi-generational co-residence is gradually giving way to nuclear households, with a reduction in informal caregiving (Varadharajan, 1989; Brink, 1998).

Some community-based services have been created, primarily during the last decade or so, by non-governmental organizations (NGOs) but usually without direct governmental assistance. Among them are day-care centers, where elders can go for meals and social activities, similar to senior centers in the United States. While it is difficult to pinpoint where or when these centers first started, they probably arose in the late 1970s or early 1980s in Bombay (Mumbai), Madras (Chennai), and Hyderabad (Nair, 1995). The centers were created to meet the need for elders to be in a safe and wholesome environment during the day as more family members, especially women, worked outside the home or attended school.

Other services include Adopt-a-Granny programs. One type involves school-age children "adopting" a group of elders in a day-care center or old-age home to reduce the isolation of elders. Another service provides monthly rations of basic foodstuffs, clothing, and sometimes pocket money to poor elders to relieve some of the economic burden on families, especially in villages and urban slums.

One can also find scattered examples of other services, such as mobile medical units, in-home care, family counseling, social work with elderly patients in hospitals, and income-generating activities (Nair, 1995). The author also discovered a "friendly visitor" program in Bangalore and a hybrid meals-on-wheels program in Chennai. But families are the main source of eldercare.

INDIAN ELDERS' LIVING ARRANGEMENTS

The joint family is the basic family structure in India; parents live with one or more of their children (Ara, 1998). Housing quality of older persons tends to depend on the work and shelter patterns of household members (Brink, 1998). The quality of eldercare also depends on the family's economic capacity. Officially, 30% of India's population lives below the poverty level; the actual proportion, however, may be substantially higher. Thus, for many families, stretching resources to provide for their elders may result in shortchanging their children (Cohen, 1998).

In addition, the quality of care for elders depends heavily on the positive or negative aspects of family dynamics. The joint family is a healthy institution if it generates emotional links among members of different generations, but it can create social and psychological problems for elders, for example, conflicts between mothers-in-law and daughters-in-law (Achamamba, 1987).

Although Indians have become concerned about the gradual fraying of traditional living arrangements, co-residence is still dominant in rural areas where 70% of India's population lives (Muttagi, 1997; Ara, 1998). Many states (e.g., Rajasthan, Bihar) lack old-age homes, day-care centers, and other services for the elderly (Rajan, Mishra, & Sarma, 1994, 1999). Less than 1% of all Indian elders live in old-age homes (HelpAge India, 1995).

STUDIES OF OLD-AGE HOMES IN INDIA, 1990-1996

Research on aging in India is still in its infancy; studies of old-age homes have been relatively rare, due to the traditional living arrangements noted above. Even though old-age homes have been in existence for about 300 years, only recently have they caught the attention of researchers. The problems of inquiry also have been exacerbated by the lack of accurate information about the facilities. Three directories (Association for Senior Citizens, 1992; HelpAge India, 1995; Nair, 1995) reported between 325 and 354 homes. Kumar (1998), citing other sources, also estimated their numbers to be between 300 and 400. However, approximately 100 homes receiving government support in 1995-1996 were not listed in these directories. Thus, probably more than 500-600 homes exist, with their numbers growing, largely driven by the increase in for-pay homes in or near major cities.

In the mid-1990s, a few studies were undertaken, focusing on homes in specific states, such as Maharashtra and Andhra Pradesh (see Dandekar, 1996; Ramamurti, Jamuna, & Reddy, 1996). These on-site studies emphasized resident satisfaction, quality of care and, to a lesser degree, management issues. Others relied on mail-back questionnaires from all known homes nationwide. In the HelpAge India study (1995), of the 256 facilities responding, 162 were free, 30 were for pay, and 64 served both destitute and paying residents; 53 catered only to women. Fewer than 13,000 elders resided in these homes (HelpAge India, 1995). With the exception of Ramamurti et al. (1996), day care centers, mobile medical units, and other services for the aged were not included in these studies.

Accounts in national newspapers such as *The Hindu* have focused on problems with quality of care and what should exist, but as of today, no standards or guidelines exist for old-age homes. This is in sharp contrast to the United States, where regulation of board-and-care homes has been and remains a key issue (Hawes, Wildfire et al., 1993; Morgan, Eckert, & Lyon, 1995).

A NATIONAL STUDY OF OLD-AGE HOMES, 1997-1998

To fill some gaps left by these earlier studies, a four-month nationwide investigation was undertaken by the author in 1997-1998. While this short time barely permitted scratching the surface of a very complex and multi-faceted society, the author was familiar with India, having stayed there for several months twice before.

Nearly 50 homes and nine day-care centers were visited in six Indian states: Andhra Pradesh, Karnataka, Kerala, Maharashtra, Tamil Nadu, and West Bengal; and in two Union Territories: Delhi in the north and Pondicherry in the south. These areas were selected because they were located in different parts of India and known to have many facilities and programs for the aged. Gujarat, a western state with more than 20 homes, however, was not visited because distances precluded the additional time commitment required.

Methods

A six-page questionnaire, based on the work of Dandekar (1996), Shankardass (1995) and Morgan, Eckert, and Lyon (1995), was developed for use in structured interviews of managers, supervisors, or trustees of old-age homes and day-care centers. (Unlike the earlier on-site studies, residents were not interviewed, except in for-pay homes where managers or trustees were often residents.) The instrument was critiqued by colleagues at the Centre for Research on Ageing at Tirupati, Andhra Pradesh. A list of candidate homes was generated, using the directories and a 1995-1996 list of programs receiving Government of India (GOI) support. This was no simple task. Sometimes a home in one source was not cited by the others; addresses often were not the same or were simply lacking; and some homes appeared to have more than one name. Finally, a list of slightly more than 80 old-age homes was created. Care was taken to include different types of homes: religious vs. non-religious auspices; urban vs. rural; free vs. for-pay or both; and acceptance of both sexes or just one.

Despite some facilities' refusal to participate or occasional inability of the researcher to gain permission in a timely fashion, 48 homes were visited. Attempts were made to visit two others on the list, but they had vanished. No government-run homes, often reported as being of poor quality (Ghosh, 1998), were surveyed. Trying to gain access to two of these homes in Pondicherry and Delhi required lengthy discussions with several levels of bureaucracy that ultimately proved unsuccessful.

Access was also contingent on the ability of local "guides" to help locate the homes and assist in translation. Staff of HelpAge India, a nationwide NGO, played a major role in securing the participation of many homes in the study. They were also helpful in overcoming language barriers: the author spoke none of India's major languages and not all old-age home staff spoke English with ease. Thus, while the sample was clearly opportunistic, comprising only 12-15% of previously identified homes, and time spent in each facility was limited (approximately two to three hours per visit), the study provides a number of insights on senior housing in India.

Results

The findings are presented in two ways. First, a summary of all 48 homes is presented. Second, the differences between the old (free homes) and new (for-pay homes) approaches are briefly noted.

All homes. The 48 old-age homes differed in location, amenities, and size; common areas and services; auspices; length of operations; management issues; and resident characteristics.

Location, physical amenities, and size. Half (50%) of the homes were located in urban areas, with equal proportions (25%) found in suburban and rural areas. Not surprisingly, a home's location influenced its physical appearance and amenities. In general, rural homes tended to resemble houses in local villages and provided unsophisticated amenities. They were quite small–two or three rooms, housing a dozen or more persons, with a vegetable garden tended by the residents, to help feed themselves. Essentially, these elders were continuing the customary patterns of rural life, but outside the traditional living arrangement. With the exception of two rural homes, all homes had locked gates for safety and security reasons, regardless of the neighborhood in which they were located.

Suburban homes, primarily serving middle- or upper-middle-income aged, were of modest size and looked like typical homes in the particular part of India where they were located. The urban homes tended to be quite large-scale. Some (usually for-pay homes) resembled other apartment buildings in the same section of town, while others were large complexes of a more institutional character but with extensive grounds. The majority (85%) of homes had some kind of planting, usually consisting of potted trees and plants, characteristic of Indian residences; however, only 50% had formal gardens, and only 42% had places to sit. More than a third (37%) had gardens where residents could work, if they wished.

Bathing and toileting areas were separate; Western-style bathrooms are a relatively modern phenomenon in India. As might be expected, rural old-age homes were more primitive by Western standards; two lacked even the barest of bathing and toileting amenities. Nearly four-fifths of all homes provided buckets for bathing; the rest had Western-style showers. Only 22% provided hot water (primarily paid homes); however, cold water bathing is not unusual in India. Toilet styles were evenly split between squat (29%) and Western (27%) types, with nearly 40% of the homes having both. Only 25% had special seating and about one in five had grab bars in either bathing or toileting areas. Other important environmental supports were found: nearly half of all homes (48%) had ramps rather than stairs; 92% had sliding lever door handles that are easy to manipulate; and wide doorways and hallways were the norm in 54% and 79% of all homes, respectively.

Overall, most homes did not house huge numbers of elders. The largest facility was home to 230 residents, the smallest to four persons. Larger homes accommodated both men and women; some also housed non-elderly persons (e.g., orphans, mentally retarded). With the exception of one home in Chennai consisting of one large room with two alcoves, men and women did not share sleeping quarters. A few smaller facilities were segregated by gender: 16% permitted only women; two sponsored by the military allowed only retired officers and their wives or widows, and one home, men only.

Common spaces and services. Common spaces were relatively similar; 92% had a dining room or area, even in paid homes where residents, especially couples, often preferred to take meals by themselves. A smaller proportion (73%) had formal kitchens, because paid homes were somewhat less likely to offer a full meal service; two rural homes did not have separate rooms for either eating or cooking, but simply outdoor areas.

Similar to U. S. government-assisted housing built in the 1960s and 1970s, many homes had limited common spaces. An area for watching TV, which in some homes was also the reception area, was found in nearly 75% of all homes. A library or game room, a prayer room, and separate office or reception area were found in somewhat more than half of all homes; yoga/exercise rooms were encountered less frequently (35%). Nearly half (48%) had an infirmary, usually two to five beds. Larger homes had more beds (12-16), to separate ill residents from their dormitory-mates.

Meals were provided by most homes: 80% served three meals a day, with 60% also providing two snacks daily; paid homes often provided fewer meals. Strictly vegetarian meals were offered by 52% of the homes, in keeping with religious traditions of many Indians. Non-vegetarian meals were the usual diet in 12% of the homes, while 31% had both vegetarian and non-vegetarian menus to accommodate the different food preferences of residents.

Health care issues were important. Contrary to earlier reports (HelpAge India, 1995), these homes seemed willing and able to provide some health services, rather than asking residents to leave if they became too infirm. Nearly all (98%) homes required new residents to be ambulatory and free of contagious diseases, with 54% mandating some kind of exam or physician's certification. Access to periodic health screening was provided by 98% of the homes, as was vision care (90%) and dental care (69%), primarily extractions. Virtually all (96%) had access to a local clinic or hospital; 60% were within one kilometer of this kind of facility. Three for-pay homes were co-located with a hospital; one free home even had its own small operating room.

Nearly 80% indicated willingness to create special diets for residents to reduce their sugar or salt intake; the remainder indicated that resident non-adherence led to the staffs' reducing efforts to change behavior. Slightly more than half (52%) of the homes tried to meet nutritional requirements by adding fresh fruit.

Help with activities of daily living (ADLs) was provided by a majority of all homes, but several paid homes expected residents to make their own arrangements and pay for them. Aid with bathing and medications was provided by 73% of all facilities, followed by assistance with feeding (71%). More than half reported help with ambulation and transfer for residents needing that kind of assistance. One home had a separate Alzheimer's unit.

Auspices of the homes were of two types, with 40% run by religious groups. In the four southern states, Christian homes were dominant, but Hindu-run homes were also prominent. Only one Parsi-run home was identified. No Moslem home was found and only one home reported having ever had a Moslem resident.

The majority (60%) of homes were sponsored by charitable trusts or organizations, such as Rotary International. Only 4% required residents to have a particular religion; even in church-run facilities, no attempt was made to convert residents. However, all facilities provided opportunities for prayer and the singing of *bhajans* (hymns), and 54% made arrangements for residents to attend religious events. As noted earlier, many had special prayer rooms (in Christian homes, chapels). Because religion and spiritual life are a dominant force in Indian life, it is fitting that old-age homes included this activity. Furthermore, all homes made arrangements for cremation and burial–consonant with Hindu and Christian beliefs–if no family members were available to do so.

All homes (100%) were open to all castes, a somewhat unexpected finding. Separation by caste is still very deep-seated in Indian society, although that tradition is weakening in a few urban centers. While there was no way to determine whether Untouchables were actually being housed with Brahmins, it is unlikely this was happening.

Length of operation. The 48 homes ranged in age from four months to 190 years, with a mean age of 35 years. Fully 38% had been created within the last decade, reflecting the rising demand for age-specific housing. This growing nationwide demand was mentioned by nearly all interviewees, regardless of how long their homes had been in existence.

In general, urban homes for destitute residents tended to be the oldest facilities; for-pay urban homes were newer. The latter appeared to be responsive to the desires of older city dwellers to age in place in the communities where they had lived and worked as adults, rather than return to their villages of origin. This was true in more Westernized cities like Bangalore and Mumbai. Rural and suburban homes, in contrast with their urban counterparts, tended to be among the most recently established facilities.

Management issues included major expenditures, financing, staffing, and oversight. The largest expenditure for old-age homes (also true of day-care centers) was food; other significant costs included medical services and supplies, staff pay (with meals), and building maintenance and repair. Most homes (83%) relied on in-kind donations of materials and/or services (e.g., doctor's visits); more than half (56%) said general donations were their most important source of financing. Thus, the majority of homes were dependent on the fund-raising skills of staff or trustees or on the results of local community outreach. They relied heavily on a tradition of charity among all religions in India and on NGO assistance, aided by income tax policies for charitable deductions. About one-third received government funding, with 17% citing this public assistance as their most important source. But most preferred to avoid bureaucratic red tape and thus did not seek government aid.

Staffing in 83% of the homes consisted of a matron/on-site supervisor (generally living in the home); cooking and cleaning staff (77%); safety/maintenance workers (69%); and gardeners or drivers (48%). In general, homes had limited personnel due to the expense, and their staffs were not highly trained. Only 36% of the homes, usually those run by Christian orders, had staff with a nursing or social work background.

Similarly, with few exceptions, home administrators had only on-the-job training; career training is non-existent. In most homes, the matron/senior staff handled resident complaints; only 6% had a grievance group. Staff members were characteristically hired from the local community by word-of-mouth and received minimal training about older people. Their attitudes towards the aged, however, were an important consideration in their being hired and retained. The ability to provide tender loving care (TLC) for people in their final years was uniformly expressed by all interviewees as the primary reason for their home's existence.

In contrast with the United States, 96% of these homes expected their residents to provide care to each other, partly to compensate for the lack of staff but primarily to keep them involved in the life of their community, that is, the old-age home. In addition, 69% expected their residents to be productive, consonant with their capabilities, by engaging in various household tasks (e.g., food preparation); by helping plan activities (40%); through income-generation (e.g., making garlands or snacks for sale) to help sustain the home (23%); or by providing services to the outside community (17%). A few (10%), primarily in rural areas, expected the residents to grow food for the home.

Nearly 70% of the homes used volunteers, usually drawn from specific organizations or schools, rather than the general community. These groups often sponsored special events, such as holiday celebrations or entertainment. General community support, including financial help, was reported by 83% of all respondents. Support and interest of government officials at any level was reported less frequently (60%).

Fully 83% of the homes had formal governing councils or advisory groups, comprising professionals in various walks of life. These councils generally ranged in size from five to 10 members and existed to help ensure quality of care and to raise funds. Because only half of the homes were ever visited by any government official to monitor care quality, the councils' oversight role was extremely important. All homes kept some kind of case records on individual residents, primarily admissions information, but only 52% noted individual progress. Death records were maintained by 77% and discharge records by 19%. Thus, data were kept on the comings and goings of residents rather than on their changes in status or needs over time.

Resident characteristics. The ages of the residents ranged from 60– the usual age of admittance–to 105; however, in three homes, exceptions were made for family reasons to accommodate younger individuals. Age 60 is the customary marker of old-age in the Hindu religion, in public policy determinations, and the age of mandatory retirement for workers covered by pensions.

Three common reasons were given for residents being in the homes: inability of the family to care for the person (96%); reasons of economic need (56%); and the desire to live with peers (12.5%). Inability to care for oneself was a minor issue. Indeed, with the exception of one facility primarily serving the homeless, all homes required prospective residents to be ambulatory and in good health when admitted and also mandated some kind of pre-admission interview, often with family members, to ensure compatibility with other residents.

More than half of the homes (54%) required prospective residents to have some kind of physical exam or certification by a doctor. It was particularly important, especially in the larger homes for destitute people, that prospective residents not have any communicable diseases like tuberculosis. However, once residents were admitted, they stayed until they died (the norm) or chose to leave, a rare occurrence. Home administrators indicated they rarely found it necessary to summon a family member to remove the resident because he/she was too ill to be cared for by the facility any longer. Because medical and discharge records were not examined, no measures of residents' frailty were made; however, while many had problems with ambulation, most appeared to be able to care for themselves with some assistance. Few were totally bedfast. Consistent with the literature (see, for example, Dandekar, 1996), many administrators reported residents were depressed or sad due to their not being cared for in the traditional manner, as expected.

Paid vs. free homes. While for-pay and free homes were similar in many respects, they also differed, as shown in Table 1. As noted earlier, for-pay homes are a relatively recent phenomenon. For older couples and widowers, a place of their own is sometimes preferred, even if the younger family resides nearby. Strong affectional ties, however, are still maintained. For those elders whose children live elsewhere in India or abroad, or elders without children, these homes ensure they will be looked after.

Nearly six in 10 of these homes (58%) served destitute people, in keeping with long-held values of helping those lacking economic and other kinds of family support. One-third served those who could pay, while the remainder (9%) housed both destitute and for-pay residents. In this last group of homes, paying residents partly subsidized the non-payers. Monthly payments ranged from 450-3000 rupees (approximately $13-$85) and covered housing, access to some services, some meals, and security. In 16% of the paid homes, charges varied for couples and the use of more/special services. At a few homes, medical, dental, and sometimes housekeeping services were out-of-pocket expenses for residents.

Unlike the United States, where "programs for the poor are poor programs," many of the homes for the destitute people were well-constructed and well-maintained. They often embraced a philosophy of the home as a therapeutic environment, focused on rehabilitation and opportunities for residents to contribute to the common welfare of the home. It was normative to help each other, often as companions for the very frail, and engage in tasks promoting the welfare of all residents, for example, baking and mending. Women were likely to help with food preparation and men participated in gardening, while both sexes were active in income-generation activities. Most day-care center attendees also helped with meals and income-generation to help sustain the program and enhance their sense of usefulness and purpose.

By contrast, for-pay homes were less likely to stress the common welfare of the home. Instead, some residents (almost exclusively men) became engaged in local community affairs, such as teaching in the local school or sponsoring the local youth cricket team. Two *ashram*-sponsored homes required participation in the broader social welfare programs of those spiritual communities.

Other contrasts between the two types of homes were notable: free homes tended to be larger, had been in operation longer, and were often multipurpose. They served not only the aged, but other "marginal" groups: orphans, mentally retarded, and battered or abandoned women in a series of buildings or under the same roof. The different age/disability groups often mingled, with the elderly often acting as surrogate grandparents or abused women serving as caregivers for the elders.

The smallest number of residents (4) was found in a paid home for women that had been open for only four months; another resident was to move in the following week, bringing it almost to full capacity. The largest number of residents (230) was found in a facility sponsored by the Little Sisters of the Poor, who run what is essentially a "chain" of old-age homes in India, all providing very high levels of TLC for destitute residents. Five of the largest homes for the poor were undergoing

TABLE 1. Comparisons of Free and For-Pay Homes

	FREE	FOR-PAY
PHYSICAL PLANT / STAFFING/ SIZE / CAPACITY	LARGE, UP TO 200+ AT / OVER CAPACITY	SMALL, 6-50 AT / UNDER CAPACITY
AMBIENCE/AMENITIES COMMON AREAS	ADEQUATE AMENITIES, MAINTENANCE, MOST WITH GARDENS, INDIAN SOME WESTERN TOILETS, COMMON KITCHENS, SOME INFIRMARIES, PRAYER ROOM/CHAPEL	BETTER AMENITIES, MAINTENANCE, MOST WITH GARDENS, WESTERN BATHROOMS, USUALLY SEPARATE KITCHENS
STAFFING	MANAGER, COOK, CLEANING, SECURITY, & DRIVER, LAUNDRY, PERSONAL CARE AS NEEDED, SCHEDULING OF DOCTOR VISITS, SOME FORMAL TRAINING, ON-JOB TRAINING	MANAGER, SECURITY, MAINTENANCE, CLEANING, HIRE OWN PERSONAL CARE, MEDICAL SERVICES, ON-JOB TRAINING
PRIVACY	MINIMAL, GROUP SLEEPING ARRANGEMENTS (DORMITORIES), FEW DOUBLES, TRIPLES COMMON, MEALS, FEW PRIVATE POSSESSIONS	MORE WESTERN-STYLE PRIVACY, PRIVATE OR SEMI-PRIVATE ROOMS, MORE PRIVATE MEALS, MANY PRIVATE POSSESSIONS
AUSPICES	PRIMARILY RELIGIOUS	RELIGIOUS, CHARITABLE TRUSTS
RESIDENT CHARACTERISTICS		
ECONOMIC	POOR, LOW/NO PENSION, NO FAMILY ECONOMIC SUPPORT	MIDDLE CLASS, SOME PENSION, SOME FAMILY ECONOMIC SUPPORT
COMMUNITY SERVICE EXPECTATIONS	HELP CARE FOR OTHER RESIDENTS, ENGAGE IN INCOME GENERATING ACTIVITIES, GARDENING	MAY PROVIDE SERVICE TO LOCAL COMMUNITY PROJECTS (e.g., SCHOOLS)
AGE RANGE	YOUNG-OLD TO OLDEST-OLD, SOME WITH ORPHANS, BATTERED WOMEN, MENTALLY RETARDED	YOUNG-OLD, OLD-OLD, OCCASIONAL FAMILIES
MARITAL STATUS	SINGLES, WIDOWS	SINGLES, WIDOW(ER)S, COUPLES

major expansions to meet the growing need for homes for the poor. The oldest facility (190 years) was a home for destitute people in Mumbai; it was multistory, had an elevator–a major expense in India–and an extensive occupational therapy program, a type of service found almost exclusively in free homes. As anticipated, the paid homes tended to be in brand new or newer buildings and were usually one- or two-story structures.

Overall, the high premium placed on individual privacy in Western societies is less valued in India. Privacy was less available in free homes. With their lower socioeconomic status, these residents were more likely to have lived in crowded housing or on the streets than their higher-income counterparts. All free homes had dormitory sleeping rooms; only 12% had triple rooms. Facilities combining paid and free residents were more likely to have double rooms and dormitories. Paid homes had singles and doubles with their own bathrooms, and many with their own kitchen. All rooms were personalized, often with small shrines and family pictures and afforded a lot of privacy. By contrast, in free homes, a bed, without a partition or curtain, a table or locker to hold possessions, and perhaps a chair were the norm. Bathing and toileting facilities were shared. But, as one administrator observed, for many residents, these accommodations were often considerably better than what they had had throughout their lives.

From the forgoing, it can be seen that old-age homes in India cover many of the important needs of Indian elders. Many are "basic," often lacking Western-style amenities, but are in keeping with housing for various economic levels. But larger issues loom on the horizon. Given the growing numbers of elders age 60+, estimated to be 326 million in the year 2050, and the weakening of the traditional support system for older persons, Indian society and its national and state governments are facing enormous challenges. Concerns continue to be raised about the extent to which old-age homes and other age-based services can meet elders' needs (Shah, Veedon, & Vasi, 1995; Shankardass, 1995). The establishment of "pay-and-stay" homes has exacerbated concerns about the breakdown of traditional family eldercare. While all interviewees (old-age home administrators, state and national ministers, and NGO heads) expressed dismay about these 20th century developments, in nearly the same breath they all asserted that Indian families still take care of their own and this traditional pattern should be strengthened.

SOCIETAL AND POLICY IMPLICATIONS

Two major issues have surfaced: the validity of various (including Westernized) solutions to meet the needs of India's aged (see, for example, Cohen, 1998); and the definition of appropriate roles for government (national and state) and non-governmental organizations (NGOs) in an aging society, as set forth in the National Policy on Older Persons (NPOP) of 1999.

Values Issues

What is the proper role of old-age homes in India? Responses tend to fall into four categories. The first is as follows: Attempts by the government to create senior housing, although it would meet some of the elders' physical needs, are likely to weaken family responsibility towards care of their elders and are unlikely to fulfill emotional needs of the aged (Kurup 1989). Studies indicate that life satisfaction in old-age homes is low (for example, see Dandekar, 1996; Ramamurti et al., 1996) and, as shown in the West, institutional settings promote social isolation of elders from the rest of society. Thus, additional development of old-age homes should not be encouraged.

A second approach focuses on elder-housing as a last resort, which has been the historical approach. In the absence of family support and the ability of elders to care for themselves, old-age homes can meet some of the unmet needs of the elderly, but they should exist only under limited circumstances. This argument also questions whether building special homes for elders is a good use of scarce resources, when the needs of women and children are paramount to India's economic development agenda. Thus, old-age homes should be established only within defined areas and designed to provide short stays as a respite service to the family or as shelters for those who are physically and mentally incapacitated, with no one to take care of them (Nair & Ramana, 1989). Suggestions include using the network of *dharamashalas* (temporary living quarters for pilgrims) as homes for the aged, especially when constructing old-age homes is not economically feasible (International Federation on Ageing [IFA], 1992, 30).

Under this scenario, day-care centers are seen as more suitable for India since they help enhance the capacity of the elderly for independent social functioning and facilitate integration with the family and a wider social network. These centers can (and often do) offer medical care, nutritional support, recreation, non-formal education, remunerative vocational opportunities, and peer companionship (Nair & Ramana, 1989).

A third argument suggests that the demand for elder-housing is growing and needs to be met, because elders often fall through the "safety net" of family care. The only viable solution lies in establishing homes for the aged, in keeping with increased requests for information about the locations of old-age homes and admission criteria (HelpAge India, 1995). This need for more old-age homes and formal services was further indicated by advertisements and blueprints seen in late 1997 for the Indian equivalent of assisted living facilities in Bangalore, Pune, and Hyderabad, and by the activities of senior advocacy groups in Mumbai, New Delhi, and Trivandrum to develop new old-age homes elsewhere in India.

A final argument centers more on the need for quality. Much of what has been written in the popular press (e.g., *The Hindu*, *India Currents*) focuses on the wretched conditions in some facilities, similar to reports on U. S. nursing homes. However, with the exception of Shankardass (1995) and Dandekar (1996), few standards for quality of care relevant to *Indian* homes have been proposed. Given the enormous economic pressures on free homes just to stay operating, the dearth of training for old-age home personnel at any level, the lack of a well-developed regulatory structure, and different socioeconomic circumstances, Western standards and enforcement procedures hardly seem applicable. In addition, the U. S. model of board and care regulation is not particularly salutary and is very expensive (Hawes, Wildfire et al., 1993). Still, the demand for old-age homes is exerting heavier pressures on government to ensure availability and higher quality.

Role of Government

The provision of various services to the aged, such as old-age pensions, medical care, housing, and recreation, constitutes an important aspect of modern welfare states. In less developed countries, including India, there is no universal security against common risks such as unemployment, disablement, and sickness, to say nothing of social security for the aged (Pethe, 1995). India's constitution requires the national government, subject to its economic capacity, to make provision for public assistance to the elderly. The Eighth Five-Year Plan sought to encourage the provision of old-age homes and services such as day-care centers via small grants-in-aid to NGOs (Kumar, 1998; Shankardass, 1995). But these efforts hardly fill the burgeoning need, and programs can and do disappear once grants expire.

All states have initiated limited welfare measures, primarily old-age assistance, similar to early 20th century welfare programs in the American states. Some also have provided grants to create and maintain old-age homes and day-care centers and have given land (along with localities) to NGOs for building homes and centers (Nair & Ramana, 1989). Those entities receiving state government assistance are largely unregulated; an annual monitoring visit by the state social welfare department is the extent of oversight. A few municipalities and states also run old-age homes, often of low quality (Ghosh, 1998); occasional visits by the media are generally the extent of monitoring provided.

Given the limited capacity of India's governmental structure to monitor or fund homes and services for the elderly, more indirect methods are utilized. India's tax laws permit setting up charitable trusts and allow deductions for charitable giving by individuals. Trusts are usually created by individuals or small groups, some of them affiliated with international organizations such as HelpAge or Rotary, which can ensure better quality. There is no long-standing tradition of corporate giving as in the United States and, with rare exceptions (e.g., Tata), large foundations do not exist. Thus, relatively small, often local, NGOs are the main source of homes and services for the elderly, but often without much monitoring.

Role of NGOs

The national government has attached considerable importance to the role of NGOs in extending social welfare services. In the realm of aged care, NGOs are associated at different stages of planning and implementation. They set up old-age homes and, to a lesser extent, train personnel (Kurup, 1989). However, many of these efforts are small-scale and local in nature, serving very limited numbers of elders. Furthermore, most NGOs have focused on the creation of old-age homes, rather than on day-care centers and other non-institutional services, in part due to demand but also because larger subsidies are provided for homes.

The author, in her interviews of nearly 25 national and state government officials and heads of NGOs, found few respondents had given much thought to what might be done to get the voluntary sector to do more, even though all agreed that NGOs must take the lead in meeting the needs of the aged. Some NGOs indicated they were best off without any government funding or interference for their senior programs, wanting nothing from the public sector except municipal services such as police, water, and sanitation. None perceived any problems with the commercial, for-profit sector entering into the elderly services arena; many thought this was likely to happen soon and could help meet the needs of upper-income elders. The negative concerns often raised in the United States about for-profit service provision were not voiced.

THE FUTURE OF OLD-AGE HOMES IN INDIA

In 1999, the GOI established the NPOP, an action that had been underway for nearly 15 years. The "Shelter" section of this document concentrates more on general housing issues of elders rather than age-specific housing, such as old-age homes. Policies include earmarking 10% of all homes or home-sites in lower-income housing programs for older persons; providing elders with easy access to loans and easy repayment schedules for home purchases or major repairs; and ensuring that housing developments respond to elders' needs: safe and easy accessibility to shopping and parks and no physical barriers to mobility. Preferences for first floor occupancy are to be given to older persons, and public utilities should give top priority to elders' complaints.

More broadly, the NPOP declares special consideration should be given to elders in all property matters. In addition, education and training should be provided for housing professionals (e.g., architects, housing administrators) about the needs of older persons, and older persons and their families should get information about accident prevention and safety measures.

Relative to old-age homes and day-care centers, the NPOP sets forth the following principles: Housing segregation of older persons is to be avoided if it prevents community integration. Group housing for elders should consist of flatlets (presumably like studio apartments in the United States) with common service facilities and easy access to community services, recreation, cultural events, and health care. Sites for multipurpose senior centers (note the U. S. designation) should be earmarked in all housing developments. Few specifics are included with regard to how these aspirations might be implemented, and no specific government responsibility is defined.

To expand senior housing and services, Rajan, Mishra, and Sarma (1994) have suggested the public sector should bring in more international groups to expand financing; increase its current subsidy program; provide incentives to local governments and senior associations to develop community-based services, possibly with HelpAge India assistance; help NGOs get international grants; expand and increase levels of tax deductions for NGOs; and convert closed schools to old-age homes and day-care centers.

Local village councils (panchayats) also have roles to play in oversight of old-age homes and day-care centers. They can set guidelines to ensure facilities meet community standards for wholesomeness. Local groups of women that have proved so effective in grass-roots economic development can be assisted, perhaps by HelpAge or some other NGO, to develop an ombudsman program and train family members about eldercare.

Supporting families and NGOs is a vital activity for the state and national governments, if the social isolation of old-age homes is to be avoided. Adopt-a-Granny programs that relieve families of some economic burden of caring for their elders, as well as day-care centers that provide respite care, should be the lynchpins for ensuring community-based solutions to India's demographic challenge. Increased subsidies should be earmarked for these programs. Day-care centers also can play an important role in providing family education about the aging process, similar to successful programs about infant care.

Finally, all levels of government, working with the media and NGOs, can promote discussion about the challenges of population aging in India and what standards should apply to the efforts of individuals, families, and organizations to meet the needs of Indian elders in the 21st century. By decisive action within these parameters, India can avoid some of the mistakes of Western nations in housing for the elderly (see Pynoos & Liebig, 1995) and forge policies that reflect and are deeply rooted in the values of Indian society.

AUTHOR NOTES

Phoebe S. Liebig is Associate Professor of Gerontology and Public Administration at the University of Southern California. She is the author of numerous articles in policy-related journals and a Fellow of the Gerontological Society of America.

Dr. Liebig can be contacted at Andrus Gerontology Center, University of Southern California, University Park MC0191, Los Angeles, CA 90089 (E-mail: liebig@usc.edu).

REFERENCES

Achamamba, B. (1987). Social and emotional problems of men and women in joint and nuclear families. In K. S. Rao & V. Prabhakar (Eds.), *Aging–A multifactorial discussion* (pp. 97-102). New Delhi: Association of Gerontology (India).

Ara, S. (1998). Housing facilities for the elderly in India. In S. Brink (Ed.), *Housing older people: An international perspective* (pp. 87-93). New Brunswick, NJ: Transaction Publishers.

Association for Senior Citizens (1992). *Senior citizens in India: A handbook of information*. Bombay: Author.

Brink, S. (1998). Overview: The greying of our communities worldwide. In S. Brink (Ed.), *Housing older people: An international perspective* (pp. 5-20). New Brunswick, NJ: Transaction Publishers.

Cohen, L. (1998). *No aging in India: Alzheimer's, the bad family, and other modern things.* Berkeley: University of California Press.

Dandekar, K. (1996). *The elderly in India.* New Delhi: Sage.

Ghosh, G. (1998). *The Hindu Sunday Magazine*–Special Issue on Ageing, October 18.

Gokhale, S. D. (1992). Toward productive & participatory aging in India. *Caring*, 86-89.

Hawes, C., Wildfire, J. B. et al. (1993). *The regulation of board and care homes.* Washington, DC: American Association of Retired Persons.

HelpAge India (1995). *Directory of old age homes in India.* New Delhi: Author.

International Federation on Ageing (1992). *The report of the first global conference on ageing.* Bombay: Author.

Kumar, S. V. (1998). Responses to the issues of ageing: The Indian scenario. *Bold*, 8(3), 7-26.

Kurup, A. M. (1989). Policy and programmes for the elderly. In T. K. Nair & K. V. Ramana (Eds.), *Ageing and welfare of the elderly in India* (pp. 107-120). Madras: Madras Institute on Ageing.

Morgan, L. A., Eckert, J. K., & Lyon, S. M. (1995). *Small board-and-care homes: Residential care in transition.* Baltimore: Johns Hopkins Press.

Muttagi, P. K. (1997). *Aging issues and old age care.* New Delhi: Classical Publishing Company.

Nair, T. K. (Ed.) (1995). *Care of the elderly: Directory of organisations caring for the elderly in India.* Madras: Centre for the Welfare of the Aged, Madras Institute on Ageing.

Nair, T. K. & Ramana, K. V. (Eds.). (1989) *Ageing and welfare of the elderly in India.* Madras: Madras Institute on Ageing.

Pethe, V. P. (1995). Social security and society's duties towards senior citizens. In S. Joshi & A. Shah (Eds.), *A home for the senior citizens* (pp. 15-21). Pune: R. Parundekar.

Pynoos, J., & Liebig, P. S. (Eds.) (1995). *Housing frail elders: International policies, perspectives and prospects.* Baltimore: Johns Hopkins University Press.

Rajan, S. I., Mishra, U. S., & Sarma, P. S. (1994). *A survey of elderly in India.* Trivandrum: Center for Development Studies.

Rajan, S. I., Mishra, U. S., & Sarma, P. S. (1999). *India's elderly: Burden or challenge?* New Delhi: Sage Publications.

Ramamurti, P. V., Jamuna, D., & Reddy, L. K. (1996). *Evaluation of old-age homes and day care centres in Andhra Pradesh: A report to the government of India.* Tirupati: Centre for Research on Ageing.

Shah, G., Veedon, R., & Vasi, S. (1995). Elder abuse in India. *Journal of Elder Abuse & Neglect*, 6(3/4), 101-118.

Shankardass, M. K. (1995). Towards the welfare of the elderly in India. *Bold*, 5(4), 25-30.

Varadharajan, D. (1989). Elderly in the changing Indian family. In T. K. Nair & K.V. Ramana (Eds.), *Ageing and welfare of the elderly in India* (pp. 19-30). Madras: Madras Institute on Ageing.

The Role of Non-Governmental Organizations for the Welfare of the Elderly: The Case of HelpAge India

Maneeta Sawhney, MPhil, PhD candidate

Institute for Economic Growth, New Delhi

SUMMARY. Since there has been a gradual increase in the population aged 60 and older, a developing country like India is unable to cope with the needs and problems of its aged populations. While the government continues its efforts to introduce programs for the elderly, the non-governmental organizations (NGOs) have played a key role in bringing to the forefront the socioeconomic and health problems of older people in the society at large. This paper looks at the role of the NGOs through their various welfare activities and beneficial programs in carving out a place for the elderly in India. The work of HelpAge India is highlighted to examine how voluntary organizations have worked in the field of aging in India and made an impact on the lives of the senior citizens, especially those below the poverty line who are economically and socially deprived. *[Article copies available for a fee from The Haworth Document Delivery Service: 1-800-HAWORTH. E-mail address: <docdelivery@haworthpress.com> Website: <http://www.HaworthPress.com> © 2003 by The Haworth Press, Inc. All rights reserved.]*

KEYWORDS. Elderly, nongovernmental organizations, health, social, economic, poverty, care

INTRODUCTION

The concerns of the Government of India (hereafter, the Government) for the welfare of its elderly citizens began with India's participation in the World Assembly Conference in Vienna in 1982, when it adopted the United Nations (UN) International Plan of Action on Aging. The UN plan focused on the governmental role in adopting programs for the care and protection of the elderly, synchronizing these with the changing socioeconomic conditions of each society.

From the mid 1980s, the Government began to recognize the aged as a social category of persons who need specialized attention. Under several Five-Year Plans, various policy-oriented programs were introduced, but these often ignored rural-urban differences as well as the local disjunctions of class and power. An old-age assistance pension, applicable to a minority of the elderly, also was introduced, along with other welfare measures. More recently, under the Eighth Five-Year Plan, the Government sought to encourage nongovernmental organizations (NGOs) to provide old-age homes and non-institutional services via a limited grants-in-aid program (Shankardass, 1995). A comprehensive policy for the aged, however, was missing.

After many years of debate, the Government finally declared the National Policy on Older Persons in January 1999, the same year as the UN-designated International Year of the Older Person. The policy highlights the rising elderly population and the urgent need to understand and deal with the medical, psychological, and socioeconomic problems faced by the elderly. In particular, the policy emphasized the dominant role NGOs should play to assist the Government in bringing forth a society where the needs and priorities of India's elderly are taken into account. Thus, NGOs are expected to play a crucial role in welfare for India's aged as in many parts of Asia, the United States, and other developed nations (Bhatt, 1995; Stoesz, Guzzetta, & Lusk, 1999).

THE ROLE OF NON-GOVERNMENTAL ORGANIZATIONS (NGOS)

While the Government has continued its efforts to introduce programs for the welfare of the elderly, NGOs have played a key role in bringing to the forefront the problems of India's older people in the society at large; they have also provided some solutions. Through various activities and services, NGOs have established a forum whereby the voices and concerns of the elderly can be addressed.

Presently, there are many national and international NGOs working for the cause of India's elders. Most have concentrated their work among lower-income groups and the disadvantaged and underprivileged sections of the society. This is mainly because one-third of these sections are identified as "capability poor," which means they do not have access to minimum levels of health care or education for earning a decent living. Because the Government is unable to deal with such a huge dependent population, it is the nonprofit, non-governmental sector–also known as the Third Sector (Stoesz, Guzzetta, & Lusk, 1999)–that has, in the last few decades, begun to work actively for the welfare of the lower-income and dependent strata of Indian society, including the elderly.

In the first few years of NGO growth, the emphasis was placed on the abuse of women due to the gender discrimination prevalent in Indian society. For example, the Government and hospitals concentrated their attentions and resources on the needs of women and children, rather than on the elderly, leading to separate departments of pediatrics, but not geriatrics.

Only in the last few years, since demographers began providing alarming statistics about the growth of the elderly population, has a need been felt to work in this area. This lack of focus on the aged occurred because it was assumed that the elderly were well taken care of, safe in the custody of the well-integrated family system in India. But recent ethnographic case studies have indicated that the so-called "joint family system" is a myth. (See "Issues of Elder Care and Elder Abuse in the Indian Context" by Dr. D. Jamuna in this volume.) Many elderly, though living with their sons and their families, are often neglected and uncared for.

This scenario has led to the mushrooming of various NGOs working on the concerns of the elderly, especially in urban areas. Examples include Rotary International clubs, which have helped improve services for the elderly by supplementing existing services at governmental primary health-care centers and by contributing to or sponsoring old-age homes; and Age Care India, which has provided residential and institutional services to people age 50 and older, created social, cultural, educational, recreational, and spiritual programs, and has arranged for medical check-ups and part-time employment to supplement incomes of older people.

Despite this recent activity, an NGO focus on India's elderly initially emerged in the 19th century, but those efforts were small and isolated. In 1840, The Friend-in-Need Society of Madras (Chennai) was the first organization to devote itself to the care of the aged, and the Little Sisters of the Poor (LSOP) of Calcutta followed suit in 1882. The LSOP opened a home to provide shelter, clothing, and medical care to the old. Both organizations still operate old-age homes today (HelpAge India, 1995, 2001).

HELPAGE INDIA

One of the premier NGOs that began work on the cause of India's older population is HelpAge India, a secular, apolitical, non-profit organization. Formed in 1978 with the active help of Cecil Jackson Cole, a founder/member of Help the Aged, United Kingdom, it was registered on April 28 of that same year, under the authority of the Societies' Registration Act of 1960. HelpAge India is affiliated with HelpAge International, a global NGO that has been particularly active in Asia for the past several years through research and advocacy (HelpAge International, 2001). In its more than two decades of existence, the organization has expanded its efforts on behalf of India's elders.

In its newsletters and brochures and on its website (www.helpageindia.com), HelpAge India has charted its goals and objectives: to work for the cause and care of older persons, with the ultimate aim of empowering them to make decisions pertaining to their own lives. It seeks to

- improve the welfare of the aged in India, especially the needy;
- create an understanding of the changing situation and the needs of the elderly in India and to promote their cause;
- establish within the younger generation an awareness about the problems of older persons in India; and
- raise funds for the creation of infrastructure through the medium of voluntary social service organizations that help the elderly, regardless of caste or creed.

HelpAge India is a funding organization that looks for partner agencies that are able to implement its various projects and programs. Over the past decade, it has changed its orientation from implementing welfare projects to a greater focus on development. The new emphasis stresses income-generation and micro-credit projects and programs that strengthen the participation of older persons in the mainstream of Indian society, also an objective of the National Policy on Older Persons. HelpAge India's approach reflects the basic philosophical and structural elements of community development, increasingly viewed as a key to international economic development, with emphases on equity, hope, care, and social justice and on leadership, planning, management, and resource allocation (Stoesz, Guzzetta, & Lusk, 1999).

Structure

The structure of the organization enables it to carry out its several objectives and activities. HelpAge India's main office is located in New Delhi; 24 regional and area offices are located throughout the country. The regional offices are located in major cities, such as Bangalore, Chennai, and Calcutta. Mr. K. R. Narayanan, President of India, and Mr. R. Venkataraman, former President of India, are patrons of HelpAge India, lending their prestige to the organization.

The governing body, made up of 13 eminent persons from different walks of life, oversees its activities. Mr. D. R. Kohli, ICS (Retired), is the current President, and Mr. Arun Seth, Vice President. Major-General S. S. Sandhu (Retired) is the immediate-past Director General. The current Director General, Air Marshal Vinod Patney (Retired), assumed his position on October 1, 2001. All recent Directors General have been retired military personnel. They look after the forward planning and implementation of all policies and programs, with the support of six functional directorates or divisions at the head office (Figure 1).

Activities

The major activities of HelpAge India are driven by its goals and objectives and are reflected in its organizational structure. They include fundraising, sponsoring programs and special events, research and development, and communications and publications. All of these activities support the organization's advocacy role.

Fundraising. A primary activity of the organization is fundraising and resource mobilization. In one approach, a team of dedicated fundraisers works closely with school children, helping them raise funds for the cause of the elderly. This scheme results not only in collecting major donations; it also raises awareness of the elderly among the younger generation. This awareness then gets absorbed into the families of the

FIGURE 1. HelpAge India's Organizational Structure

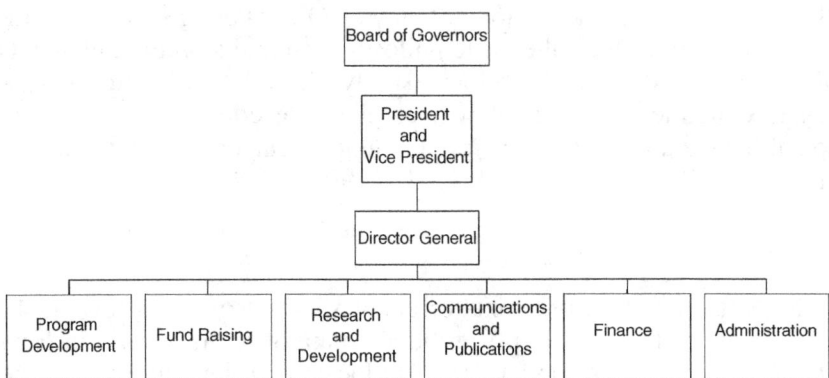

children, leading to a wider appreciation of the problems faced by older people.

Another approach is through different types of solicitations or sales. One successful approach is the "Amrit Varsha" or the payroll-giving scheme, which is for officers who contribute a part of their monthly salary to the cause of the organization; many major corporate offices in India have opted for such a scheme. Other methods of fundraising include donation boxes on the counters of hotels and shops, the solicitation of donations in the form of checks and cash, and the sales of greeting cards.

Besides its own fundraising, HelpAge India also is involved with projects co-funded by Help the Aged, United Kingdom. As noted earlier, the participation of international Third Sector organizations with Indian organizations is important for ensuring the well-being of India's elders. The dedication and commitment to raising money is embedded in HelpAge India's values and stated in its annual report and other publications: to foster the welfare of the aged, especially the needy, by raising funds for projects that assist them, regardless of caste or creed.

Through its fundraising, HelpAge India has been able to shape the practice of gerontology in Indian society by introducing programs to meet specific needs of senior citizens. Through its Five-Year plans, it aims at fulfilling different requirements in the field of aged care.

Program development. In all regional offices, the program division looks for partner agencies to help conduct the welfare services that HelpAge India provides. It also supervises the services provided, as well as funding from the main office in New Delhi.

The types of programs are not numerous, but they are carried out on a large scale throughout the country to meet the urgent basic needs of elders. The major programs are ophthalmic care, leprosy care, mobile medical care, income generation, day-care centers, Adopt-A-Gran, and homes for the aged. School education programs are another major HelpAge India activity.

Ophthalmic care. Old age is associated with a number of health problems, including decreased or impaired vision. This disability results in the aged person being dependent on family for help as he or she tries to carry out normal activities of daily living. Many older persons in India suffer from cataract-related blindness, which is treatable; fully 85% of India's 12 million visually impaired need cataract surgery (www.helpageindia.com). Thus, this type of eye surgery is the most important eye-care service provided by HelpAge India (as well as other NGOs serving the elderly). HelpAge India focuses on rural elders because of their difficulties in accessing treatment. Eye care has been a very successful and popular project. HelpAge India conducts over 50,000 cataract surgeries every year. In 1999, the organization sponsored 4% of all cataract operations in India (www.helpageindia.com).

Leprosy care. It is estimated that 2% of India's elders are affected by leprosy. Leprosy is a chronic disease transmitted by direct contact, and it can be controlled but not cured by prolonged treatment with sulfa drugs or antibiotics. In Indian society, the victims of leprosy of all ages are abandoned by their families and are forced to reside in segregated areas for persons suffering from this disease. Due to social stigma, they live with poverty and unemployment. In spite of welfare measures adopted by the Government and voluntary agencies to ameliorate their lot, most live in abject misery.

HelpAge India addresses the problems of aged lepers from the perspective of long-term care through rehabilitation. Providing residences for those with the disease, along with providing monthly incomes to subsidize basic needs, HelpAge defines a new dimension of care in the Indian context: rehabilitation of the diseased victim. In this way, it moves Indian gerontology toward a focus on the self-sufficiency of the elderly.

Mobile medical care. HelpAge India sponsors mobile medical units (MMUs) that practice social and preventive medicine and provide primary health care for senior citizens. The MMUs were started because a majority of the rural aged and urban slum dwellers were unable to go to hospitals. Villagers were especially disadvantaged by the scarcity of hospitals in rural areas. As a result, many rural aged and urban slum dwellers had medical problems that went undetected and undiagnosed. HelpAge India (as well as other NGOs, some with Government grants) initiated the use of MMUs; it now supports 100 units that go to remote rural areas and urban slums to cater to the health needs of the frail aged.

In providing basic health services, MMUs became forums where the voices of elderly people could be heard. For the first time, low-income aged advocates were expressing themselves in public places. Thus, through its programs, HelpAge India indirectly creates forums where the aged can voice their concerns. What emerges is a social category of the aged with an independent status and group awareness.

A second set of programs emphasizes community development, thereby ensuring the involvement of the elderly in society.

Community development. HelpAge India provides "overall care" for the elderly through numerous community development programs, for example, by providing health-care facilities; providing clean drinking water by installing hand pumps; improving agricultural yields through high quality seeds, resulting in increased vegetable production; providing livestock to the elderly to help generate a regular income from the sale of milk and also to improve their diets; and encouraging poultry farming as a means of income and improved nutrition.

Income generation. Poor families in India often have difficulty caring for their elders economically, socially, and psychologically. Elders unable to contribute to family welfare are less likely to share in limited family resources. To help remedy this situation, HelpAge India has supported more than 300 income-generating projects that include rearing goats; the making of candles, envelopes, and sweets; and weaving rugs. In addition, it has set up micro-credit banks, which provide small, low-cost loans to the elderly to set up small enterprises, similar to programs initiated to help women in India and other developing nations to become self-sufficient. By providing such services, HelpAge India defines aging as involving not only long-term care but also community development.

The destitute aged who are not physically incapacitated do not require short-term relief measures to meet their immediate needs for subsistence; they need long-term assistance that can sustain them to spend the "evening of their lives" with dignity. Through income-generating activities specifically designed for the aged, HelpAge India encourages the aged to be self-supporting, independent individuals and helps to remove notions of dependence among the elderly. The importance of dignity is reflected by a quote by an elder in a recent HelpAge newsletter:

"Now I do not have to plead with my sons to get me medicines or tobacco. I can buy them myself."

HelpAge India sows the seeds for others in this field to look at welfare programs for the elderly in terms of long-duration projects that can be sustained by the elders themselves.

For instance, community development programs are designed initially to require the impetus and resources from HelpAge India, but once in progress, can be carried out by the elderly themselves. This is also the case with small income-generating projects. In this way, the organization constructs an image of the elderly as independent and, to some extent, economically self-sufficient and productive family members.

Old-age homes and day-care centers. The status and role of the elderly have changed over the years with changes in Indian society. It is no longer assumed that they are dependent on the family, which may be unable to care for elder members. Although the traditional place for the aged is with their families, HelpAge India provides alternatives with a professionally managed system of care.

HelpAge India has sponsored the construction and maintenance of old-age homes in many parts of India. These homes meet the needs of those elderly who are unable to live by themselves or who have been abandoned or neglected. The old-age homes cater to the various needs of the elderly so they can live with dignity and respect and not feel a burden to society. There are over 800 old-age homes in India; nearly half of them are sponsored and funded by HelpAge India.

Besides the homes, HelpAge India also supports day-care centers where the elderly come for a few hours every day or on certain days of the week. The centers help combat the loneliness elders face and create a sense of solidarity. Some of the rural centers supported by HelpAge India also support income-generating activities. (See "Old-Age Homes and Services: Old and New Approaches to Aged Care" by Dr. Phoebe S. Liebig in this volume.)

Adopt-A-Gran. This type of program is also sponsored by HelpAge India. It involves schools "adopting" nearby old-age homes. The children visit these facilities on holidays and other special occasions and provide entertainment for the elderly residents.

This kind of intergenerational programming reduces elders' sense of isolation and makes younger persons aware of aging issues.

School education programs. Another HelpAge program designed to forge intergenerational linkages is its school education program, which involves more than 6000 schools across the country. Activities include visits to old-age homes; essay competitions based on the theme of aging; inviting grandparents to school activities; sponsoring talks, discussions, and audiovisual presentations on aging; and involving school age children in HelpAge-sponsored programs.

HelpAge India aims for all programs to become self-sustaining. The organization usually does not manage projects on its own but encourages other local voluntary organizations to provide technical assistance and financial help.

To forge these partnerships, local organizations develop proposals to receive HelpAge India aid. A team of experts then evaluates the prospective collaborator and its proposal. If the proposal meets HelpAge India requirements, the regional or local office sends it to the head office in New Delhi. The Director of Programs then gets allocation of the money for that project from the Board. The funds are given in installments, and reviews are done on a regular basis to ensure the efficacy of the project.

Research and development. Working in close association with the program division is the division of Research and Development, located at the main office in New Delhi. Its main task is to analyze the needs of the elderly and help HelpAge India's programs meet those needs. It does this by conducting research projects designed to result in policy- and project-oriented results. During the last two years, it conducted two large-scale studies: one on the role of the family and the elderly in India, the other, an evaluation of old-age homes.

Besides HelpAge India's own research activities, this division encourages social scientists and academicians to do gerontological research. It provides wide circulation of their work through its quarterly journal, *The Research and Development Journal,* which contains articles on the needs of India's elderly and the research being conducted. The subscription to the journal is subsidized at 75 rupees for an individual, 150 rupees for institutions, and 35 rupees for senior citizens.

The Research and Development division is also actively engaged with the Government and international organizations in advocacy issues for the elderly. For example, it was actively involved with the ministry to set up the National Policy for the Older Person by sponsoring four nationwide forums. To promote advocacy, it has a Forum for the Empowerment of the Elderly and sponsors monthly lectures on issues affecting elders. This has received widespread recognition and has helped create awareness of these issues among the citizens of Delhi.

Finally, the division recently released the second edition of the *Directory of Old Age Homes in India* (HelpAge India, 2001). This directory lists the addresses of all homes, the nature of the homes, and types of services provided. This directory is available at a subsidized price of 35 rupees.

Communications and publications. This division has the major task of creating awareness among the public at large about the issues of the elderly. It does this by tapping into the media and encouraging them to publish articles on aging in India. It also taps into television to raise awareness about the urgent need to feature issues of the elderly.

This division also publishes HelpAge India's annual report and a quarterly newsletter. These publications give major donors information about how and where their money is being utilized. The division also puts out a few special publications, such as Dr. Kalyan Bagchi's book, *Elderly Females in India.*

Advocacy. The efforts of these several divisions all underlie HelpAge India's advocacy on behalf of older Indians. Its goal, similar to other age-focused groups, is to promote and make a case for gerontology. HelpAge India sponsors World Elders Day in Delhi every fall to which governmental and private sector dignitaries and the media are invited. Select older individuals are honored at this gala gathering.

In this and other ways, the HelpAge India has become a major, if not *the* major, advocate for India's elders, sometimes on its own, but often in collaboration with other entities. Some examples follow:

- HelpAge India maintains an active liaison with both the Central and state governments for advocacy purposes.
- It was represented on the Working Group that recommended the Government's thrusts and policies of the Eighth and Ninth Five-Year Plans.
- It successfully pressed for travel and tax concessions and other benefits for the elderly.
- It was closely associated with the formulation of the National Policy of Older Persons.
- It is represented in the Working Committee of the National Council to implement that policy.

HelpAge India also has several important international connections that enable it to carry out its advocacy functions:

- It is one of the founding members of HelpAge International, a high-profile body of 51-member countries advocating for causes of the elderly at the United Nations.

- It has received a special United Nations testimonial for "dedicated service and support of the United Nations Programs on Aging."
- It is a full member of the International Federation on Aging.

CONCLUSIONS

HelpAge India, a Third Sector service organization, through its various projects and policies, has made and still makes a case for gerontology in Indian society–a gerontology that gives the elderly an important place in society, rather than being treated as a burden. The organization enhances the status of the aged by aiding and encouraging them to continue to be productive members of the society in which they once played active roles.

HelpAge India has also provided the Government with a set of recommendations for providing better services to the elderly. For example, it has been pressing for years for geriatrics to be taught as a separate subject in medical colleges. Thus far, only one medical college offers geriatrics as a post graduate course.

HelpAge India also has paved the way for other organizations to work for the cause of India's senior citizens. These groups include the Alzheimer's and Related Disorders Society of India, Age Care India, and Agewell, among others.

Proper and sensitive care for the aged will "add life to years" for the many neglected and forsaken Indian elders. Both the Government and the voluntary sector are trying to make Indian society friendlier for its senior citizens. However, NGOs such as HelpAge India are the primary actors in this endeavor, with the active help and support of the Government. Without NGO efforts, the National Policy will not come to fruition. HelpAge India and its sister organizations will continue to play major roles in enhancing and empowering India's elders well into the 21st Century.

AUTHOR NOTES

Maneeta Sawhney is Research Associate at the Institute of Economic Growth, New Delhi. She formerly was a Research Associate in the Research and Development Division of HelpAge India, at which time she wrote this article.

The author can be contacted at the Health Policy Research Unit, Institute of Economic Growth, University Enclave, Malka Ganj, Delhi-110007, India (E-mail: maneeta@ieg.ernet.in).

REFERENCES

Bhatt, A. (1995). Asian NGOs in development: Their role and impact. In H. Heyzer, J. V. Riker, & A. B. Quizon (Eds.), *Government-Non-Governmental Relations in Asia*. New York: St. Martin's Press.

HelpAge India (1995). Directory of Old Age Homes in India. New Delhi: Author.

HelpAge India (2001). Directory of Old Age Homes in India (2nd ed.). New Delhi: Author.

HelpAge International (2001). *Ageing in My Own Place: Home Care for Older People in the Asia-Pacific Region*. Chiang Mai, Thailand: Author.

Shankardass, M. K. (1995). Towards the welfare of the elderly in India. *Bold*, 5(4), 25-30.

Stoesz, D., Guzzetta, C., & Lusk, M. (1999). *International Development*. Boston: Allyn and Bacon. *www.helpageindia.com*

ADVOCACY AND POLICY

Senior Grassroots Organizations in India

P. K. B. Nayar, PhD

Centre for Gerontological Studies
Kochulloor, Trivandrum, India

SUMMARY. Organizations for the elderly at the grassroots level began to function in India from the third decade of the 20th century. They belong to two major types: Pensioners' Associations (PAs) and Senior Citizens' Associations (SCAs). PAs claim a membership of approximately 13 million and are structured and vertically organized. The SCAs are loosely organized and most are unitary. They have together a membership of less than 5 million. Programs of PAs are mainly confined to members; those of SCAs are wider but mainly urban-biased and middle-class oriented. Neither of them is powerful in lobbying. Of late, Government of India's (GOI) policy on the elderly (NPOP, 2000) has given a fillip to the SCAs which are gathering strength, and some, at least, are vying for availing GOI program benefits. *[Article copies available for a fee from The Haworth Document Delivery Service: 1-800-HAWORTH. E-mail address: <docdelivery@haworthpress.com> Website: <http://www.HaworthPress.com> © 2003 by The Haworth Press, Inc. All rights reserved.]*

[Haworth co-indexing entry note]: "Senior Grassroots Organizations in India." Nayar, P. K. B. Co-published simultaneously in *Journal of Aging & Social Policy* (The Haworth Press, Inc.) Vol. 15, No. 2/3, 2003, pp. 193-212; and: *An Aging India: Perspectives, Prospects, and Policies* (ed: Phoebe S. Liebig, and S. Irudaya Rajan) The Haworth Press, Inc., 2003, pp. 193-212. Single or multiple copies of this article are available for a fee from The Haworth Document Delivery Service [1-800-HAWORTH, 9:00 a.m. - 5:00 p.m. (EST). E-mail address: docdelivery@haworthpress.com].

© 2003 by The Haworth Press, Inc. All rights reserved.
http://www.haworthpress.com/store/product.asp?sku=J031
10.1300/J031v15n02_12

KEYWORDS. Pensioners' associations, senior citizens' associations, PA, SCA, InFA, NAOP

INTRODUCTION

Senior organizations functioning at the grassroots level are of recent origin in India. In fact, age-care organizations themselves are a recent phenomenon in the country. Even though the first institution for the care of the old (the Monegar and Rajah of Venkatagiri Chaultries) was established in Chennai (old Madras) in 1782, it took nearly a century and a half for other old-age homes to appear. Similarly, even though pensions were introduced for Government of India (GOI) employees as early as 1871, the first pensioners' association (Postal Pensioners' Association) came into existence only in 1934. The first association of senior citizens (Respect Age International) was formed in 1950, but it was formally registered only in 1962. Because population aging was not an issue in India until the second half of the 20th Century and because government and the academic community were preoccupied with population control issues and strategies in the 1950s and 1960s, aging received only residual attention during these two decades. However, from the 1970s onwards, the subject began to attract considerable attention. Later, the World Assembly on Aging (Vienna, 1982) and the resulting Vienna International Plan of Action on Aging stimulated action in the field. Along with welfare programs for the elderly, programs for their empowerment also began to become part of the agenda for age care. Development of the elderly began to be recognized and accepted as an important element in old-age policies and programs.

Grassroots organizations engaged in promoting the cause of the aging in India fall under two broad categories:

1. Pensioners' Associations, and
2. Senior Citizens' Associations.

PENSIONERS' ASSOCIATIONS

Pensioners' associations were first started among the retirees from the Government of India (GOI) services. This was because in the beginning only GOI employees had pension benefits after retirement. In the Indian states, which numbered over 500 before 1947 and where bureaucratic structures differed widely, pensions were introduced only much later and at different times in different states. In 1934, the first association of pensioners was formed. This was the Postal Pensioners' Association (PPA) founded by the pensioners from the Postal Department in Mumbai (old Bombay). Later, it was expanded to include pensioners from the Telegraph Department when the Post and Telegraph Departments were combined by the GOI. The Association was accordingly renamed the All-India Post and Telegraph Pensioners' Association (AIPTPA). Mumbai continued to be the headquarters of the Association. Currently, AIPTPA has over 30,000 members spread all over India. It has the largest number of branches, with a large proportion of its members in Maharashtra State. Indeed, each major city in Maharashtra has a branch of this Association. The PPA was formed primarily to protect the interests of the pensioners from the Postal Department, and these centered around the retirement benefits to members and their families. The PPA soon inspired pensioners from other GOI services–the Indian Railways, Central Services, etc. After the country's independence (1947), there was a spate of associations of pensioners from the various government and semi-government organizations–Departments of Income Tax, Information and Broadcasting, Audit and Revenue, etc., as well as different public undertakings. The goal continued to be the maximization of retirement benefits of all sorts.

Besides these sectional and functional associations of pensioners, other associations came into existence that cut across sections and functions and that drew members from all GOI services and statutory agencies. The All India Organization of Pensioners (New Delhi), the Bharat Pensioners' Samaj (New Delhi), the Central Government Retired Employees' Association (Mumbai), and the All India Central Government Pensioners' Association-North India Region (Jalandhar) are some of the major organizations of this type. Federations of pensioners' organizations at the national level also came into existence. Important among them are the Coordination Committee of the Central Government Pensioners' Associations (New Delhi), the All India Central Council of Pensioners' Associations (New Delhi), and the Federation of Central Government Pensioners' Associations (Chennai). All these associations–sectional/functional, national, and federal–are mass membership organizations that claim to represent all the pensioners in their catchment areas. However, only a small proportion of pensioners are actually on their rolls. For example, the All India Central Government Pensioners' Association (North India Region), one of the latest entrants in the field (formed in 1995), has only around 650 members, and all of them are confined to a few cities in northern and western India. There are over 3.2 million GOI pensioners and family pensioners but only a small proportion are members of any association; still smaller proportions are active members. But this lack of representation of the associations is more than compensated by the motivation and commitment of their leadership. The best example is the All India Central Government Pensioners' Association (AICGPA). By sustained work extending over only four years, it was able to catch the central government's "eye" and to get membership in the recently constituted National Council of Older Persons (NCOP).

Although there are many and various pensioners' associations–unitary, federating, regional, and national–all have very important roles to play because of their members' heterogeneity of interests. Usually, the associations become active when the Government of India (GOI) appoints a Pay Commission (called Central Pay Commission or CPC). The major responsibility of the CPC is to recommend revision of emoluments and service conditions of GOI employees *in service*, but their terms of reference also include consideration of GOI pensioners' cases. CPC holds meetings with representatives of pensioners' associations where the latters' demands are discussed. Associations acting on behalf of their members write and present memoranda to the CPC, making a strong case for their demands. Generally, the CPC is liberal in its recommendations to the GOI, but the government may not accept many of their crucial recommendations for want of money. In this situation, the axe falls more heavily on the pensioners than on those in service because the latter can enforce their demands by trade union action. The resulting differential treatment of those in service and those who have retired from service creates a feeling of relative deprivation among the latter group. This is the point at which the associations begin lobbying–pressuring the Prime Minister and concerned Union Minister, Members of Parliament, and other significant persons–with different degrees of success for different organizations. Usually, there will be a common demand and sectional demands, the latter representing the demands of different categories of pensioners. Their complaints/demands find an important place in their annual conferences and newsletters.

Pensioners' associations of all types and categories are primarily concerned only with the furtherance of the interests of their own members (pensioners and family pensioners). This is evident from the goals and objectives of these associations. The Election Manifesto, prepared by the Coordination Committee of the Central Government Pensioners' Associations (CCCGPA) in January 1988 on the eve of the General

Election to the 12th Lok Sabha (Lower House of the Indian Parliament), provides a sample of their major demands:

1. Replacement of the Pension Act of 1871 by a new Pension-cum-Social Security Act, treating the pension as a statutory, inalienable right;
2. Creation of a Pension Fund by an Act of Parliament to ensure an honorable and proper living for pensioners;
3. Implementation of the recommendation of the 5th Central Pay Commission *in toto*;
4. Raising of the pension and family pension to the level of the last pay drawn;
5. Free Medicare to the pensioners on a par with the current employees;
6. More powers to the Pension Ministry to deal with pension cases independently;
7. Pensioner Bhavans (houses) in major towns; and
8. Utilization of the services of pensioners in civic duties, election duties, and disciplinary cases of government departments.

In its Memorandum submitted separately to the Prime Minister of India in January 1999, the AICGPA put forward a few more demands, the most important of which are:

1. conferment of the status of "Senior Citizen" on all pensioners irrespective of age;
2. recognition of Pensioners' Associations for settlement of cases taken up by them;
3. setting up of "Pension Adalats" (Courts) for speedy disposal of pension cases; and
4. the nomination of a central government pensioner to Parliament to safeguard the interests of pensioners.

GOI pensioners' associations are grassroots organizations working and, at times, lobbying for the cause of their members who make up one of the most organized groups among the elderly population in the country. They advance and advocate the cause of the pensioners before the Government, and though not always successful, they certainly get a fair deal from the government.

Ex-Service Men's Associations

Ex-service men's associations consist of persons retired from the country's armed forces. Since the armed forces retire their ranks at a fairly young age, not all members are old. Some of them take up civilian jobs after retirement, but they continue to be members of an association. The organizations are highly structured and their members enjoy many privileges that civilian pensioners do not have. There are approximately 3.2 million ex-service men–about the same number as there are civilian pensioners, including family pensioners. GOI periodically appoints special commissions to enquire about their problems and needs and usually grants benefits to them without much private lobbying.

State Pensioners' Associations

State service pensioners' associations exist in all the Indian states. Since pension rules and benefits vary from state to state, these associations are not only relevant; they are also necessary. Besides associations of state service pensioners, there are also associations of pensioners from state public enterprises, universities, and other autonomous bodies that are created by statutes of the state legislature (statutory bodies). Compared to GOI pensioners' associations, state pensioners' associations have a larger proportion of active members, and they are more integrated and cohesive. State service pensioners are more strongly organized, with district level units, and in some states, local units.

The style of these associations resembles that of the central pensioners' organizations. Activities center mainly on the State Pay Commissions' Awards and state governments' responses to them. Usually, the pensioners are marginalized when Pay Commissions' recommendations are implemented. As in the case of the GOI, state governments can afford to be indifferent towards the demands of pensioners compared to those in service, because the latter's organizations are strong, and governments are afraid of estranging them. In this situation, the state pensioners' associations become active champions of their members. They resort to a great deal of pressure on the government, but their position is weak and direct actions are not influential. Hence, lobbying is the major strategy that they use. Holders of power in the government are the focus of their lobbying. Bosses of the ruling political party (parties) are sometimes found to be more amenable to the problems of state pensioners than the state governmental machinery, even though it is the state machinery that must act in the final analysis.

In terms of membership and activities, Maharashtra state pensioners' associations are in the forefront. This state has over 60 different pensioners' associations. The larger and most active associations in Maharashtra are:

1. Mumbai Municipal Corporation Pensioners' Association;
2. Greater Mumbai Government Pensioners' Association;
3. Maharashtra Government Pensioners' Association; and
4. Maharashtra State Federation of Retired University/College Teachers' and other Employees' Associations.

One interesting point in the demands of state service pensioners is that retirement benefits of state pensioners should be raised to the level of GOI pensioners.

SENIOR CITIZENS' ASSOCIATIONS

These voluntary associations of senior citizens are formed spontaneously with limited membership. Unlike pensioners' associations whose membership is confined to pensioners only, senior citizens' associations are, in principle, open to all those who attain the eligible age (usually 60, but in some associations, 55), irrespective of whether or not they were once in government service. However, senior citizens' associations in India are almost entirely elitist bodies with members drawn mainly from the middle- and upper-income groups. The origin of many of these associations from sponsorship by Rotary Clubs may be one reason for this situation. These associations consist of urban, educated, and economically secure individuals who pay a not-so-small membership fee. There are usually two kinds of members–Life Members and Ordinary Members. Fee for Life Members ranges from a one-time payment of Rs. 500 to Rs. 2500 or more, and for Ordinary Members between Rs. 50 to Rs. 150 per year (US$ = Rs. 45). The Kerala Senior Citizens' forum has one of the lowest membership fees, Rs. 10/-per year. But its structure and style of functioning are different from other senior citizens' organizations.

According to available records, the first association of senior citizens was the Respect Age International formed in 1950 in Agra, near Delhi, by a local philanthropist, H. K. Gupta. It was formally registered as a charitable, nonpolitical, secular, social welfare society in 1962. The stated objectives of the society are as follows:

1. to inculcate the feeling of respect and honor for senior citizens;
2. to create awareness by organizing seminars, workshops, etc.;
3. to provide security and support including income earning opportunities;

4. to establish and conduct day-care centers, aged homes, and night shelters in India and abroad;
5. to provide medical aid, health and hygiene, adult literacy, education, recreation, and spiritual and consultancy programs for the benefit of senior citizens, widows, and the disabled; and
6. to establish information centers, offices, and branches of the society in India and abroad.

Funds for the society come from grants-in-aid from the central and state governments, membership fees, charity programs, collection drives, etc. The society works in association with the International Senior Citizens' Association Inc., U. S. A., and the Organization for Industrial, Spiritual, and Cultural Advancement International, Japan. Although claiming international status and though it has international, national, and regional advisory committees, the activities and membership of the society are confined to Agra and its environs.

After the birth of Respect Age International, there was a lull in the formation of further senior citizens' associations for nearly two decades. Isolated informal groups were established in Delhi, Bombay, Pune, Calcutta, and many other metropolitan cities, but they were mainly cultural and spiritual organizations of elderly people formed to provide a forum for interaction and friendly get-togethers. Often, experts at these gatherings presented lectures on subjects of interest. A typical example is the "Vruddha Sabha" (meaning assembly of old people), started in Pune by an Ayurvedic physician, Girish Shastri Shendye in 1967. It was formally shaped into an association in 1975, but not registered. It functions as a cultural and spiritual organization and meets every Monday in a temple precinct.

Senior citizens' associations in India, as a popular movement, owe their origin to Rotary International. In 1977, Rotary International gave direction to all Rotary districts and clubs in India to work for senior citizens in order to give life to their years. Acting on this suggestion, the Governor of the Bombay Rotary District took the initiative and formed the first Senior Citizens' Club at Dombivali in Bombay City in November 1977. The example was followed by other Rotary Clubs in the Rotary District, and soon several senior citizens' clubs sprang up in Maharashtra. By 1980, their number had risen to 20, and it was found desirable to have a body to coordinate their activities. Accordingly, the Federation of Senior Citizens' Organizations Maharashtra (FESCOM) was formed in 1980 by the existing 20 clubs. Currently, FESCOM has 175 units spread all over Maharashtra, and membership of 30,000 senior citizens–both men and women (the latter, mainly wives of male members). The major goals of FESCOM are:

1. formation of new senior citizens' clubs;
2. the organization of day-care and day-care centers;
3. social integration;
4. consumer guidance;
5. assistance to old age homes;
6. organization of health programs and recreational activities; and
7. approaching central and state governments for redress of grievances.

The Federation publishes a quarterly magazine called *Manayuva*.

Next to Bombay, Pune is the nerve center of senior citizens' activities in Maharashtra. Pune has as many as 52 senior citizens' clubs, and they are organized into the Association of Senior Citizens' Organizations of Pune (ASCOP). This Association, formed in 1991, is part of FESCOM. Among its objectives is the creation of unity among various senior citizens' clubs and motivating them to struggle for the cause of senior citizens. ASCOP has established a wing called Academy of Senior Citizens to undertake activities and programs in education, training, and research. The motto of ASCOP is "Empowerment of the elderly for healthier, serene, and independent living."

The state of Maharashtra leads India in senior citizens' organizations, in both quantity and quality. Two of the senior citizens' associations of this state need to be specially mentioned because they have stepped out of the stereotype role of a senior citizens' club: the Kothrud Senior Citizens' Association of Pune and the Association of Senior Citizens of Mumbai.

The Kothrud Senior Citizens' Association (KOSCA) was established in 1988. The eligible age for membership is 55. Spouses of members are admitted even if they are below this age. Besides the routine activities performed by senior citizens' associations, KOSCA has organized a Gerontological Research Program and was a co-sponsor and active supporter of ASCOP's Academy of Senior Citizens. The Gerontological Research Program organizes workshops and seminars, besides carrying out research activities and publishing reports. KOSCA also established a Senior Citizens' Forum in September 1997, which consists of qualified social workers in the field of gerontology to extend special assistance and service to the very old and to those living alone. KOSCA has been adjudged the best association of senior citizens in Maharashtra and also at the national level by the Indian Federation on Ageing (InFA).

The Association for Senior Citizens (ASC) Mumbai was established in 1986 and is affiliated with the International Senior Citizens' Association (ISCA) of Los Angeles. Among its non-routine activities are the organization of an International Seminar on Senior Citizens and Society in 1987 and the publication of selected papers of this seminar under the title, "The Aging in India"; the compilation of a brochure containing information regarding "Facilities Available to Senior Citizens in Different Countries" (1988); the publication of a book entitled *Senior Citizens in India–A Handbook of Information* (K. L. Khandpur, Bombay, 1992); and the organization of a seminar on "Family and Elderly Women– Their Status, Role and Problems" and publication of the seminar's report (1995). ASC was judged as the third best association of senior citizens in India and the best in Bombay by the Indian Federation on Ageing (InFA).

While the pride of first place in organizing senior citizens' clubs and raising them to new heights goes to Maharashtra, other Indian states also were moving in this direction, though with reduced speed. Here again, the inspiration for many of them was the Rotary International. Among these states, Kerala was most active. The first Senior Citizens' Association was formed in this state in 1982 at Trivandrum.

There are at present 133 senior citizens' organizations in Kerala. From the point of view of background of members and style of functioning, the organizations may be broadly grouped into two categories. The first category is the conventional type with a highly formalized structure and elitist character. Currently, there are 13 of them, and they are organized into the Federation of Senior Citizens' Associations, Kerala. The second category is more common-man-oriented and structurally different from the first. Called Kerala Senior Citizens' Forum, it was started in 1995. Immediately after formation, it went about organizing units of which there are 120 at present. There is a strong concentration (65) of these units in Kannur District. The units are small in number, with membership of most ranging from 30 to 75. The Forum is engaged in an aggressive membership and unit-building drive. It has a highly centralized structure with a State Committee and District Committees. There is active and continuous interaction between the two layers. A newsletter, the *Kerala Senior Citizen*, keeps members and units abreast of the developments in the Forum and its units and provides interesting news items relevant to the aged.

It is pertinent to mention two senior citizens' groups that have a new (and common) nomenclature: the Indian Association of Retired Persons (IARP) at Mumbai (IARP-M) and the IARP at Calcutta (IARP-C). Both were inspired by and modeled on the American Association of Retired Persons (AARP). Of these, IARP-M is older. It was founded in 1973 by the late P. T. Gokil, who resided in the United States for a long time and was a member of AARP. His interest in older persons persuaded him to take a course in gerontology in the University of Wisconsin at the age of 70. At one time IARP-M had a membership of about 1200, but now there are about 600 members. The fall in numbers is due to deaths of enrolled members without new members joining. In spite of its name, both membership and activities are confined to Mumbai City. The IARP-M is engaged more or less in the same types of activities as other senior citizens' organizations: It runs a day-care center, provides medical, legal, employment, and other services, and publishes a bulletin.

The IARP-C was founded by a medical doctor, Sisir K. Gupta, in 1997. Again, the inspiration was the AARP. It has chapters in Delhi, Chandigarh, Hyderabad, Ludhiana, and even in Mumbai, but with no apparent collaboration with IARP-M. The major aims are to provide health care, transportation, social, cultural and intellectual stimulation, and alleviation of loneliness and isolation among the elderly. IARP-C publishes a quarterly journal, *The IARP Journal*. The association is negotiating with AARP for affiliation/collaboration. Unlike its Mumbai namesake, IARP-C is more dynamic, resourceful, and aggressive in carrying out its activities. In just two years, IARP-C has made its existence felt and is a voice heard in decision-making circles in New Delhi. Its Director, Dr. S. K. Dutta, has been nominated by the GOI to the National Council of Older Persons.

Indian Federation on Ageing

A survey of senior organizations would not be complete without a description of the Indian Federation on Ageing (InFA). This organization is perhaps the largest in the field, and was started in December 1988 at Dondaicha in the District of Dhule in Maharashtra. The driving force was Dr. S. D. Gokhale, later President of the International Federation on Ageing (IFA). InFA also had the good fortune to receive generous financial assistance from an industrial firm, the Rawal Group of Companies. InFA has many elder empowerment programs–training in gerontology and geriatrics, promoting research in gerontology and geriatrics, workshops for updating knowledge and skills of the elderly, and in other ways contributing to the health and happiness of the elderly. In early 1998, InFA organized an International Training Program in Gerontology and Geriatrics at Pune in collaboration with the UN International Institute on Ageing (INIA), Malta. The major objectives of InFA give an indication of the direction in which the senior citizens' movement in India is proceeding: (1) Improve the health-care status and general welfare of senior citizens by health education, holding medical check-ups and treatment camps, and by promoting studies in gerontology. (2) Strive for the full participation of senior citizens in the socioeconomic and cultural life of the community, and provide recreation, education, social security, etc., to them. (3) Create a talent bank for senior citizens volunteering for work and provide placement services for part-time or full-time occupation–remunerated or not–as per demand. (4) Initiate, promote, and develop organizations of senior citizens in various localities and bring them all under one umbrella for the coordination of activities and united efforts to achieve due recognition and rights from Indian society and the government.

InFA is designed to work as an apex federation of aging and age care institutions, comprising senior citizens' associations, pensioners' organizations, research institutions, etc., and to organize them regionally. Currently, four such regions are planned; some are already in operation. The four regions together will cover the whole of India. If InFA succeeds in this, it will be a paramount institution of and for the elderly. The noteworthy achievements of InFA within a decade of its existence point to a leadership role for it in the field of aging in India. Moreover, InFA is the only organization that has as its declared objective the bringing together of all the senior citizens' associations in India, and it has achieved some amount of success in reaching this objective.

A new development in the field of senior citizens' associations is the emergence of the Federation of Associations of Senior Citizens (FASC), New Delhi, started on February 8, 1999, immediately after the GOI announcement of the National Policy of Older Persons (NPOP) in January 1999. Few of the nine members of FASC represent any senior citizen association (SCA), though it has provision to admit representatives of SCAs from eight Indian states to justify its name. The FASC's aims and objectives, in some cases, run parallel to those of the NPOP (see later), namely, "to help to organize and set up Associations of Senior Citizens (ASCs) in various sectors and to affiliate the ASCs on a common bond." FASC's objectives also include "helping the state/central governments in the matter of devising suitable mechanisms so as to ensure that the funds allocated for the welfare of senior citizens are actually reaching the target groups" and "to conduct independent audit/evaluation of nongovernmental organizations (NGOs) when called upon to do so by the state/central governments, with a view to prevent the misuse and diversion of funds allocated for the welfare of senior citizens." Since most of the promoters are highly influential ex-senior bureaucrats, FASC has been able to influence the GOI in a substantial manner in the implementation of the NPOP. Two of FASC's promoters have been nominated to the NCOP and, of these, one is also nominated as a member of NCOP's Working Group of seven members. FASC's aims, objectives, and structure are designed to enable it to act as an apex body of NGOs to help the GOI in its elder welfare programs.

SENIOR ORGANIZATIONS– AN OVERVIEW AND ASSESSMENT

A survey of senior organizations in India shows two major strands working on parallel lines–the government pensioner's associations (PAs) and the senior citizens' associations (SCAs). The PAs are quite indigenous and spontaneous in their origin and style of functioning and have limited objectives and action programs, while the SCAs have been inspired by exogenous agencies (like Rotary International and AARP) and have different structures and styles of functioning. Objectives and programs of the latter group are more general and not intended for members alone. A comparison of the structure and process in these two sets of organizations will heighten their similarities and differences.

Membership

Membership in PAs is limited to retirees from government organizations, including the armed forces and statutory bodies. All the different strata of the bureaucracy are eligible to be members of these organizations. Because of this, membership in these organizations is more representative of all the regions and socioeconomic groups of the country. All members are covered by adequate social security in the form of pensions and other retirement benefits. However, although the PAs cater to the needs of over 3.2 million GOI pensioners, an equal number of military pensioners and family pensioners, and another 7 million state pensioners, the actual number of paid members in PAs is quite small. This is especially true at the GOI pensioners' level, where members are widely scattered throughout the country.

In contrast, membership in SCAs is open to all senior citizens regardless of their employment backgrounds. However, the vast majority of SCA members are middle, upper-middle, and upper-class persons who retired from different walks of life. SCAs have a highly structured style of functioning. Meetings are held monthly, and all members endeavor to attend these meetings. However, SCAs are not representative of older people in India in either demographic or regional terms. They are urban-centered, and except for Maharashtra, are thinly spread over the country. The federations of SCAs are also not all-India federations in real terms. Again, Maharashtra has a near-total coverage of SCA and federational activity. In light of the goal of India's newly declared policy on the elderly, all the SCA federations are launching all-India membership drives to claim national status. In this, the InFA and FASC are moving fast. It is not possible to give a correct estimate of the number of senior citizens covered by the SCAs, but the number is probably not more than 5% of India's 80 million old persons.

Objectives and Programs

The differential objectives of the two groups of associations have already been pointed out. The PAs have very limited objectives: to pursue and protect the interests of pensioners vis-à-vis those in service. For this purpose, and to the extent possible, they lobby and pressure the central and state governments from time to time. Usually, they become active when the Pay Commissions are at work or when the governments implement the Pay Commissions' recommendations. It is only rarely that their activities go beyond the interest and welfare of their members.

In contrast, the SCAs have a wider perspective, and they have objectives and programs of all sorts for both members and other senior citizens, and occasionally for others. The Federation of Senior Citizens of Maharashtra (FESCOM) has programs of environment protection, social integration, consumer guidance, libraries, health programs and the like, which are aimed at all categories of people. Recently, the Indian Association of Retired Persons, Calcutta, also has entered such fields. The UN emphasis on "a society for all ages" has accelerated this process among SCAs and their federations. However, where the constituents of federations are spread far and wide, as is the case with many, such programs are difficult to implement except in isolated pockets.

Finance

There are two major sources of revenue for senior organizations. One is the membership fee. The other consists of donations from members and non-members, funds raised for special programs, and contributions from government and private agencies including business and industry. PAs usually have only membership dues. Because their numbers are very small, income from this source is also small. The programs of these agencies are also modest and less expensive.

The SCAs are better placed financially. They function as independent local agencies and meet at frequent intervals; membership fees are easily collected. Decisions regarding additional funds needed for programs are made democratically, and members are involved at both the collection and expenditure stages. Hence, mobilization of funds is easy, although the amount may have to be small. Federations of SCAs are also better placed than PAs in raising funds because of their wider image in the community. They undertake bigger and more community-oriented programs (e.g., FESCOM's), and they can mobilize public and government funds more easily. The support received by the InFA from the Rawal business group has already been mentioned. Individual units of SCAs and their federations apply for the GOI grant-in-aid programs for the welfare of the aged such as day-care centers, mobile clinics, and the like.

Senior Empowerment

If power is conceptualized as the mobilization of senior political strength through organizations that act upon government in a pressure group capacity (Pratt, 1976, 1993; Tout, 1993), senior organizations in India are very weak compared to their American, British, and Canadian counterparts (Day, 1990; Gifford, 1990). At best, the role of the Indian organizations has been that of petitioner. However, when concessions are evoked, they are done so more through the personal influence of leaders than through the strength of numbers, bargaining strategies, or pressure group techniques. PAs and their federations are more strongly organized than SCAs or their federations for getting concessions. Even so, two of the major rights of pensioners were asserted through court cases filed by private agencies and individuals. Thus, the right to pension for all categories of employees, sometimes hailed as "the Magna Carta of the Pensioners," was established through decrees given by the Supreme Court of India in petitions filed by *Common Cause*, "an organization for ventilating common problems of the people," and by Devakinandan Prasad vs. State of Bihar and D. S. Nakra vs. Union of India.

The SCAs are further down the ladder in empowering their ranks through organizational means. Regional, ethnic, and linguistic differences have made a common forum or strategy for all SCAs or their federations quite difficult. The circumscribed base of many of the federations of SCAs, even when claiming all-India status, has made a national approach and agitational tactics difficult. The urban middle-class base of the SCAs in a country where 70% of the people are rural and live below the poverty line also acts as a handicap in their empowerment efforts. The fact that the Indian journey from the World Assembly on Ageing (1982) to the International Year of Older Persons (IYOP) in 1999 was uneventful, long, and laborious shows the lack of political power of senior organizations. Even the Government of India's belated and unceremonious declaration of the National Policy on Older Persons (NPOP) in January 1999 shows that government has approached the problem of aging in a routine manner. Ironically, when the government did act, it thought of creating a new NGO to empower the country's senior citizens, rather than strengthening or relying on the existing ones or their network. In fairness to the senior organizations and NGOs working for seniors, it must be acknowledged that they have been continuously urging the Government of India to evolve a national policy for its older citizens. Age-Care India, under its dynamic director N. L. Kumar, demanded a policy on aging as early as 1981 when the United Nations was preparing for the Vienna Congress. The Centre for Gerontological Studies of Trivandrum approached the GOI with the Draft of a National Policy and Plan of Action for the Elderly in January 1998, on the eve of the IYOP 1999 (Nayar, 1998).

THE EMERGING SCENARIO

The GOI Declaration of the National Policy on Older Persons (NPOP) and the creation of a National Committee on Older Persons (NCOP) are landmarks in the history of senior organizations in India. The NPOP seeks to "assure older persons that their concerns are national concerns and they will not live unprotected, ignored or marginalized. The goal of National Policy is the well-being of older persons. It aims to strengthen their legitimate place in society and help older persons to live the last phase of their lives with purpose, dignity and peace" (NPOP, Sec. 15).

From the point of view of senior organizations, sections 75 and 95 are most relevant. Section 75 says "older persons will be encouraged to organize themselves to provide services to fellow senior citizens . . ." Initiatives taken by them in advocacy, mobilization of public opinion, raising of resources, and community work will be supported. Section 95 is more specific in the matter: "An autonomous registered National Association of Older Persons (NAOP) will be established to mobilize senior citizens, articulate their interests, promote and undertake programs and activities for their well-being, and to advise the government on all matters relating to older persons. The Association will have National, State and District level offices and will choose its own office bearers. The Government will provide financial support to establish the National and State level offices, while the District level offices will be established by the Association from its own resources, which may be raised through Membership subscription, donations, and other admissible means. The government will also provide financial assistance to the National and State level offices to cover both recurring as well as non-recurring administrative costs for a period of 15 years and thereafter, the Association is expected to be financially self-sufficient."

An autonomous National Council for Older Persons (NCOP) envisaged under Sec. 95 of the NPOP was established by the government in May 1999. The major objectives of the NCOP are:

1. to advise government on policies and programs for older persons;
2. provide feedback to government on implementation of the NPOP as well as on specific program initiatives for older persons;
3. advocate the best interests of older persons; and
4. lobby for concessions for older persons, etc.

Among the 39 members of the committee, six are from federations of SCAs and one from a PA. Among the six SCA representatives, two are from one association–the FASC, which was started in 1999, one month after the declaration of NPOP. Obviously, the appointment does not reflect any influence of either the PAs or SCs except in a marginal way. Again, in the seven-member Working Group constituted from among the NCOP "to make NCOP functional," one is from FASC.

The bypassing of existing senior organizations in the establishment of a new one (NAOP) with state and district level units is an indication of the government's lack of confidence in the representation of existing organizations and their ability to reach out to the mass of older persons. In one sense, this is not unjustified, since the existing organizations do not have any real mass basis. As mentioned earlier, the organizations are mainly urban, while the vast majority of the elderly live in villages–the areas really needing support. Some of the SCAs represented in the NCOP are making efforts to establish branches in other regions to overcome this lacuna. Even so, their urban roots will take a long time to proliferate in the rural areas. At the same time, rural associations of the elderly are slow to get established. To the author's knowledge, only one such organization exists, the Kerala Senior Citizens' Forum, with over 120 units concentrated in North Kerala.

CONCLUSION

Senior organizations in India cannot be compared to similar organizations in the western industrialized countries like the AARP in the United States or Senior Citizen's Forums in Canada or Age Concern in the United Kingdom. These are mass organizations whose memberships run into millions. Their origins could be traced to some government policy on pensions or social security that, in these countries, covers the entire population. As such, everybody has a stake in it. Moreover, these organizations command huge resources; hence, they can act as powerful lobbies.

This situation does not apply in India. To begin with, those covered by pension/social security benefits account for less than 20% of the elderly. Even here, only a small number of people have membership in senior organizations, and the spread is not uniform throughout the country. They are concentrated in urban areas. Secondly, the bulk of the elderly are uneducated and poor and live in rural areas. Mobilizing them around an intangible issue will be difficult (see Mukund Rao, 1993, pp. 302-3). Replication of the AARP example in India has not been successful. In fact, both Indian Associations of Retired Persons, started in Mumbai and Calcutta, have remained elitist organizations, and the IARP-M has faced a dwindling membership over time. It is possible that the newly-established FASC, with strong grounding in the NCOP, may emerge as the paramount organization of senior citizen associations in India. But enjoying patronage from GOI while lacking a mass base, FASC may develop oligarchic tendencies unless proper safeguards are taken. The intervention of the GOI in this area to start the NAOP may not affect the existing seniors' organizations because the clientele of the two are different. Further, the government may feel the need to seek the services of these existing organizations, which could strengthen its hands by providing the expertise and experience accumulated by them over long years of service.

However, it will be several years before mass organizations of the AARP type emerge in India. Currently, the vast majority of the Indian elderly is uneducated, disorganized, and without any provision for adequate social security. In the future, most elderly people will have received more education and will be more participative in social, economic, and political activities. As the elderly become more aware of their rights, the demand for a reallocation of resources in their favor may become a rallying point, mobilizing them into a political force.

AUTHOR NOTES

P. K. B. Nayar is Chairman, Centre for Gerontological Studies, Kochulloor, Trivandrum, India (also Chairman, Kerala State Education Advisory Board). Dr. Nayar was chair, Department of Sociology, and Dean, Faculty of Social Sciences, at the University of Kerala, where he also was Director, Population Research Centre and the Centre for Women's Studies. Dr. Nayar was educated in India and the United States and holds five Master's Degrees. He was Fulbright Professor and recipient of the French Government's Award for Internationally Renowned Scientists; he is also a member of several national and international academic and professional bodies. Dr. Nayar is the author of over 100 research papers and seven books.

Dr. Nayar can be contacted at the Centre for Gerontological Studies, Kochulloor, Trivandrum 695 011, India (E-mail: pkbnayar@bigfoot.com).

REFERENCES

All India Central Government Pensioner's Association (1999). *Our Directory 1999*. Ludhiana: AICGPA.
Common Cause (n.d). *Record of Services*. New Delhi: A-31West.End.
Day, C. L. (1990). *What Older Americans Think: Interest Groups and Ageing Policy*. Princeton: Princeton University Press.
Gifford, C. G. (1990). *Canada's Fighting Seniors*. Toronto: James Lorimer.
Government of India (1999). *National Policy on Older Persons*. New Delhi: Ministry of Social Justice and Empowerment.
Government of India (1999). "National Council for Older Persons," (Office Memorandum No. 22-3/99-5D dated May 10, 1999) New Delhi: Ministry of Social Justice and Empowerment.
Indian Association of Retired Persons (1998). *IARP Journal*. First Issue January- March, 1998.
Indian Association of Retired Persons (1999). *Bulletin for Senior Citizens: Souvenior*, *17*(2).
Indian Federation on Ageing (1999). *Ageing India*, *1*(3).
Khandpur, K. L. (1992). *Senior Citizens in India–A Handbook of Information*. Bombay: Association for Senior Citizens.
Kothrud Senior Citizen's Association (KOSCA) (1988). *Information Brochure*. Pune: Kothrud.
Nair, S. B. (1990). *Social Security and the Weaker Sections*. New Delhi: Renaissance Publishing House.
Nayar, P. K. B. (1991). "Social Security and the Family in the Asia-Pacific Region." Invited Paper at the 9th Regional Conference of International Social Security Association, Jakarta.
Nayar, P. K. B. (1998). A policy and plan of action for the elders of India. *Aging and Society*, *11*(3 & 4).
Nayar, P. K. B. (2000). "The Evolution of Social Safety Net as Related to Demographic, Economic and Political Trends with Special Reference to Pensions in India." Paper presented at the International Seminar on Building the Social Safety Net for Asian Societies in Transition. Louvain-la-Neuve, Belgium, April 27-29, 2000.

Pratt, H. J. (1976). *The Gray Lobby*. Chicago: University of Chicago Press.
Pratt, H. J. (1993). Senior organizations and seniors' empowerment: An international perspective. In Tarik M. Shuman et al. (Eds.), *Population Aging: International Perspectives*. San Diego, CA: University Center on Aging, 321-360.
Rao, M. (1993). Older persons: Issues concerning their empowerment and participation in development. In Tarik M. Shuman et al. (Eds.), *Population Aging: International Perspectives*. San Diego, CA: University Center on Aging, 293-320.
Tout, K. (1993). Empowerment: An aging perspective. In Tarik M. Shuman et al. (Eds.), *Population Aging: International Perspectives*. San Diego, CA: University Center on Aging, 221-292.

Towards a Policy for Aging in India

S. D. Gokhale, PhD, MSW

President, CASP

SUMMARY. India has been engaged in developing the National Policy for elderly for the last two decades. The efforts to establish a policy began building on traditional values, a small number of pre-independence enactments. Lawgivers of India spoke of the rights of the elderly and the responsibility of the state towards them almost 2000 years ago. Additional factors such as culture, social norms, and influence of international organizations, particularly the Vienna Plan of Action, have been responsible for shaping the Policy. The Plan of Action agreed upon at the end of the Vienna meeting could not come into being due to several reasons such as the size of the country and its federal structure. This article takes an overview of the efforts made by the federal government and the NGOs to create a National Policy. The article describes the process by which the National Policy came into being and provides an overview and critique of the present Policy. The author makes a summary of the major areas of action suggested by the Policy, the strategies designed, and the implementation roles of different Ministries. The author describes the steps taken since 1999 and provides the concluding remarks. *[Article copies available for a fee from The Haworth Document Delivery Service: 1-800-HAWORTH. E-mail address: <docdelivery@haworthpress.com> Website: <http://www.HaworthPress.com> © 2003 by The Haworth Press, Inc. All rights reserved.]*

KEYWORDS. India's aging policy, Five-Year Plan, National Policy on Older Persons, Provident funds, pension plan

INTRODUCTION

India has been engaged in developing a national policy for aging for a little over two decades. Other Asian countries, large and small, such as China, Indonesia, Hong Kong, and Singapore, also worked to create more coherent policies for their growing numbers of elders during the 1980s and 1990s. Similarly, Western nations modified their national aging policies during the same time period. In most, policy development consisted of a framework of principles as the basis for desired service delivery outcomes. For example, Australia established a National Strategy for an Aging Australia, based on four principles or concepts: (1) age vs. need, (2) coordination of effort with state governments, (3) crisis vs. prosperity, and (4) integration and participation. Canada and the United States also engaged in reforming their policies for the elderly, with special emphases on the roles of provinces/states and, in the case of the latter, of the for-profit sector, in areas such as income maintenance, health care, and housing.

India's efforts in the late twentieth century began far earlier, building on traditional values, a small number of pre-independence enactments, and a post-independence developmental period lasting into the early 1980s. Like other countries, population aging has helped shape India's national policy, but other factors, including the influence of international organizations (e.g., the United Nations, the International Federation on Ageing) and the insertion of age-related concerns into the Seventh, Eighth, and Ninth Five-Year Plans, were also key. Unlike Hong Kong and Singapore, the process was not guided by top-down initiatives but by a more open, democratic process. This ultimately led to the announcement of the National Policy on Older Persons (NPOP) in 1999.

This article on national policy development for aging in India consists of six sections. The first provides a quick overview of traditional values concerning old age and treatment of the aged. This is followed by two sections that briefly describe major enactments for aged welfare during the British colonial period and in the three decades after independence up to the early 1980s (see "Economic Security for the Elderly in India: An Overview" by S. V. Kumar in this volume for greater detail). The fourth section describes the process by which the National Policy on Older Persons (NPOP) came into being in the mid- to late

1990s, during which time two major initiatives (a national old-age pension and a food security program) were enacted. This is followed by an overview of the principles and values underlying the NPOP and a summary of its major areas, including strategies and implementation roles of different sectors. The last section describes the steps taken since 1999, with some concluding remarks.

TRADITIONAL VALUES CONCERNING THE AGED

While a number of factors influence the development of public policies, it is generally conceded that values are a vital foundation on which those policies rest (see Achenbaum, 1983; Aaron, Mann, & Taylor, 1994). This is even more evident in countries with a federal system of government, such as India and the United States. States and regions have differing value traditions that lead to interstate variations in policy (see Tracy, 1991; Kincaid, 1995; Shankardass, 1995).

The major factors influencing India's aging policy are social values and behavioral norms transmitted from generation to generation. According to Indian culture, the family and self-sustaining village communities are the backbone of the social infrastructure. The debate whether the family system has been withering away is over, and Indian society has accepted the idea that the modern family in India may change its face and form, but it will persist. Although the old definition of a family as a group of people living under the same roof, eating at the same hearth, and related to each other by blood or law has changed, the basic qualities of family relationships expressed through caring for each other and sharing remain. People may live apart and eat separately, but as long as they feel they belong to a family, the family as a system will be sustained. Consequently, any program in India for the elderly cannot overlook the role of the strong family relationship as a crucial social determinant of aging policy.

The values in Indian society, such as respect for elders, love for and devotion to the family name, and acceptance of the responsibility to transmit culture from one generation to another, are other cultural factors with an impact on policy for the aged. The Indian family is not restricted only to parents and children but extends to persons who would normally be considered distant relatives in western societies. It is defined by a wide range of distinct relations who are all included as parts of the integrated Indian family. Each relationship has a different name in most of the Indian languages. For example, while "uncle" is a common word in English used for the brother of one's father or mother, in India, they have different names. Similarly, the father's sisters and mother's sisters are designated separately; the former as "Atya" in Marathi or "Fufi" in Hindi, and the latter as "Mavshi" in Marathi or "Masi" in Hindi. These represent a few examples of cultural factors expressed in everyday language underlining the concept of respect for elders and their positions in the family system, which are reflected in the national policy established at the end of the twentieth century.

Respect for the aged was established early. The "Law Givers" of India provided social norms for coping with the subject of aging. For example, in about 2000 B.C., Manu the first Law Giver spoke about the responsibilities of society towards the old. Similarly, in the post-Vedic period, Kautilya spoke about government's role in treating the elderly with respect and laid down various rules for the regulation of guilds, designed to provide collective security for life, prosperity, and freedom from want and misery (Rajan, Mishra, & Sarma, 1999, 140). In the 8th century A.D., Shukracharya in *Sukraniti* discussed sickness, pension, and old age benefits and family pension and maintenance allowances. The original Sanskrit quotations eloquently speak to the positive outlook of government and society towards India's aged in the last 2000 years or so.

Traditionally, Indian society accepted four important life stages. The first, Bramacharya, consists of a period of learning for the child, followed by Grishastha, the time when the adult is married, settled, and looks after his familial and societal duties. The third, Vanaprastha, consists of withdrawal from day-to-day material activities at age 60, while the fourth, Sanyasa, is the time when the person withdraws totally and is engaged only in his relationship to God and service to society. In a somewhat similar fashion in industrial societies, old age corresponds with retirement from the active work force, traditionally at age 65. In today's India, the central government has used age 60 as the demarcation of "old," a measure first promulgated by the United Nations at the 1982 World Assembly on Aging. However, different states have different age standards for old-age pensions and other benefits related to the later years. They range from between ages 55 and 74 for men and ages 55 to 75 for women.

Because India is a federal government, the subject of aging is on a concurrent list. That is, the Government of India (GOI), as well as the state governments, can plan and develop programs for the elderly; however, the GOI can develop programs that require state participation. India is a very large country composed of 25 states and seven Union

Territories (similar to the District of Columbia and U. S. territories), each with its own political and social context. Thus, their approaches to aging policy vary, as do the types of programs that have been created for the benefit of the elderly and their families. In many instances, as in the United States and other federal nations, efforts initiated by one state often lead to adoption by others and to new national policies.

AGING POLICIES IN THE COLONIAL PERIOD

During the period from the mid-18th to the mid-20th centuries, the British government was primarily concerned with maintaining law and order, which included the development of a bureaucracy composed of both British and Indian civil servants. During the colonial period, the British concept of dealing with social issues through the instruments of institutionalization and legislation was introduced in India. The British government established laws relating to security in old age, such as pensions and Provident funds restricted to the formal employment sector (e.g., government) and a system of old-age homes supported via grants. The traces of this legacy are found in various new laws enacted since 1950; some of these earlier laws were retained after independence in 1947.

Four major pieces of legislation were introduced from the 1870s to the 1940s. The Pension Act of 1871 set up a pension plan for colonial administrators that was made available to all government employees, including Indians in government employment. It was administered by the Royal Commission on Civil Establishment. Amendments were enacted by the British in 1919 and 1935. Today, Part XIV, Article 309 of the Constitution, sets forth recruitment and conditions of service, including compulsory retirement at age 60. It applies both to central and state government pensions; with respect to the latter, state legislatures alone have the authority to make amendments to any legislation.

Other social welfare legislation was passed in the 1920s and 1930s. In 1923, a Worker's Compensation law was passed for government workers; it, too, was retained after independence. Among other provisions, the amount of compensation could be recovered by the elderly parent in case of death of a child during the course of employment. Two other laws revolved around inheritance issues and reflected the need to create appropriate legislation for both Hindus and Moslems. The Indian Succession Act allowed the father to succeed to the property of an intestate who dies without lineal descendants. In the absence of a father and any lineal descendants, the property would devolve to the mother. The Shariat Act of 1937 allowed for property to be distributed among the heirs of the deceased Moslem–which could include elders–after the payment of funeral expenses, of any payment due for services preceding death and of any amounts for the repayment of debt.

The issue of social security became more salient during the early 1940s. The Adarkar Commission Report was submitted on August 15, 1944 to outline the foundation for a social security scheme, based on several principles. These principles included: administrative simplicity, flexibility, financial viability, expandability, and compulsory and contributory requirements. The Adarkar Commission Report laid the basis for the creation of various retirement income schemes and other social welfare programs after independence in 1947. In particular, the health insurance scheme proposed by the Commission materialized in the scope of the Employees' State Insurance Act of 1948; it was thoroughly amended in 1966.

AGING POLICY FROM 1947 TO 1980

With independence, the Constitution of India was established, mandating the well-being of elders as a government responsibility. Article 41, a Directive of State (i.e., government) Policy, requires that the State shall, within the limits of its economic capacity and development, make effective provision for securing the right to public assistance in cases of old age, unemployment, sickness, disablement, and other cases of underserved want. Other constitutional provisions include directions for government's role, both at the national and state levels, through its various schedules. For example, entry 24 in list III of Schedule VII deals with the welfare of labor, including work conditions, Provident funds, workers' compensation, invalidity (disability), and old-age pensions and maternity benefits. Similarly, item 9 of the State lists and items 20, 23, and 24 of the concurrent list relate to old-age pensions, social security, social insurance, and economic and social planning. The right to equality guaranteed by the Constitution as a fundamental right applies equally to elders. Several laws were enacted in the 1950s to 1980s to enhance the security of the aged. These included the Employee's Provident Fund and Miscellaneous Provisions Act of 1952, a step towards making welfare provisions for the future of industrial workers after retirement or for the benefit of their dependents, in case of early death. The Family Pension program, passed in 1971, helped extend much-needed long-term protection for families of industrial workers who die prematurely. Without this program, the accumulations in the Provident fund were too meager to render adequate family protection for industrial workers. These provisions benefitted government and industrial workers in the "organized sector," about 10% of India's entire work force. Workers in agriculture and small business (the "unorganized sector") are not covered.

In keeping with the tradition of family economic solidarity, the Hindu Adoption and Maintenance Act and the Hindu Succession Act were both enacted in 1956. Parents are entitled to inherit the property of sons and daughters, irrespective of their claims for maintenance from their children. The law on inheritance and succession does not create any special right for the elderly parents, but they are entitled to a benefit, along with other beneficiaries, from the property of their deceased child. Further reflecting the Indian cultural attitude of children's obligations towards their parents, Section 125 of the Code of Criminal Procedure created, in 1973, a duty on every person having sufficient means to maintain his father and mother when the parents are unable to maintain themselves.

A number of states, including Himachal Pradesh, Maharashtra, and Goa, also passed parents' maintenance laws, similar to parent responsibility laws passed by some American states with mixed success in implementation. These laws introduced a simple procedure to make it obligatory for errant wards to care for their aged parents. To bring relief to older persons without loss of time, the Civil Divisional Office fixes the amount and a Commissioner acts as the appellate authority. Various Indian states also established old-age pensions for destitute elders in the late 1950s and 1960s; Uttar Pradesh was first in 1957, followed by Andhra Pradesh and Kerala. Administered by state social welfare departments, these benefits ranged from 30 to 100 rupees per month. As of today, all the states and Union Territories have implemented old-age pension schemes for the poor elderly. The plans are drawn up by each political entity according to its financial resources; no statutory sanction exists, nor can these pensions be claimed as a matter of right. The rate of pension, eligibility criteria, residency conditions, and coverage vary from state to state.

Other legislation passed in the first decades after independence included a special tax benefit for elders age 65+ under the Income Tax Act of 1961 and the Payment of Gratuity Act of 1972, an additional retirement benefit for industrial workers. Pensions for Freedom Fighters who had fought for independence and retired servicemen also were enacted.

Similar to the GI Bill in the United States, servicemen were supported to resettle in civilian life through opportunities for training and education. Two life insurance schemes, Jeevan Akshay and Jeevan Dhara, were enacted to provide financial security after the age of 50.

Some states also started giving grants to voluntary organizations for the maintenance of destitute elders in old-age homes. In some cases, the old-age pensions paid to residents of these homes are paid to the voluntary organizations running the homes for their upkeep and care. These several efforts helped lay the foundation for a national policy on aging.

DEVELOPING A NATIONAL POLICY FOR AGING IN INDIA

Several factors led to the movement for a national policy on aging during the 1980s and 1990s, including population aging, changing customs, and earlier governmental efforts noted above. Activities on the international front also built momentum for a national policy on aging. Although the concept of individual aging had been recognized for many millennia in India, the impact of population aging was not well-understood until well into the last quarter of the 20th century and was not accepted as a subject for planning policy formulation. From only 12 million persons aged 60+ in 1901, the numbers of the aged became 20 million in 1951, and 57 million in 1991. The proportion of elders steadily rose from 5.1% in 1901 to 6.8% of a rapidly expanding population in 1991. UN projections indicate that India will have 198 million persons age 60+ in 2030 and 326 million in 2050, more than the entire U. S. population today.

Increasingly, other aspects of demographic aging became clearer, due to research and the tracking of census data by the National Sample Survey Organization in the late 1980s and 1990s: for example, the effects of migration on the age structure of the population and the pattern of most Indian elders continuing to live in rural areas, with urban elders constituting a second generation. In turn, other societal changes became more apparent: the changing roles of women, differences in the traditional status of women in rural areas compared to urban educated and employed women, and changes in the face and form of the family, with value systems undergoing a rapid change. Yet, the elderly continued to expect their children to support them and still do.

At the same time, organizations of elders, which had formerly sought help and small favors from government, began to talk about their rights and develop an advocacy role. Population aging in a democratic state leads to increased proportions of older voters who have the right to determine public policies. It has often been said child welfare policy is neglected because children are not voters. By contrast, elders are often vocal and determined to express their will through the ballot box. By the late 1990s, most political parties had included aging as part of their election manifesto. In the 1999 elections, the Indian Federation on Ageing (IFA) wrote all political parties and their leaders, requesting clarifications of their positions on aging issues. Thus, the political situation was ripe for a national policy on aging.

Understanding of the characteristics of India's elders also increased. The GOI began to realize that not only did the destitute elderly need economic support and care, but a large portion of economically secure and physically fit aged also required emotional and psychological security and community support for a wholesome existence. This growing understanding by national policymakers was influenced by the 1982 World Assembly on Aging, by the U. N. Principles for Older Persons adopted by the General Assembly in 1991, and by the Proclamation on Ageing and Global Targets on Ageing for the Year 2001, adopted by the General Assembly in 1992. The leader of the Indian delegation was Shri Atal Behari Vajpayee, the current Prime Minister of India, who outlined the progress towards India's national policy on aging. Furthermore, the international discussions on economic security of older persons in developing countries generated by the World Bank study (1994) became the subject of national debate in India. It was clear that the various programs of economic security for the elderly needed to be reviewed and that a search for a new system for such provision might be necessary. An urgent need to supplement traditional family support systems also gained greater recognition, with emphasis on developing supportive services at the local level, rather than at the national or state levels.

It thus became necessary for the GOI through its tradition of Five-Year Plans and its National Planning Commission (NPC) to introduce welfare schemes directed at making the lives of elders more livable. India had borrowed the concept of planning from the former Soviet Union; for the last 50 years or so, the planning process has been initiated with Five-Year Plans. The NPC's role has been to prepare those plans and monitor their implementation. The Prime Minister of India serves as chairman; a Deputy Chairman, usually a politician nominated by the government with the rank of a cabinet minister of the national government, also serves on the NPC. The Commission has several advisors on specialized topics, such as education, health, aging, and development.

These advisors function as a "think tank" for the NPC that operates through a cadre of national bureaucrats.

The NPC prepared an approach to the Ninth Five-Year Plan that stated: (1) A high priority would be given to empowering Special Groups (e.g., the aged) economically and socially to enable them to join the mainstream of national development. This would be accomplished by creating an environment of freedom and dignity to enhance the exercise of their rights and privileges like all citizens, and by passing necessary legislation, consistent with the concept of economic growth with social justice. (2) Efforts would be made to minimize the gap between these groups and the rest of society, by enhancing their development in both quantitative and qualitative terms and by taking advantage of inputs from governmental and non-governmental agencies. (3) A National Policy on Aging would be created to address four broad areas: pensions, affordable health services, affordable shelter, and other welfare measures. The Policy on Aging would also recognize the productive role the aged can play through active involvement in developmental activities, not just as beneficiaries. (4) Professionally-trained personnel would be needed to ensure formulation of needs-based policies and programs with effective implementation in response to local needs. Monitoring programs and evaluating them qualitatively would be required.

Several welfare programs were initiated in the 1980s and 1990s, some specifically to benefit elders (or age-based policies and programs), while others helped various groups of individuals, including the elderly (age-related–see Hudson, 1995). Providing a minimum package of primary health and medical services through the expansion of healthcare infrastructure has been India's first priority. Being an integral part of the overall population, the elderly in rural and tribal areas and urban slums have benefitted from this expansion. Health insurance schemes, such as Bhavishya Arogya, and Mediclaim, administered by the General Insurance Corporation of India, were established. Pensioners are among those who can purchase this insurance.

In the area of age-based programs, Central Government Health Scheme facilities were made available to retired national government pensioners. Furthermore, the GOI assisted non-governmental organizations (NGOs) to run special programs (e.g., Mobile Medical Units [MMUs]) for the health of the elderly. The Eighth Five-Year Plan sought to encourage NGOs to provide old-age homes and non-institutional services, such as day-care centers, via grants-in-aid (Shankardass, 1995). Beginning in 1983-1984, the Ministry of Welfare started to provide this grant assistance. The program became very popular with NGOs, and recipient organizations grew rapidly from 134 in 1992-1993, to 218 in 1993-1994, and to 346 during 1994-1995 (see Table 1). Proposals for setting up new homes and day-care programs continued to be received from various new NGOs, and the grant program was expanded in keeping with the recognition in the Ninth Five-Year Plan that elder services are an integral part of the developmental policies of the nation.

These grant programs have not been evenly distributed among India's states and Union Territories or various regions. The NGOs in Andhra Pradesh have been particularly active in developing programs for elders. The majority of GOI-supported old-age homes, day-care centers, and MMUs are found in the southern states of Andhra Pradesh, Karnataka, Maharashtra, and Tamil Nadu (Table 2).

Legislative activity at both the state and national levels for the very poor elderly also occurred during the middle and late 1990s, accompanied by growing advocacy for a national policy on aging. State old-age pensions were liberalized, partly due to the rise in the cost of living; however, these funds are still quite meager and their disbursement often problematic. Similar issues arose with the National Old-Age Pension Scheme enacted in 1995 as part of the National Social Assistance Program. Designed to assist destitutes aged 65 and older on a nationally uniform basis, this program provided a monthly amount of 75 rupees (or about $2), but with a ceiling on the number of recipients allocated to each state and Union Territory. Four years later, a food security program (called Annapurna) was enacted, similar to programs created earlier in Kerala and Tamil Nadu. Again, the restrictions on the numbers of recipients and problems of the elderly establishing their eligibility have made the program less effective.

Earlier efforts toward developing a more comprehensive national policy on aging were delayed for a number of reasons. Foremost was the federal structure of Indian government. A national policy, if it is to be developed in consultation with all the states, is bound to take some years, especially in a vast country like India. Important roles in impacting both state and national policymakers were played by several age-based advocacy organizations, such as HelpAge India and the Indian Federation on Ageing (IFA), both affiliated with larger international entities, as well as Age Concern India and the Centre for Gerontological Studies in Kerala. The IFA played a major role and made the first effort to frame a national policy by drafting a memorandum to which the Minister of Welfare agreed in principle. Subsequently, the Ministry prepared a draft proposal that was circulated to all state governments for their feedback. A revised draft was the basis for inter-Ministerial (interagency) discussion before an outline of a policy statement

TABLE 1. Growth of Grant Programs for Elders, Early-Mid 1990s

	1992-1993	1993-1994	1994-1995
#s of NGOs	134	218	346
#s of Homes	62	126	209
#s of Day Care	157	180	236
#s of MMUs	2	11	29
#s of Non-Institutional Services	-	1	4
Expenditures in rupees	1.06 crores	3.06 crores	5.28 crores

(1.00 crore = 10 million)

was prepared. In a special session at the first World Conference on Ageing organized by the IFA in Bombay and Pune, representatives from governments and national NGOs in aging established a consensus on the main components of the policy.

Subsequently, many experts from within and outside, including the UN and the International Federation on Ageing, were consulted. Data from many countries were collated and reviewed. A consultant, Dr. A. B. Bose, was nominated by the Ministry of Social Justice and Empowerment to draft the policy statement, and a committee of experts convened to review the first draft. The committee met in Delhi and deliberated on the draft statement for two days. The IFA worked with pensioners' associations and affiliated organizations (e.g., the Federation of Senior Citizens' Clubs in Maharashtra) in about 10 states and submitted a detailed memorandum on this policy statement. The final draft was then discussed at forums in several parts of India in late 1997 to early 1998, several (of the forums) convened by HelpAge India, the IFA, and other aging advocacy groups, and in the national parliament. The voice of the elderly through these efforts certainly made a dent on the thinking of policymakers; all political parties took note of this advocacy. The National Policy on Older Persons (NPOP), comprising three sections (Background, National Policy Statement, and Implementation) was finally adopted on August 15, 1999.

THE NATIONAL POLICY ON OLDER PERSONS (NPOP)– AN OVERVIEW

Background

The first section of the NPOP describes population aging in India and its positive and negative implications; the status of older women, espe-

TABLE 2. Number of Government-Supported Programs in 1994-1995, by State/ Union Territory

Name	#s of Homes	#s of Day Care	#s of MMUs	# Others
Andhra Pradesh	68	45	11	1
Assam	1	1	-	-
Bihar	22	-	-	1
Gujarat	1	1	-	-
Himachal Pradesh	-	1	1	-
Haryana	3	8	-	-
Karnataka	10	-	-	-
Kerala	3	2	-	-
Madhya Pradesh	7	3	-	-
Maharashtra	4	7	-	-
Manipur	9	17	-	-
Orissa	23	28	1	-
Punjab	-	1	-	-
Rajasthan	-	4	1	-
Tamil Nadu	22	34	7	-
Tripura	2	5	-	-
Uttar Pradesh	30	47	-	-
West Bengal	23	34	4	2
UTs				
Dadra/Nagar Haveli	-	1	-	-
Delhi	-	1	2	-
Pondicherry	1	-	-	-
Totals	209	236	29	4

(Source: Revised list, Ministry of Welfare, May 19, 1995)

cially widows, is emphasized. Mention is made of the constitutional requirement for GOI responsibility for older persons' well-being: the demand for a policy statement to ensure that elders know where they stand in the overall national perspective and the need to facilitate a humane, age-integrated society. In this respect, the NPOP followed the lead of the UN and the IFA in appreciating the contributions of older persons to society and recognizing that fundamental human rights do not diminish with age. The rights of the elderly must be clearly identified and respected; without rights to independence, participation, self-fulfillment, dignity, and to be cared for, elders cannot meet their desired responsibilities.

National Policy Statement

The goal of the NPOP is to strengthen the legitimate place of older persons in society and help them live their last years with purpose, dignity, and peace, similar to the "quality of life" goals espoused by the Older Americans Act. Intervention areas include financial security, health care, shelter, welfare, and other needs of elders; protection against abuse and exploitation; opportunities for developing the potential and participation of elders; and services to improve quality of life of elders.

Several guiding principles are stated:

1. the need for affirmative action for elders, especially older females so they do not become victims of triple neglect and discrimination on account of gender, age, and widowhood;
2. a focus on the empowerment and active and productive involvement of older persons to ensure their continued contribution to family, community, and society;
3. an age-integrated society in which family capacity for caregiving is strengthened;
4. the necessity for partnerships of individuals, families, communities, and other institutions with government to carry out NPOP objectives; and
5. expanded social and community client-oriented and user-friendly services for the aged, with special attention to those in rural areas.

Furthermore, the NPOP views the life cycle as a continuum, of which the post-age 60 phase is an integral part. Age 60+, rather than a cut-off point for beginning a life of dependency, is seen as a phase when individuals should have choices and opportunities for creative, productive involvement. "Productive aging" (see Gokhale, 1992) is the NPOP's philosophical keystone.

Financial Security. A major focus of dealing with principal areas of intervention and action strategies is financial security, particularly for different income groups. This includes an emphasis on inflation effects, administrative issues of the NOAPS, better returns from Provident fund accumulation, the expansion of pension coverage under strong regulatory authority, and tax relief for medical deductions and for co-resident families with elders. Income-generating activities after retirement, the promotion of long-term savings instruments, and the rights of elders to be supported by their children are also part of financial security.

Health Care/Nutrition. Similarly, health care and nutrition constitute a major NPOP focus, with an emphasis on long-term management of illness at home. Elders' health-care needs are a high priority, with a goal of good affordable health services, heavily subsidized for the poor and a graded system of user fees for others. A mix of public health services and insurance, combined with not-for-profit and private health-care services, is envisioned. Differing governmental roles are described: public sector promotion for health insurance with subsidies for lower-income groups; encouraging non-profit roles via assistance, concessions, and relief; and encouraging and regulating for-profits, preferably by private care provider associations. The primary health-care system is key, with greater orientation to the health-care needs of older persons. Geriatric facilities at secondary and tertiary levels, with special counters for elders at public hospitals, are to be developed. In addition, medical/paramedical personnel will be trained in health care for the aged; NGOs will provide mobile health services and special health camps; and hospice programs are to be funded by a public-private mix.

Another emphasis is on self-care and family care materials on nutritional needs in old age, the promotion of healthy aging, the strengthening of health education programs by using mass and folk media, and targeting information to younger and middle-aged groups about the effects of life-styles during the early years on health status in later life. Families will be provided counseling and information on the care and treatment of elders with mental health problems. NGOs are expected to play major roles.

Shelter. A third major emphasis is elder housing, with a 10% earmarking of urban and rural lower-income housing for the aged. Elders will be given easy access to housing purchase and repair loans and to ground floor apartments; housing developments will be expected to be responsive to their community-based amenity needs, including multipurpose senior centers; and information concerning accident prevention will be provided to elders and their families. Group housing of older persons, with common service facilities, will be encouraged, but age-segregated housing that prevents interaction with the rest of the community is to be avoided. Institutional care in old-age homes is seen as the last resort. Education and training of housing professionals will include modules on older persons' needs.

Education/Welfare/Protection of Life and Property. Other areas of intervention include education, welfare, and protection. Information, continuing education, and educational materials relevant to older people's lives will be developed and disseminated; curricula at all levels will incorporate materials to strengthen intergenerational bonds; schools will develop outreach programs to interact with seniors on a regular basis; and contributions of the elderly will be highlighted in the media. Welfare programs will focus on the most vulnerable elders, and non-institutional services by NGOs will be promoted to strengthen the coping capacity of the aged and their families. Older persons will be encouraged to form informal neighborhood groups to satisfy social and recreational needs. A Welfare Fund for elders will be created, with tax-deductible funding from corporations, trusts, charities, and individuals combined with government funds. States will be expected to establish similar funds.

Protective services against fraudulent dealings and physical and emotional abuse, especially of widows, will be provided, with NGOs playing major roles. Police will keep a friendly eye on older couples and individuals living alone. Elders also will be provided with advice on maintaining contacts with family and friends and taking precautions against crime.

Affirmative Action. Other interventions involve affirmation actions on behalf of elders. These include concessions (discounts) for travel and entrance fees; preferential seating and easy access to services; speedy disposal of elders' complaints; the designation of the year 2000 as the National Year for Older Persons; and featuring issues relevant to elders on National Older Person's Day, similar to National Older Americans Month. A listing of central and state government programs for elders will be compiled, updated regularly, and disseminated widely to associations of older persons.

Strategies. The last part of the National Policy Statement section focuses on strategies. Of utmost importance is the role to be played by NGOs. Governmental reliance on NGOs for economic development and for social welfare programs in India and other Asian nations has been characteristic (Riker, 1995). The primary mechanism described in the NPOP is grants-in-aid, an approach also used in the United States. Promotion of NGO networking and information exchange and training of NGO personnel are also to be used. Elders will be encouraged to organize and deliver services to their fellow senior citizens (similar to meals-on-wheels delivery in the United States), to set up and participate in volunteer programs, and to mobilize public opinion on behalf of seniors. Trade unions and employer organizations will be encouraged to promote and organize programs on aging issues and services for retirees.

Other strategies include tapping the potential of older persons to play key roles in more effectively transmitting India's sociocultural heritage to their grandchildren; undergirding the familial support system through support services (e.g., respite care); and sensitizing the young to the importance of meeting filial obligations and intergenerational bonding. In particular, the sensitizing of all to accept the role of married daughters in elder caregiving, as opposed to the more traditional role of daughters-in-law, is seen as vital. Encouraging traditional co-residence via tax relief, medical expense rebates, and housing preference, as in other Asian nations, is another proposed strategy.

Finally, other mechanisms include promoting research and training on aging by setting up regional centers for geriatric and gerontological studies, providing research grants, creating a national institute and an interdisciplinary coordinating body on research, and strengthening professional associations in aging. Manpower training will focus on geriatric specializations in medical colleges, training institutes for nurses, and in-service training centers. Curriculum development assistance, especially in schools of social work and other university departments, and training of NGO personnel are seen as vital approaches, as is sensitivity training for persons in the legislative, judicial, and executive branches of government at all levels. Finally, the media are recognized as very important players in highlighting the changing situation of elders and in identifying emerging issues and areas of action.

Implementation

The third and final section of the NPOP deals with an outline of its implementation. Wide dissemination is seen as the basis for an action plan. Collaboration by government, other institutions, and individuals is the primary mechanism. Organizations of older persons have special responsibilities such as watchdogs, mobilizers of public opinion, and generators of pressures for NPOP implementation.

The Ministry of Social Justice and Empowerment (MSJE) is the lead agency to coordinate all matters relating to implementation of the NPOP, via a new separate Bureau of Older Persons and the participation of different national departments of the GOI through an Inter-Ministerial Committee. The MSJE role is similar to that played by the Administration on Aging in the Unites States. States are also encouraged to set up separate Directorates (departments) of Older Persons for coordination and monitoring at the state level.

Each national ministry is required to prepare Five-Year Plans and annual action plans about their implementation of aspects of the NPOP that fall into their jurisdiction. Targets, time frames, and implementation responsibilities will be specified to ensure that both age-related and age-based programs benefit elders; each ministry's annual report will indicate progress achieved during the year. The NPC and Finance Ministry will facilitate budgetary provisions required for implementation. In addition, the MJSE will prepare a detailed review of NPOP implementation every three years. The preparation of the report is to draw on non-official sources and to be discussed at a national convention. To ensure effective implementation at different levels, on occasion experts in public administration will be called on to consult on details of administrative structure, coordination, and monitoring of the NPOP.

At the subnational level, state governments and Union Territory administrations will be urged to undertake similar actions. Similarly, Panchayati Raj institutions (village councils) will be encouraged to participate in NPOP implementation by addressing local level issues and needs of the elderly and developing programs for them, and by providing forums, which ensure adequate representation of older women, to discuss elders' concerns and actions to be taken. They are expected to mobilize and utilize the talents and skills of older persons through specific plans, with the help of panchayat Social Justice Committees.

Beyond the use of existing central governmental structures, two new autonomous entities will be created: the National Council for Older Persons (NCOP) and the National Association of Older Persons (NAOPS). The NCOP, headed by the Minister of Social Justice and Empowerment, is composed of 39 members and a seven-member working committee. It includes representatives from the NPC and relevant central ministries, from five states on a rotating basis, and from other institutions: NGOs, academic bodies, media, and from diverse experts on aging. Basic NCOP objectives include: advise the GOI on specific initiatives and on the NPOP; advocate for the aged; lobby for concessions, rebates, and discounts for the elderly; represent the collective opinion of the aged to the GOI; and suggest steps and measures to enhance the quality of intergenerational relations and productive aging.

The NAOPS, similar to the U. S. Federal Council on Aging, is designed to mobilize senior citizens, articulate their interests, promote and undertake programs and activities to benefit elders, and advise the GOI on all matters related to older persons. It will have national, state, and district-level offices and choose its own officers. The GOI will provide financial support for national and state-level offices to cover recurring and non-recurring administrative costs for 15 years. Thereafter, the NAOPS is expected to be financially self-sufficient. District offices will be funded by the NAOPS from its own resources raised from a variety of means, for example, dues and donations.

An Advisory Council also has been constituted to provide advice to the MSJE by reviewing the policy from time to time and providing expert advice to the Minister. It is an expert group that can link the government with NGO activity through discussion and networking. The people serving on this Council are not necessarily those who met with the Minister during the development of the NPOP, although several are, including the author.

CONCLUDING REMARKS

The NPOP is clearly ambitious in the breadth of its areas of intervention and action strategies that seek to mobilize all levels of government, NGOs, families, and older persons themselves in helping meet the challenges and opportunities of India's population aging. The NPOP is a very comprehensive piece of work and provides a context for planning and programmatic action by government, society, and its citizens. One important feature of the NPOP is that it gives enough freedom to each state and Union Territory to generate programs that will serve different geographical areas, different ages groups, and different needs, depending on the social and cultural background of various regions. The states are not of equal size nor do they have the same rural-urban division or socioeconomic status. Some states have a large urban base like Delhi, Maharashtra, and Tamil Nadu, while some, such as Bihar, Madhya Pradesh, and Rajasthan, have a very large rural component. The programs set up for the aged by these states are bound to differ so they can cater to the diverse needs of diverse elders. For example, planning health services in Madhya Pradesh and Rajasthan will have to take into account such factors as reaching out to tribal populations living far apart from each other.

Similarly, the age structure of each state varies. In states like Kerala, a large number of the elderly are dependent on their younger family members who are living and earning abroad. In Andhra Pradesh, the proportion of those aged 80+ is higher compared to other states. Thus, the programs for rural-urban, young-old, and old-old must be different in those states and every other state. A second distinguishing feature is the NPOP's focus on strengthening the family system, the most cherished social institution in India and the most vital, non-formal social security for the old. While similar to national policies in other Asian nations, this emphasis is in contrast to U. S. policies on aging, with their focus on the aged individual. Only recently has specific policy recognition been accorded to the role of the family in the National Family Caregiving Initiative now being implemented by the U. S. Administration on Aging, 57 State Units on Aging, and approximately 670 Area Agencies on Aging, with grants-in-aid assistance to numerous not-for-profit entities.

A final important feature is the heavy reliance on NGOs, both social welfare organizations and associations of older persons. While caution has been voiced concerning the transfer of government responsibility to voluntary organizations (O'Connell, 1996), this issue seems less germane in the case of India and other Asian nations lacking a well-developed historical and comprehensive social welfare role of the kind encountered in more industrialized nations. NGOs play vital roles in aged care in all nations (Beer, 1994). Economic development concerns, while touching on the roles of elders in the Ninth Five-Year Plan, are still paramount. The current level of the economic capacity of the GOI and state governments and widespread poverty in rural areas, especially among the elderly, make reliance on and assistance to NGOs a wise strategy. However, the uneven distribution of NGOs focused on the elderly across India means that some regions will lack this capacity. Interventions and support from external organizations, such as HelpAge International, the International Federation on Ageing, Rotary International, the Grameen Bank, and AARP's international program, could play instrumental roles in NGO capacity-building through funding support and technical assistance, especially at the local level, in cooperation with India-based organizations such as HelpAge India, the Indian Federation on Ageing, and clusters of senior organizations (e.g., the Federations of Senior Citizens' Clubs in Maharashtra and in Kerala).

Several criticisms, however, have been leveled at the NPOP by the author and others. Most broadly, the NPOP looks like a "wish list," similar to Title I of the Older Americans Act, rather than a meaningful document for action. A much higher priority must be given to the crucial issue of economic security for elders. The welfare of the unorganized sector, fully 90% of the work force, is completely neglected, as are trends that affect their well-being. Partly due to globalization, casual employment is more widespread, with implications for old-age poverty. Increasing widowhood places older women, particularly those age 80+, in great jeopardy, an issue that should be addressed by the national government on a pilot basis, rather than leaving it to local government initiatives. In addition, the family is the safety net for the aged, but the NPOP does not adequately address how to strengthen familial abilities, including economic capacity, to carry out this vital role. The problems with the administration of the national old-age assistance and Annapurna programs must also be corrected.

Other administrative and coordinating issues need attention as well. While the MSJE is the lead agency, the plan of action for distributing responsibilities among other Ministries, for example, Health, Education, Labor, is insufficient. For example, the national health policy of 2001 does not refer to geriatric and gerontological problems and issues or even refer to the NPOP. An effective coordinating mechanism clearly needs to be instituted. This same problem has been experienced by the U. S. Administration on Aging since its creation in 1965.

Furthermore, because the NPOP is only a statement of intent, it is missing a plan of action with a financial statement, as is required of all policy statements in India. For example, the national policy on education had an action plan and a program of expenditures; this was not the case with the NPOP. In addition, the effort to create a voluntary organization, more or less run by the national government, seems contradictory as a mechanism to promote more participation.

Additionally, overreliance on governmental grants-in-aid to NGOs needs to be reexamined. The growth of the program attests to its popularity with NGOs, but there are no established ongoing mechanisms for monitoring the progress and viability of the programs or of the organizations running them. Especially in regions where no stable NGOs are operative, thought must be given to building up that kind of capacity.

Finally, the present policy appears to be dominated by demographic considerations, rather than the personal experience of aging. The NPOP needs to have a human face and to recognize the importance of spirituality in coping with aging. This is especially germane for men who experience major role changes due to mandatory retirement and is in keeping with the traditional four stages of life. In short, as the basis for its future success, the NPOP needs to retain traditional values, put a higher priority on economic security in old age, and forthrightly address issues of implementation.

AUTHOR NOTES

Dr. S. D. Gokhale, former President of the International Federation on Ageing (1992-1997), was a U. N. Advisor on Aging. He is currently President of the Community Aid & Sponsorship Programme (CASP). A PhD from Banaras University, India, and trustee Editor of *Kesari* daily newspaper, he was Executive Secretary of the Indian Council of Social Welfare. In 1975, Dr. Gokhale became Assistant Secretary General of Asia and Western Pacific Region of the International Council on Social Welfare.

Professor, author, researcher, editor, and administrator, Gokhale is currently a member of various U. N., government, and university committees. A distinguished social scientist, he is known both nationally and internationally.

Dr. Gokhale can be contacted at (E-mail: caspune@pn2.vsnl.net.in).

REFERENCES

Aaron, H., Mann, T., & Taylor, T. (eds.) (1994). *Values and public policy.* Washington, DC: The Brookings Institution.
Achenbaum, A. (1983). *Shades of gray: Old age, American values and federal policies since 1920.* Princeton, NJ: Princeton University Press.
Beer, C. (1994). Non-governmental organizations: Their role in aged care. *Bold,* 4(2), 2-5.
Gokhale, S. D. (1992). Toward productive and participatory aging in India. *Caring,* 86-89.
Hudson, R. B. (1995). The history and place of age-based public policy. *Generations,* 19(3), 5-10.
Kincaid, J. (1995). Values and value trade-offs in federalism. *Publius: The Journal of Federalism,* 25(2), 29-44.
National Policy on Older Persons (1999). New Delhi: Ministry of Social Justice and Empowerment.
O'Connell, B. (1996). A major transfer of government responsibility to voluntary organizations? Proceed with caution. *Public Administration Review,* 56(3), 222-226.
Rajan, S. I., Mishra, U. S., & Sarma, P. S. (1999). *India's elderly: Burden or challenge?* New Delhi: Sage Publications.
Riker, J. V. (1995). From co-optation to cooperation and collaboration in government-NGO relations (pp. 91-130). In N. Heyzer, J. V. Riker, & A. B. Quizon (Eds.), *Government-NGO relations in Asia.* New York: St. Martin's Press.
Shankardass, M. K. (1995). Towards the welfare of the elderly in India. *Bold,* 5(4), 25-30.
Tracy, M. B. (1991). *Social policies for the elderly in the third world.* New York: Greenwood Press.
World Bank (1994). *The old age crisis, policies to protect the old and promote growth: A policy research report.* New York: Author.

Index

AARP. *See* American Association of Retired Persons (AARP)
AARP's international program, 232
Abuse, elder
 in India, 6
 in Indian context, 135-140. *See also* Elder abuse, in Indian context
Academy of Senior Citizens, 201
Activities of daily living (ADLs), 92
 in national study of (1997-1998) old-age homes, 166
AD. *See* Alzheimer's disease (AD)
Adarkar Commission Report of 1944, 49, 218
ADLs. *See* Activities of daily living (ADLs)
Adopt-a-Gran program, 161
 in HelpAge India, 187
Age, as factor in disabilities in India, 92-95
Age Care India, 181,190
Age Concern
 India, 223
 United Kingdom, 210
Age-Care India, 208
Aged, traditional values concerning, 215-217
Agewell, 190
Aggarwal, V., 115
Aging
 in Asia, 14-16,15t
 care for, old and new approaches to, 159-178
 global scenario of, 13-16,14t,15t
 in India
  demography of, 69-77,71t,74t-76t
  2001-2051, 11-30. *See also* India, elderly in
 foundations of, 4-5
 geriatrics and, 144-147
 healthy, determinants of, 71-72
 policy for, 213-234
  in colonial period, 217-218
  development of, 220-224,224t
  introduction to, 214-215
  1947-1980, 218-220
 research on
  behavioral, 36-37
  biomedical, 35-36
  early, 33-34
  future of, 39-40
  perspectives on, 31-43
   introduction to, 32-33,32t
  social sciences, 36-37
  strengths of, 37-39
  trends in, 34-37
  weaknesses of, 37-39
"Aging, Disability, and Disabled Older People in India," 5
Aging populations, in China, 2
AICGPA. *See* All-India Central Government Pensioners' Association (AICGPA)
AIPTPA. *See* All-India Post and Telegraph Pensioners' Association (AIPTPA)
Aligarh Muslim University, 35
All-India Central Council of Pensioners' Associations, 195
All-India Central Government Pensioners' Association (AICGPA) (North India Region), 195
All-India Institute of Medical Sciences, 147
 Delhi, 36

© 2003 by The Haworth Press, All rights reserved. *235*

All-India Organization of Pensioners, 195
All-India Post and Telegraph Pensioners' Association (AIPTPA), 195
Alzheimer's and Related Disorders Society of India, 190
Alzheimer's disease (AD), 94
Alzheimer's Society of India, 154
American Association of Retired Persons (AARP), 203, 210
"Amrit Varsha," 184
Annapurna program, 45, 60, 61, 62, 223
Artificial Limbs Manufacturing Corporation, 103
ASCOP. See Association of Senior Citizens' Organizations of Pune (ASCOP)
ASCs. See Associations of Senior Citizens (ASCs)
Asia, aging in, 14-16, 15t
Assam tea plantation Provident fund, 53
Association of Gerontology, 34
Association of Parents of Mentally Retarded, 102
Association of Senior Citizens (ASCs) of Mumbai, 201, 202
Association of Senior Citizens' Organizations of Pune (ASCOP), 201
Associations of Senior Citizens (ASCs), 204
Ayurveda, 144

Bagchi, K., 189
Balya, 33
Bangalore University, 95, 98
Barnes, J.A., 111
Bartholomew, J.J., 101
Bass, S.A., 14
Behavioral research, in India, trends in, 36-37
Benares Hindu University, 35

Bhajans, 167
Bharat Pensioners' Samaj, 195
Bhavishya Arogya, 222
Bhavishya Jeevan plan, 57
Biomedical research, in India, trends in, 35-36
Biswas, S.K., 79
Bonus Scheme Act, 53
Bowe, F., 100
Brahmacharya, 33, 216
Brymer, C., 156
Bultena, G., 88
Bureau of Older Persons, 229

CAC program. See Call-a-Car (CAC) program
Call-a-Car (CAC) program, 152
Canada, Senior Citizens' Forums in, 210
Caregiver(s), in India, 127-135
  family, 128-129
  institutional care services, 131-134
  state, 128-129
  stress among, 134-135
Caregivers Club, 151-152
Caregiving, mechanics of, 129-131
CCCGPA. See Coordination Committee of the Central Government Pensioners' Associations (CCCGPA)
CCRCs. See Continuing care retirement communities (CCRCs)
CEFRA. See Center for Research on Aging (CEFRA)
Center for Research on Aging (CEFRA), 34, 36
  S.V. University, at Tirupati, 1-2
Central Board of Trustees, 54
Central Civil Service Pension Rules of 1972, 50
Central Government assistance, 146
Central Government Employees Group Insurance program, 52

Central Government Health Scheme, 222
Central Government Retired Employees' Association, 195
Central Government Welfare Department's survey, 132
Central Services, 195
Central University of Hyderabad, 35
Centre for Gerontological Studies
    in Kerala, 223
    in Trivandrum, 208
Centre for Research on Aging, at Tirupati, Andhra Pradesh, 163
Chadha, N.K., 6,109,115,116,117,118
CHD. *See* Coronary heart disease (CHD)
China, aging populations in, 2
Civil Divisional Office, 219
Civil service employees, retirement benefits for organized sector, 50-52
Coal Mines Provident Fund, 53,54
Code of Criminal Procedure, 219
Cole, C.J., 182
Colonial period, aging policies in, 217-218
Common Cause, 207
Communication(s), of HelpAge India, 189
Community development, by HelpAge India, 186
Constitution of India, 102,218
Continuing care retirement communities (CCRCs), 146
Contributory Provident Fund, 50,52
Coordination Committee of the Central Government Pensioners' Associations (CCCGPA), 195,196-197
Coparcener(s), defined, 120
Coronary heart disease (CHD), in India, 89-90
Council of Teaching Hospitals, 156

DAD program. *See* Dial-a-Driver (DAD) program

Dandekar, K., 90-91,91t,163, 174
Das, 137
Dave, S., 68
Day-care centers, HelpAge India and, 187
Death, in old age, causes of, 73,74t
Decalmer, P., 135
Dementia, in India, prevalence of, 94
Demographics
    of aging in India, 69-77,71t,74t-76t
    of aging India, 2001-2051,11-30.
    See also India, elderly in
"Demography of Indian Aging, 2001-2051," 4
Department of Audit and Revenue, 195
Department of Income Tax, 195
Department of Information and Broadcasting, 195
Department of Welfare, of Government of India, 35
Devakinandan Prasad v State of Bihar, 207
Development, community, by HelpAge India, 186
DFLE. *See* Disability-free life expectancy (DFLE)
Dharmashastra, 33
Diabetes Club, 143,152
Diabetic Hospital and Research Center, 156
Dial-a-Doctor program, 153
Dial-a-Driver (DAD) program, 152
Directive Principles of State Policy, 49
Director of Programs, in HelpAge India, 188
Directorates (departments) of Older Persons, 229
Directory of Old Age Homes in India, 188-189
Disability(ies), in India
    age-related mental morbidity and, 92-95
    gender as factor in, 99-102
    older persons and, 86-87,89-95,90t,91t
    people growing old with, 87-89

types of, 97
Disability profile, in older persons, 72-77,74t-76t
Disability-free life expectancy (DFLE), 71
Disabled persons, invisible, 97-99
Disabled women, reproductive rights of, 101-102
Double Endowment policy, 57
Dr. Reddy's Foundation for Human and Social Development, 154
Dr. Reddy's Heritage Foundation, 148
Draft of a National Policy and Plan of Action for the Elderly, 208
D.S. Nakra v Union of India, 207
DST, 38
"Dust Busters" training program, 154
Dutta, S.K., 203

Easwaramoorthy, M., 116
Eckert, J.K., 163
Economic(s), aging in India and, 5
Economic characteristics, of elderly in India, 20-24
Economic security, for elderly in India, 45-65
"Economic Security for the Elderly in India: An Overview," 5
Eighth Five-Year Plan, 174,180,222
Elder abuse
  in India, 6
  in Indian context, 135-140
    case studies, 136-137
    historical background of, 126-127
    introduction to, 126
Elder care, in Indian context, 125-135
  family's role in, 128-129
  historical background of, 126-127
  introduction to, 126
  primary caregivers in, 127-135. See also Caregiver(s), in India
  state's role in, 128-129
  types of, 127-135
Elderly
  death of, causes of, 73, 74t
  disability and, 86-87
  disabled, in India, 5
  GOI's policy on, 193
  health of, defining of, 71
  in India, 11-30
    advocacy and policy related to, 7-8
    demographic profile of, 16,17t 2001-2051,11-30
    described, 16-20,17t,19f,20t
    economic security for, 45-65
      introduction to, 46
      traditions of, 46-47
    economic status of, overview of, 47-48
    emerging aging scenario (2001-2051), 24-27,25t,26t
    gender as factor in, 6, 16
    health care services for, 77-81
      future projections for, 80
    health status of, 5,67-77
    introduction to, 12-13
    links with non-kinship groups, 6
    literacy among, 20-21
    marital status of, 21-22
    morbidity among, 72-77,74t-76t, 89-92,90t, 91t
    national government actions in 1990s, 59-62
    old-age homes for, 6-7
    policies and programs for, 102-105
    policy changes due to, 27-28
    prevalence of, 11-12,16
    research on, 4-5
    retirement of, traditions of, 46-47
    social and economic characteristics of, 20-24
    social networks in, 109-124. See also Social networks, of old people in India
    work status of, 22-24
  living arrangements of, 161-162
  mortality, morbidity, and disability profile among, 72-77,74t-76t

services for, 159-178. *See also* Old-age homes
welfare of, NGOs in, 179-191. *See also* HelpAge India; Non-governmental organizations (NGOs)
Elderly Females in India, 189
Election Manifesto, 196
Ellett, F., 156
Employee Provident Fund, 54
Employees' Deposit-Linked Insurance program, 54
Employees' Family Pension program, 54, 55
Employees' Provident Fund, 218
Employees' State Insurance Act, 53
Employees' State Insurance Corporation, 54
Empowerment, senior, SCAs and PAs and, 207-208
Ex-service men's associations, 197-198

"Facilities Available to Senior Citizens in Different Countries," 202
Familial relations, aging in India and, 5-6
"Family and Elderly Women–Their Status, Role and Problems," 202
Family Pension program, 218-219
FASC. *See* Federation of Associations of Senior Citizens (FASC)
Federation of Associations of Senior Citizens (FASC), 204-205
Federation of Central Government Pensioners' Associations, 195
Federation of Senior Citizens' Associations, Kerala, 202
Federation of Senior Citizens' Organizations Maharashtra (FESCOM), 200-201, 206
FESCOM. *See* Federation of Senior Citizens' Organizations Maharashtra (FESCOM)
Foster Child program, 155

Foster Grandparent program, 155
Friend-in-Need Society of Madras, 182
Fundraising, by HelpAge India, 183-184, 184f

Gangadharan, K.R., 6, 143
Gangrade, K.D., 112-113
Gender, of elderly in India, 6, 16
 as factor in disabilities, 99-102
 as factor in social networks, 117-118
General Assembly, 221
General Insurance Corporation of India, 222
General Provident Fund, 50, 52
Geriatric(s), aging in India and, 144-147
Geriatric Clinic of the All-India Institute of Medical Science, 113
Geriatric hospitals, in India, 143-158. *See also* Heritage Hospital (HH)
"Geriatric Hospitals in India, Today and in the Future," 6
Geriatric Research, Education, and Clinical Care Centers, 146
Geriatric Society of India, 34
Gerontological Research Program, 201
Glendenning, F., 135
Global Strategy for Health for All by the Year 2000, 68
Goddess Sita, 119
GOI. *See* Government of India (GOI)
GOI employees. *See* Government of India (GOI) employees
Gokhale, S.D., 7, 8, 203
Gokil, P.T., 203
Golden Couple contest, 143, 153
Goswami, U.A., 93
Government, role in old-age homes, 174-175
Government General Hospital, Madras, 36
Government of India (GOI), 73, 145, 163, 180, 196, 216
 Department of Welfare of, 35

Ministry of Welfare of, 35,98
Government of India (GOI) Act of 1935, 3
Government of India (GOI)
   employees, 194
Government of India (GOI) policy on
   the elderly, 193
Government of India (GOI) services, 194
Grameen Bank, 232
Grandparent-Grandchild Bridge Program,
   153-154
Grandparent-Grandchild quiz competition,
   154
Grishastha, 33,216
Group Superannuation program, of LIC,
   56
Gupta, H.K., 199
Gupta, S.K., 203
Guru Nanak Dev University, Amritsar, 35

Health
   aging in India and, 5
   of older persons, defining of, 71
Health care services, for older persons
   in India, 77-81
   future projections for, 80
Health life expectancy (HLE), 71
Health status, of older persons in India,
   67-77
   introduction to, 68-69
   "Health Status and Health Care
      Services Among Older
      Persons in India," 5
Help the Aged, United Kingdom, 182
HelpAge India, 7,36,37,154,164,175,
      182-190,223,224. *See also*
      Non-governmental
      organizations (NGOs), in
      welfare of elderly
   activities of, 183-190
   Adopt-a-Gran in, 187
   advocacy by, 189-190
   communications of, 189
   community development by, 186
   day-care centers and, 187

described, 182-183
Director of Programs in, 188
fundraising activities of, 183-184,184f
income generation by, 186-187
leprosy care in, 185
mobile medical care in, 185-186
old-age homes and, 187
ophthalmic care in, 185
program development by, 184-185
publications of, 189
research and development in, 188
school education programs of,
   187-188
structure of, 183,184f
HelpAge India study, 132,133,162
HelpAge International, 182,189,232
Heritage Caregivers, 151
Heritage Diabetes Clubs, 151
Heritage Home Care Services, 152
Heritage Home Care Services
   Program, 152
Heritage Hospital (HH), 6,143
   community outreach of, 153-154
   consultation at, 155
   establishment of, 147
   example of, 147-158,149t
   in India, development of, 146-147
   medical facilities and services of,
      149-151
   as model of geriatric care, 156-158
   new programs at, 155-156
   patients in
      numbers of, 148, 149t
      problems of, 148-149
   service clubs in, 151-152
   site of, 147
   training activities of, 154-155
Heritage Pharmacy Services, 152
Heritage Senior Citizen's Festival, 153
Heritage Senior Net, 151
HH. *See* Heritage Hospital (HH)
Hindu Adoption and Maintenance Act,
   134, 219
Hindu Succession Act,
   119,120,121,122,219

HLE. *See* Health life expectancy (HLE)
Hyderabad foundation, 154

IADLs. *See* Instrumental activities of daily living (IADLs)
IARP. *See* Indian Association of Retired Persons (IARP)
IARP-C. *See* Indian Association of Retired Persons (IARP), at Calcutta (IARP-C)
IARP-M. *See* Indian Association of Retired Persons (IARP), at Mumbai (IARP-M)
ICDS. *See* Integrated Child Development Scheme (ICDS)
ICMR. *See* Indian Council of Medical Research (ICMR)
ICMR Task Force Geropsychiatric study, 93
ICSSR. *See* Indian Council of Social Science Research (ICSSR)
IFA. *See* International Federation on Ageing (IFA)
ILO. *See* International Labor Organization (ILO)
Income generation, by HelpAge India, 186-187
Income Tax Act of 1961, 219
India
　aging in. *See* Aging, in India; Elderly, in India
　caregivers in, 127-135. *See also* Caregiver(s), in India
　CHD in, 89-90
　dementia in, prevalence of, 94
　elder abuse in, 135-140. *See also* Elder abuse, in Indian context
　elder care in, 125-135. *See also* Elder care, in Indian context
　elderly in. *See* Elderly, in India
　expectation of life at ages 60 and 70 for, 18,20t
　geriatric hospitals in, 143-158
　institutional care services in, 131-134
　joint and nuclear family residence in, 118
　"Law Givers" of, 216
　life expectancy in, 70,71t
　life insurance in, 45
　mental morbidity in, age-related disability and, 92-95
　old-age homes in, 159-178. *See also* Old-age homes
　older persons in
　　with disabilities, 89-95,90t,91t
　　health status of, 67-77
　population pyramids of, 18,19f
　Sample Registration System in, 24
　savings-linked insurance in, 45
　senior grassroots organizations in, 193-212. *See also* Senior grassroots organizations, in India
　social and economic security policies in, 48-59
　　in colonial period, 49
　　economic security for unorganized sector, 55-59
　　for non-civil service employees, 53-55
　　in post-independence period, 49-50
　　retirement benefits for organized sector, 50-52
Indian(s), annual per capital income of, 48
Indian Association of Retired Persons (IARP), 206, 210
　at Calcutta (IARP-C), 202
　at Mumbai (IARP-M), 202
Indian Constitution, 3, 134
Indian Council of Medical Research (ICMR), 34-35,36,38,73
Indian Council of Medical Researches (ICMR), 89
Indian Council of Social Science Research (ICSSR), 35,38

Indian Federation on Ageing (InFA), 7,201,202,203-205,223
Indian Medical Association, 102
Indian Railways, 195
Indian Society, life stages of, 216
Individual Retirement Accounts (IRAs), 52,58
InFA. *See* Indian Federation on Ageing (InFA)
INIA. *See* UN International Institute on Ageing (INIA)
Institutional care services, in India, 131-134
Instrumental activities of daily living (IADLs), 87
Insurance, savings-linked, in India, 45
Integrated Child Development Scheme (ICDS), 104
Inter-Ministerial Committee, 229
International Federation on Ageing (IFA), 190,203,224,232
International Labor Organization (ILO), 50
International Seminar on Senior Citizens and Society, 202
International Senior Citizens' Association (ISCA) Inc., U.S.A., 200
  of Los Angeles, 202
International Third Sector organizations, 184
International Training Program in Gerontology and Geriatrics, 203
International Year of Older Persons (IYOP), 180,208
International Year of the Elderly, "Vienna Declaration" of, 34
Invisibility, of disabled population, 97-99
IRAs. *See* Individual Retirement Accounts (IRAs)
ISCA. *See* International Senior Citizens' Association (ISCA)
"Issues of Elder Care and Elder Abuse in the Indian Context," 6

IYOP. *See* International Year of Older Persons (IYOP)

Jajmani system, 47
Jamuna, D., 6,125
Jarvik, L.F., 70
Jawaharlal Nehru University, 35
Jayaram, 136-137
Jaycee, 79
JCSSR, 36
Jeevan Akshay, 56-57,220
Jeevan Dhara, 220
Jeevan Griha plan, 57
Jeevan Mitra policy, 57
Jeevan Suraksha plan, 57
Joint and nuclear family residence, in India, 118
Journal of Aging & Social Policy, 1
Journal of the American Geriatrics Society, 156

Kerala, Centre for Gerontological Studies in, 223
Kerala Senior Citizen, 202
Kerala Senior Citizens' Forum, 199,202,209
Kesari, A., 120
Kesari, U.P.D., 120
Khandelwal, 95
"Knowledge is power," 32
Kohli, D.R., 183
KOSCA. *See* Kothrud Senior Citizens' Associations (KOSCA)
Kothrud Senior Citizens' Associations (KOSCA), 201
Krishnamurthy, K., 95
Kumar, N.L., 208
Kumar, S.V., 5,45
Kumar, V., 5,67,114,115,117

"Law Givers," of India, 216
Leprosy care, in HelpAge India, 185

LEWD. *See* Life expectancy without chronic disease (LEWD)
LIC. *See* Life Insurance Corporation (LIC) of India
Liebig, P.S., 1,6
Life expectancy
  disability-free. *See* Disability-free life expectancy (DFLE)
  healthy, 71
  in India, 70,71t
Life expectancy without chronic disease (LEWD), 71
Life insurance, in India, 45
Life Insurance Corporation (LIC), of India, 56
  Group Superannuation program of, 56
Literacy, among elderly in India, 20-21
Little Sisters of the Poor (LSOP), 170,182
Local village councils, 177
LSOP. *See* Little Sisters of the Poor (LSOP)
Lyon, S.M., 163

Madras Medical College, 36
Malhotra, R., 116,117
Management issues, in old-age homes, 167-169
Manayuva, 201
Mangla, A.P., 115
Manu, S., 33,216
Marital status, of elderly in India, 21-22
Mathur, S., 96
McDonald, J., 116
Meals-on-Wheels program, 143,152
Medicare system, 104
Mediclaim, 222
Mental morbidity, age-related disability and, in India, 92-95
Mini Mental State Examination (MMSE), 95
Ministry of Food and Civil Supplies, 61
Ministry of Health, 40
Ministry of Human Resource Development, 40

Ministry of Rural Development, 61
Ministry of Social Justice and Empowerment (MSJE), 68, 103,134,154,224,229,230
Ministry of Welfare, 35,98,102,103, 133,222-223,223
Miscellaneous Provisions Act of 1952, 218
Mishra, U.S., 4,11,176
Mitakshara, 120,121
MMSE. *See* Mini Mental State Examination (MMSE)
MMUs. *See* Mobile medical units (MMUs)
Mobile medical units (MMUs), of HelpAge India, 185-186
Mobile Medicare Units, 133
Money Back policy, 57
Morbidity
  mental, age-related disability and, in India, 92-95
  in older persons, 89-92,90t,91t
Morbidity profile, in older persons, 72-77,74t-76t
Morgan, L.A., 163
Morris, R., 14
Mortality profile, in older persons, 72-77,74t-76t
MSJE. *See* Ministry of Social Justice and Empowerment (MSJE)
Mumbai, Association of Senior Citizens of, 201,202
Municipality of Hyderabad, 154

Nandi, P.S., 93
NAOP. *See* National Association of Older Persons (NAOP)
Narayanan, K.R., 183
National Association of Older Persons (NAOP), 7,208-209,230
National Council on Older Persons (NCOP), 7,35,40,196,208, 209,230
National Family Caregivers Initiative, 157

National Financial Commission, 3
National Institute of Public Cooperation and Community Development (NIPCCD), 36
National Medicare Program, 139
National Old-Age Pension (NOAP) scheme, 60-61,223
National Older Americans Month, 228
National Older Person's Day, 228
National Planning Commission (NPC), 221-222
National Policy for Elderly, 213-234. *See also* Aging, in India, policy for
National Policy on Aging, 222
National Policy on Older Persons (NPOP), 4,5,60,68,85,102, 151,154,160,180,183,188, 204,208,214,224
  GOI Declaration of, 208
  historical background of, 224-225
  implementation of, 229-231
  national policy statement of, 226-229
  overview of, 224-231
National Sample Survey Organization (NSSO), 23,68,97,133,220
National Sample Survey Organization (NSSO) report, 127,128
National Social Assistance Program, 102,223
National Social Assistance Scheme, 60
National Strategy for an Aging Australia, 214
National Year for Older Persons, 228
Nayar, P.K.B., 7,193
NCOP. *See* National Council of Older Persons (NCOP); National Council on Older Persons (NCOP)
New Jeevan Dhara plan, 57
NGOs. *See* Non-governmental organizations (NGOs)
1982 World Assembly on Aging, 221
Ninth Five-Year Plan, 223,232

NIPCCD. *See* National Institute of Public Cooperation and Community Development (NIPCCD)
NOAP scheme. *See* National Old-Age Pension (NAOP) scheme
Non-civil service employees, retirement benefits for, in India, 53-55
Non-governmental organizations (NGOs), 79,125,146,159, 161,173,175-176,204,222
  role of, 180-182
  in welfare of elderly, 179-191
  introduction to, 180
NPOP. *See* National Policy for Older Persons (NPOP)
NPS. *See* National Planning Commission (NPC)
NSSO. *See* National Sample Survey Organization (NSSO)
NSSO report. *See also* National Sample Survey Organization (NSSO) report

OAP scheme. *See* Old Age Pension (OAP) scheme
OASIS (Old Age Social and Income Security), 62
Oka, M., 14
Old Age Income and Social Security, 68
Old Age Pension (OAP) scheme, 102
Old Age Social and Income Security (OASIS), 62
Old-age homes, 6-7
  residency in, 116-117,159-178
    free vs. for-pay homes, 170,171t
    future of, 176-177
    government's role in, 174-175
    HelpAge India and, 187
    national study of (1997-1998), 163-172,171t
      ADLs help in, 166
      auspices of homes in, 166-167

common spaces in, 165-166
described, 163
length of operation of homes
   in, 167
location in, 164-165
management issues in,
   167-169
meals provided in, 166
methods in, 163-164
paid vs. free homes in,
   169-172,171t
physical amenities in,
   164-165
resident characteristics in, 169
results of, 164-172,171t
services of homes in, 165-166
size of homes in, 164-165
overview of, 160-161
policy implications in, 172-176
residency in, 116-117
societal implications in, 172-176
studies of (1990-1996), 162-163
values issues in, 173-174
"Old-Age Homes and Services: Old
   and New Approaches to
   Aged Care," 6-7
Older Americans Act, 226,232
Ophthalmic care, in HelpAge India, 185
Organization for Industrial, Spiritual,
   and Cultural Advancement
   International, Japan, 200

Padmasree, V., 136
Panchal, A.K., 93
Panchayati Raj institutions, 230
Panchayats, 177
PAs. *See* Pensioners' Associations (PAs)
Patney, V., 183
Pay Commission, 196
Payment of Gratuity Act of 1972, 219
Payment of Gratuity program, 53
Pension Act of 1871, 197,217
Pension-cum-Social Security Act, 197
Pensioners' Associations (PAs),
   193,194-199

Pensions for Freedom Fighters, 219
Persons with Disabilities Bill of 1994, 98
Persons with Disability Act of 1994, 5
"Perspectives of Research on Aging in
   India," 4
PHC. *See* Primary health care (PHC)
PHC system. *See* Primary health care
   (PHC) system
Policy implications, in old-age homes,
   172-176
Population(s), aging, in China, 2
Post and Telegraph Departments, 195
Postal Pensioners' Association (PPA), 195
Powers, E., 88
PPA. *See* Postal Pensioners'
   Association (PPA)
Prabhkar, A.K., 89,90t
Prakash, I.J., 5, 85
Primary health care (PHC), 127
Primary health care (PHC) system, 80
Privilege, 151
Proclamation on Ageing and Global
   Targets on Ageing for the
   Year 2001, 221
Program development, by HelpAge
   India, 184-185
Provident Fund program, 53
Provident funds, 49
Publication(s), of HelpAge India, 189
Punia, D., 22

Rajan, S.I., 1,4,11,176
Ramamurti, P.V., 1,4,31,162
Rao, A.V., 76,78
Rawal Group of Companies, 203
Reddamma, 133
Rehabilitation Council of India, 103-104
Reproductive rights, of disabled
   women, 101-102
Research, on elderly in India, 4-5
Research and development, in
   HelpAge India, 188
Respect Age International, 199, 200
Retirement, in India, traditions of, 46-47

Retirement benefits, in India, for
    organized sector, 50-52
Rotary International clubs, 7,79,175,
    181,199,200,232
Royal Commission on Civil
    Establishment, 49,217

Sagar, R., 94
Sample Registration System, in India,
    24
Sandhu, S.S., 183
Sanyasa, 33-34, 216
Sarma, P.S., 4,11,176
Savings-linked insurance, in India, 45
Sawhney, M., 7,179
SCAs. *See* Senior Citizens'
    Associations (SCAs)
Schieman, S., 87
School education programs, of
    HelpAge India, 187-188
SEAR. *See* South East Asian Region
    (SEAR)
Senior citizens' associations (SCAs),
    7, 193, 199-205
Senior Citizens' Club, at Dombivali in
    Bombay City, 200
Senior Citizens' Forums, in Canada, 210
*Senior Citizens in India–A Handbook
    of Information,* 202
Senior empowerment, SCAs and PAs
    and, 207-208
Senior Forum, of Heritage Hospital, 153
Senior grassroots organizations, in
    India, 193-212
  ex-service men's associations, 197-198
  introduction to, 194
  membership in, 205-206
  objectives of, 206
  overview of, 205-208
  programs of, 206
  revenue for, 206-207
  senior empowerment due to, 207-208
  state pensioners' associations, 198-199

"Senior Grassroots Organizations in
    India," 7
Senior Heritage Selections, 155
Senior Net Club–Click@50, 143,151
SES. *See* Socioeconomic status (SES)
Seth, A., 183
Seventh Five-Year Plan, 68
Shah, B., 89,90t,93
Shankardass, M.K., 114,115,117,163,174
Sharma, M.L., 22
Shastipurthi, 34
Shendye, G.S., 200
Shukracharya, 216
Silver Couple contest, 143,153
Singh, S., 117,118
Sishrusha Management Consultants, 147
Sita, 136
Sitamma, 136
Small, G.W., 70
Social characteristics, of elderly in
    India, 20-24
Social implications, in old-age homes,
    172-176
Social networks
  aging in India and, 5
  analytical use of, 111
  defined, 112
  of old people in India, 109-124
    described, 110-118
    gender as factor in, 117-118
    introduction to, 110
    joint and nuclear family
      residence, 118
    life course related to, 115-116
    network size, 114-115
    networks beyond core, 115
    policy of, 118-121
    supportive care of, 115
"Social Networks of Old People in
    India: Research and Policy," 6
Social relations, aging in India and, 5-6
Social science(s), in India, trends in, 36-37
Social Science Institute, 104
Social security, in India, 45-65. *See
    also* Elderly, in India,
    economic security for

Societies' Registration Act of 1960, 182
Socioeconomic status (SES), 72
South East Asian Region (SEAR), 78,79t
Special Assistance for Research in Aging and Life Span Development, 35
Sri Venkateswara University, 34
Standing Committee on Population Projections, 74
State Pay Commissions' Awards, 198
State pensioners' associations (SPAs), 198-199
Stress, among caregivers, 134-135
Sukraniti, 216
Supreme Court of India, 207
S.V. University, Tirupati, 36
Swathi Health Care, 147

Telegraph Department, 195
"The Aging in India," 202
The Hindu, 162
The IARP Journal, 203
"The Magna Carta of the Pensioners," 207
The Panchayat Act of 1991-92, 4
The Research and Development Journal, 188
"The Role of Non-Governmental Organizations for the Welfare of the Elderly: The Case of HelpAge India," 7
The Shariat Act of 1937, 218
Third Sector, 181
Third Sector organizations, international, 184
"Towards a Policy for Aging in India," 7
Turner, H.A., 87

UGC, 38. *See* University Grants Commission (UGC)
UN International Institute on Ageing (INIA), 203
UN Principles for Older Persons, 221
UNICEF, 154
Union Territory's Social Welfare Department, 58
Unit Trust of India, 56
United Kingdom, Age Concern in, 210
United Nations (UN), 2
United Nations (UN) International Plan of Action on Aging, 180
United Nations (UN) Programs on Aging, 190
University Grants Commission (UGC), 34-35
University of Gwalior, 35
University of Wisconsin, 203
U.S. Federal Council on Aging, 230
U.S. News & World Report, 156
U.S. Veterans Administration, 146

Vajpayee, S.A.B., 221
Values issues, in old-age homes, 173-174
van Willigen, J., 6,109,118
Vanaprastha, 33,34,216
Vasudeva, 136
Venkatagiri Chaultries, 160
Venkataraman, R., 183
Vidyasagar Institute of Mental Health and Neuroscience (VIMHANS), 154
Vienna Congress, 208
"Vienna Declaration," of International Year of the Elderly, 34
Vienna International Plan of Action on Aging, 194,213
VIMHANS. *See* Vidyasagar Institute of Mental Health and Neuroscience (VIMHANS)
Volunteer Guild, of Heritage Hospital, 151
"Vruddha Sabha," 200

"War on Ages," 154

Welfare, of elderly, NGOs in, 179-191.
    See also HelpAge India;
    Non-governmental
    organizations (NGOs)
Welfare Department, 38
WHO. *See* World Health Organization
    (WHO)
Wisocki, P.A., 95
Wood, J.B., 99
Work status, of elderly in India, 22-24
Worker's Compensation law, 217
Working Committee of the National
    Council, 189
World Assembly on Aging, 194, 208, 216
World Bank, 2, 63
World Bank study, 221
World Conference on Aging, 224
World Elders Day, 153, 154, 189
World Health Organization (WHO),
    36, 71
World Health Organization
    (WHO)–coordinated
    multi-center study, on
    estimation of prevalence of
    dementia, in India, 94

Yerraiah, 133